DOMINATION AND POWER

DOMINATION AND POWER

PETER MILLER

ROUTLEDGE & KEGAN PAUL
LONDON AND NEW YORK

First published in 1987 by
Routledge & Kegan Paul Ltd
11 New Fetter Lane, London EC4P 4EE

Published in the USA by
Routledge & Kegan Paul Inc.
in association with Methuen Inc.
29 West 35th Street, New York, NY 10001

Set in Sabon, 11 on 12 pt
by Input Typesetting Ltd, London
and printed in Great Britain by
T. J. Press (Padstow) Ltd, Padstow, Cornwall

Library of Congress Cataloging in Publication Data

Miller, Peter, Ph. D.
Domination and power.

Bibliography: p.
Includes index.
1. Power (Social sciences) 2. Dominance
(Psychology) I. Title.
HM136.M486 1987 303.3 87–9848

British Library CIP Data also available

ISBN 0-7102-0624-0

For Linda

CONTENTS

•

ACKNOWLEDGMENTS

I have benefited from the support and encouragement of a number of people in carrying out this study. Particular thanks are due to Graham Burchell, Colin Gordon, and Paul Hirst. Also, to Donald MacRae who acted as supervisor for the thesis on which this book is based. The author, however, has to accept responsibility in the last instance.

A different type of thanks are due to Vera for her typing, and much else besides.

SUBJECTIVITY AND POWER

•

The significance of the phenomenon of power would appear to be self-evident. Whether it be applied to nation states, organisations, or individuals the notion has permeated the public consciousness, and intellectual discussions on the topic continue to proliferate. It is as difficult to escape from debates over power as it is to escape power itself. The question of subjectivity and of the notion of the subject is different. It appears to belong to a different field of debate, one that is more properly philosophical, even esoteric. Doubtless there are complex reasons for this state of affairs. A central one may well be that a culture is remarkably adept at concealing its constitutive features. I am less concerned, however, with explaining this state of affairs than with addressing the implications it has had for the way the phenomenon of power is understood.

My argument here draws heavily on that of Foucault – that power and subjectivity have been conceived for too long as fundamentally opposed. Power has been viewed as operating exclusively through the repression of an essential subjectivity. For power to operate it has been assumed that it must have as its effect the crushing of subjectivity. The subject in such a vision rises up from time to time in a valiant struggle against power, but is constantly turned back. Often this will be achieved bloodily, but other means are available also. Sometimes the threat of force will be enough to subdue the possible eruption of subjectivity. Foucault has suggested a directly opposed image of power, one which operates in precisely the other direction, not by repressing subjectivity, but by promoting it, cultivating it and nurturing it. This operation of power via the promotion of subjectivity, however, is not neutral. Subjectivity is always promoted under specific conditions, it is always a regulated subjectivity which emerges out of this process. The discrete mechanisms through which this operates can be termed regulatory practices of the self.

To refer to the title of this book, I suggest that we need to distinguish between domination and power. Domination indicates a particular mode of operation of power, and its identification depends also on a certain philosophical mode of conceptualising power. It is a mode of acting upon individuals or groups of individuals directly counter to their aspirations or demands. It is a phenomenon we witness often in the home, the school, the workplace, and at national and international state levels. It sometimes reaches horrific proportions and at such points may take effect by causing the death of the dominated. Therein lies its ultimate sanction.

Power, by contrast, operates through the promotion of subjectivity and is more resourceful. It is not limited to seeking to deny and to challenge, but attempts to invest the individual with a series of personal objectives and ambitions. Power in this respect is a more intimate phenomenon. It knows the individual better, it does not act on individuals at a distance and from the outside. It acts on the interior of the person, through their self. As a mode of intervention on social relations it is one in which the production of a knowledge of the subject and a mode of acting upon the subject is crucial.

To view power in this way is to suggest the need for a considerable displacement of conceptual principles. It means that we should not allow our understanding and analyses of power to be subsumed under philosophical *a priori*s. It means also that the route to an understanding of power in western societies may well be via a consideration of the notion of the subject rather than through a conceptual analysis of power.

To address the notion of the subject, however, is to enter difficult waters. The furore which the work of Althusser and his colleagues[1] provoked is one indication of the philosophical sensibilities operative in this terrain. Althusser's work addressed head-on the notion of the subject, and although the word power did not figure in his writings, the concern was a closely allied one. Althusser addressed the question of the subject in two principal respects. Firstly, in his notion that individuals do not function within Marxist theory as constitutive subjects, but only as occupants, supports (*träger*) of places and functions within the process of production.[2] The true 'subjects' were not 'concrete individuals' – 'real men', but the relations of production. But since these were relations, the category subject, the notion that relations of production were relations between men, was considered a violation of Marx's thought. This interpretation of Marx's thought followed partly from a philosophical *a priori* of Althusser's which was an anti-humanism. It followed also from Althusser's interpretation of the Marxist notion of totality as a structural totality. This totality was to be divided into different levels, and the relations between the different levels were conceived according to a model of structural, if not structuralist causality.

The other aspect of Althusser's work which confronted the notion of subject was his proposal for a theory of ideology.[3] Here Althusser sought not to lay down a 'true' Marxism from certain canonical texts, but actually to depart from a set of dominant Marxist principles. This consisted essentially of rejecting a notion of ideology posed in terms of truth/falsity, and substituting a conception of ideology as the production of subjectivity. Through the notion of Ideological State Apparatuses Althusser retained his Marxist credentials, but these were weakened by a series of theses towards a general theory of ideology. The important point of these theses for my purposes here is the general conclusion to which they lead. This was that the distinctive contribution of ideology in general is that it has the function of *constituting* concrete individuals as subjects. There is, Althusser was to argue, 'no ideology except by the subject and for subjects'.[4] All ideology was to be viewed as having the function of constituting concrete individuals as subjects.

As I have already noted, Althusser was addressing here not the question of power but that of ideology. Its significance, however, is in two respects. Firstly, in the centrality it accords to the category of the subject as something to be explained rather than assumed. Secondly, in the duality identified in the process of the constitution of subjects. This meant that individuals were produced 'as if' they were constitutive subjects, but this took place in and through their own subjection. The term Althusser utilised here was interpellation. Individuals were interpellated within ideology in order that they should accept their own subjection. This dual process was one of subjectification.

This way of attending to the category of the subject was novel within Marxism, and opened up the prospect of a theory of the production and reproduction of society without recourse to the philosophical *a priori* of constitutive subjectivity. But there was a problem. The mechanism for the production of subjects through ideology was a feature of ideology in general. It was, that is to say, outside of history, it was an eternal feature of human existence. This was, to use Althusser's own terms. 'une énorme bévue', a huge oversight. The category of subjectivity may be so pervasive within western culture that it appears eternal. But this is far from being the case. After all of Althusser's invectives against philosophical humanism,[5] he ended up attempting to found his theory of ideology on the one category which required explanation. Having provoked a florid defense of socialist humanism,[6] it turned out that it was more the declaration of intent with regard to the category of the subject than the actual gains which were notable.

There were, however, more sensitive issues at stake. They can be designated by the term 'structuralism'. In the space of a few years structuralism has passed from being the site of a debate to carrying with it an almost automatic condemnation. If certain individuals denied the relevance of the label already in the late 1960s, then today one has to search extremely hard to encounter a self-declared structuralist. It should be noted, however, that the passage of less than a decade has not produced an accumulation of evidence against structuralism. Today, it seems, the enthusiastic student need only be aware that it is the 'zone' into which he or she should not venture.

Structuralism, of course, was only a name. It came to stand as a symbol for a variety of researches carried out across the fields of psychoanalysis, linguistics, literary studies and more general cultural analyses carried out under the auspices of semiology. Understood in this way structuralism was a mode of analysis of phenomena which sought to identify a level, usually a non-empirical one, at which one would discern the basic elements of things. The number of elements was a matter of choice. It depended on what one was looking at. The interest hinged on the relations which obtained between the elements.

It was, however, not just structuralism's general methodological protocols which were to become the focus of debate. They seemed also to carry a philosophical message. This message was interpreted as having the force of a proposed conceptual genocide against 'the subject'. The 'subjects' of phenomenology, existentialism and all humanisms were to be removed in order that they might be reinstated in their rightful places, positioned as effects of structures. It is fair to say that there were grounds for this interpretation. Althusser had sought an ally in psychoanalysis in his proposals for a theory of ideology. Michel Pêcheux[7] had chosen a slightly different route, via linguistics and the study of discourse. Through these alliances it was hoped to produce an explanatory schema for ideology which would be all-embracing. It would give a new lease of life to the study of those general class-based ideologies with which Marxism had always been concerned. But it would add to these a crucial new dimension. This would be an explanation of the mechanisms through which concrete human individuals are transformed into subjects, into beings that acted 'as if' they were constitutive of their social world. This was the heart of the issue, the question of the 'real effects' of structures.

Of course Althusser was not strictly speaking making a new discovery or opening up new continents of knowledge. He was undertaking, rather, a project of combination of themes and ideas. This was something others had been engaged on for some years already. Lacan was one of them,[8] in his mammoth investigations which sought to combine linguistics and psychoanalysis. The subject was to be understood for Lacan through its position in relation to the 'symbolic system' and the relations between this and social relations. Certain interpreters took this as grounds for proposing a revitalisation of historical materialism via Lacanian theory.[9] The key issue here for my purposes concerns what this offered *vis-à-vis* the notion of the subject. Lacan had said that 'man speaks, but it is only that the symbol has made him man.' The subject was to be viewed as a network made up of the properties of language. The structure of language was to reverberate across the subject. The subject was to become the material of the relations of speech.

The projects which Althusser and Lacan were working on had an important point of contact. They both sought to examine the relations and mechanisms through which human individuals were produced as subjects. Althusser for his part sought to identify a mechanism which actually produced subjects. Lacan was more interested in the various decentrings through which the subject was positioned within the structure. Neither of them addressed the historical emergence of those discourses and practices which take the formation of subjects as their concern.

There were, however, quite different ways in which the category of the subject had been understood. The German sociologist Max Weber had explicitly addressed the question of the subject and its domination some half-century earlier. Weber's writings are a complex mixture of sociology and history and operate at a number of different levels. Two of these are relevant to my concerns here. The first relates to Weber's general protocols for the understanding of power and authority. Weber was to distinguish between power (*Macht*) and authority (*Herrschaft*).[10] The former referred to the probability that one actor in a social relationship will be able to carry out his will despite resistance. The latter referred to the probability that a command will be obeyed by those to whom it was addressed. As one commentator has noted,[11] this conception of power stems from Weber's general sociological principle that social action is an interpersonal process. The implication of this is that power is viewed as a mode of domination which obtains between subjects.

The second aspect of Weber's work of interest here is his treatment of the notion of discipline. Weber was to define discipline as the probability that habituation would lead to prompt, automatic and stereotyped obedience to commands. This conception of discipline did not reduce to a mode of interpersonal control. Rather than being dependent on a category of subjectivity, it depended on a principle of impersonality. The guiding principle here was rational discipline. Weber was to define discipline as nothing other than the 'consistently rationalized, methodically trained and exact execution of the received order, in which all personal criticism is unconditionally suspended and the actor is unswervingly and exclusively set for carrying out the command.'[12] The military, he argued, was the archetypal model for such discipline. Uniformly conditioned and trained for discipline, this 'moral' element of the endurance of the troops was to be central to the modern conduct of war. Discipline was crucial to the winning of wars. It was important also in a more general sense. It was to have lasting effects on the political and social order. It gave birth, Weber argued, to patriarchal kinship among the Zulus, and to the Hellenic *polis* with its gymnasiums. More importantly, perhaps, the rule of the modern European bureaucratic state organisations was seen to have its origin in discipline. It has always been the case, Weber argued,[13] that discipline has affected the structure of the state, the economy, and possibly also the family. The discipline of the army gave birth, Weber argued, to all discipline.[14] Large-scale economic organisation was, however, the second agency for training men for discipline. Weber acknowledged that there may be no direct historical link between Pharaonic workshops and construction work, Carthaginian Roman plantations, the mines of the late Middle Ages, the slave plantation of colonial economies, and the modern factory. The one element in common to these different forms of economic organisation was discipline. The techniques of discipline differ in each case. Military discipline, however, was to provide the ideal model for the modern capitalist factory, as it had done for the ancient plantation. But in contrast to the plantation, discipline in the factory was to be founded on a wholly 'rational' basis. This was not synonymous with the notion of rationalisation often used to characterise Weber's work. It referred instead to the empirical observation that a calculation of the optimum profitability of the individual worker was undertaken in the same way as any material means of production. 'Scientific management', Weber argued, was the greatest triumph in the rational conditioning and training of work performances. The effect of this was to adjust the psychological and physical apparatus to the demands of the machines.

Within contemporary sociology it has been common to interpret Weber's sociology as dominated by an investigation of the process of rationalisation. An alternative explanation has recently been proposed[15] which suggests that Weber's concerns are rather different. Instead of rationalisation it is argued that the key theme underlying Weber's work is the notion of *Menschentum*. A qualitative interest in the history of mankind. This was to be investigated in Weber's writings through a detailed study of the differential modes of conduct of life (*Lebensführung*). The rational conduct of life was one of the central objects of this study. The world religions were also to be understood as 'systems for the regulation of life'.

Whilst highly attractive, this revised interpretive grid for understanding Weber's work does not seem to me entirely convincing. Its principal drawback lies in its attempt to substitute one exclusive theme for the interpretation of Weber's work by another. It seems to me more likely that Weber's studies were animated by a plurality of factors. Whilst I sympathise with the wish to shift attention away from Weber's dependency on southwest German neo-Kantianism, it is hard to understand Weber's work entirely independently of an anthropology.

The reason for addressing this question of the interpretation of Weber's work here is its centrality to sociological debate over the notion of power. To the extent that Weber's studies concern the category of the subject they are doubly interesting. To put the matter in stark terms, it can be said that there are two options. Either we view Weber's analyses of power as inherently limited to the extent that they depend on an anthropology of the constitutive subject. The limitation here would be that they assume precisely that which has to be explained. Or we interpret Weber's studies as containing the elements of an analysis of power which sees it as operating through pressures and influences brought to bear on the conduct of individual lives. As I have suggested already, I think we have to resist the temptation of a clear reply to this either/or. At times Weber does appear to view the human subject as a given, as something upon which a sociology has to be built. At other times he seems to be investigating the modes of formation of differential ethical life-styles adequate to their respective social relations.

But if we are to interpret Weber's writings as equivocal in their treatment of the notions of power and the subject, the same cannot be said for two principal lines of thought which owe so much to Weber. These are the writings of Georg Lukács and critical theory.[16] Lukács was not hesitant about identifying the place which the notion of the subject was to assume in his schema.[17] Notwithstanding the different phases his work went through, the principle of essential subjectivity as an originary force in history occupies an absolutely central position. For Lukács subjectivity was a phenomenon which characterised a class rather than an individual. Through combining a Hegelian notion of dialectic with a set of rudimentary Marxist concepts, with the former dominant, Lukács sought to establish that the class-subject had a material and historical foundation. Unfortunately it had neither. Lukács's view of capitalism owed much to the Weberian concern with bureaucratisation and the phenomena of rational calculation.[18] However it lacks Weber's sensitivity to the significance of the latter. The only force which might oppose capitalist domination in his view was the emergence of a form of consciousness whose very existence was sufficient to guarantee that it would realise itself historically. But Lukács need not detain us here, for his concern with subjectivity had little to do with human individuals.

The writings of Horkheimer, Marcuse and Habermas provide a more instructive case than those of Lukács. Grouped together into that entity known as critical theory they provide a central focus for this book so I shall limit my remarks on them here. They merit attention to the extent that they all witness an attempt to offer accounts of capitalism which include a notion of the domain of the cultural as a realm endowed with its own effectivity and requiring analysis in its own terms. They merit attention here also since such analyses are overtly based on a philosophy of the subject as a foundation for the analyses of domination. It is the interconnection of these two dimensions which makes them of particular interest. To characterise critical theory according to its barest features, it might be said to combine a radicalisation of Weber's analysis and critique of rational domination with a modernisation of historical materialism through shifting attention from the economic to the cultural sphere. This intersection of

Weberian and Marxist concerns was to produce a body of writing of immense vitality which has not subsided yet. But as an analysis of power it was also to result in a project which laboured under immense restrictions imposed by the commitment to a notion of essential subjectivity. The radicalisation of Weber's analyses consisted of maintaining a persistent critique of what Weber had described as rational domination. Capitalism was to be defined as essentially effecting a rationalisation of all spheres of social life. And the effects of this were seen to be a domination which had as its point of focus the essential subjectivity of individuals. This principle of essential subjectivity was to serve as a measure of the extent of existing patterns of domination, and also as that which founds and effects the abolition of domination. The self-affirmation of essential subjectivity would be the mechanism by means of which the rule of domination would be halted.

An examination of how the analysis of domination intersects with the notion of the subject in critical theory may hopefully provide a useful route towards understanding the ways in which power relations operate by deploying rather than repressing subjectivity. To say this, however, is not to side with the outright condemnations of critical theory which have come from the varied guardians of Marxist orthodoxy. One such example can be found in the writings of Therborn.[19] Armed with full Althusserian weaponry, Therborn detected in critical theory a double reduction of science and politics to philosophy, a denial of the scientific concepts of historical materialism. Perry Anderson[20] was to detect another failing. The clue to this lay in critical theory's implication within a phenomenon identified as 'Western Marxism'. The hallmark of western Marxism, and the reasons for its impoverishment according to Anderson, was its structural divorce from political practice. Critical theory in many respects was seen by Anderson to exemplify this degeneration of Marxism, although a host of other parties were indicted too. My concern in this study with critical theory is to explore the relations which exist between power and subjectivity. It is not to condemn in its entirety a project which has too many dimensions to aspire to deal with them all. This said, however, the analyses of domination undertaken across the quite different writings of Horkheimer, Marcuse and Habermas seem to me ultimately to founder. Their inability to examine the process of historical constitution and regulation of subjectivity is, I argue, a serious weakness to their analyses of cultural domination.

There are, of course, a vast range of debates and analyses of power beyond those already referred to. The most succinct treatment of them is provided by Steven Lukes.[21] The debate amongst sociologists which was to follow the publication of this book[22] indicates that there was felt to be something at stake in the struggle which developed over the adequacy of different conceptual analyses of power. There was, it is worth noting, little analysis of the functioning of power in this debate. The stakes concerned almost entirely the conceptual foundations for any such analysis. Lukes had proposed a view of the relationship between power and 'real interests'. He was to conclude that it was possible for power to be exercised over an individual or group against its preferences, but nevertheless in its real interests. This was a possibility at least in the short-term. Much conceptual discussion followed. Alternative conceptions were proposed. One version commended itself on its avoidance of 'structuralism' and 'voluntarism'.[23] A view was offered which was systematically determinist, and causal, but which did not reduce agency to the condition of a 'bearer' of the activity of extrinsic structures. Another version challenged the notion of interests as a general model of the mobilization of agents in particular practices and struggles.[24]

These various propositions for a conceptual analysis of power bear little relationship to my concern here with power and subjectivity. One central reason for this is that I argue that an interpretation of power as a capacity which functions through the promotion of regulated subjectivity cannot be reduced to a simple conceptual proposition. It can be understood only through a detailed examination of the historically and culturally varied range of regulatory practices of the self. It is quite likely that in the long run the very term power will prove to be inappropriate for such an investigation. For the present, however, it is perhaps adequate to register that a considerable distance separates a notion of power understood as the exercise by A of power over B, contrary to B's preferences, and a notion of power as a multiplicity of practices for the promotion and regulation of subjectivity.

One particular debate over power in recent times which took as central the question of subjectivity was that between Nicos Poulantzas, an Althusserian Marxist, and Ralph Miliband, a more empirically minded British political sociologist.[25] The debate was to prove lengthy and quite heated. It animated two philosophical traditions which were at odds with each other. The debate concerned the interpretation of the state as a system of power. Poulantzas proposed a view of the state as a set of objective structures, a system within which individuals were the 'bearers' (*Träger*). The state apparatus could not be viewed, Poulantzas argued, as reducible to interpersonal relations. The fault with Miliband's analysis, Poulantzas was to argue, lay in its commitment to a 'problematic of the subject'. Attacked in this way, Miliband defended his commitment to at least a partially intersubjective view of the state elite. Structural constraints could not, he argued, be viewed as reducing those who run the state to mere functionaries. This opposition was inevitable given the theoretical starting points of the adversaries. Unfortunately this was also to serve to lock the debate in a circular argument which each had already resolved for themselves. The debate was never opened up to take account of the possibility that the subjects who were being so intensely debated were themselves the product of a lengthy process of historical formation.

Some years later Poulantzas modified his denial that there might be something to be studied at the level of the various practices of subjectivity.[26] The adversary, however, was rather different. In a discussion of the researches of Michel Foucault he suggested that these were of considerable value. They may even, he went so far to say, help to enrich Marxism in a number of respects.[27] Their merit lay in the attention they gave to the disciplinary processes of normalisation as one aspect of power techniques. This was, however, as far as he was prepared to go. Despite their merits which he was willing to concede, Foucault's researches could only ever be seen as contributing to a project which was already inscribed in Marxist theory. The notion that they entailed a different and quite legitimate project was disallowed. Judged in this way they were viewed as constantly in danger of drifting into the dangerous waters of idealism. And they failed also because they refused to acknowledge where power 'really' came from. This origin of power was of course exploitation and the class struggle. It mattered little that such terms have throughout the history of Marxist analysis received little elaboration, and their role as determining forces has proved remarkably resistant to conceptual or empirical understanding. Marxist theory, as far as Poulantzas was concerned, specified a field of truth which had as one of its principal functions to judge other systems of thought, especially in cases where they seemed likely to effect a programming of a politics at odds with that of Marxism.

These are some of the ways in which the notion that one can investigate the question of power through the category of the subject has been addressed and also avoided. It has either been assiduously ignored, or confronted, and found to be wanting. Against this we now have at our disposal an immensely rich contribution to the study of the phenomenon of the subject in western societies in the shape of the works of Michel Foucault. Together they provide us with a series of investigations covering the emergence of psychiatry, medicine, the human sciences, the prison, sexuality, and technologies for the government of the self. Together these comprise the most outstanding contribution to our understanding of how the government of individuals in western societies operates through a variety of discourses and practices which seek to constitute human individuals as subjects, and to do so according to notions of truth. This has had the effect of enabling a displacement of interminable conceptual debates concerning subjectivity or power in favour of a series of investigations of the various knowledges and practices which seek to transform human beings into subjects, and to generate true knowledges of them. This concern with the category of the subject can, I argue, be viewed as the common thread which runs throughout Foucault's studies.

This preoccupation with the different modes of subjectification of individuals can be characterised as operating in three dimensions.[28] The first of these concerns those bodies of knowledge which address themselves to the human subject. This may be the speaking subject in *grammaire générale*, philology and linguistics. Or it may be the productive, labouring subject as studied in the analysis of wealth. Or it may be the living subject of natural history or biology. The second dimension concerns those practices which install a division of subjects of differing qualities. The subject here may be divided either inside himself or from others, as for instance in the divisions established between the sane and the mad, the healthy and the sick, the criminals and the non-criminals. The third dimension concerns the knowledges and techniques by means of which an individual may seek to transform him- or herself into a subject. This may be in the domain of sexuality, and the ways in which individuals have come to recognise themselves as subjects of sexuality. Or it may concern a more general set of techniques of the self, 'arts of existence' by which individuals come to fix for themselves rules of conduct and to regard themselves as singular beings. These practices have developed in religious as well as in educational, medical, industrial, and psychological practices.

Viewed in this way one can say that *it is not power but the subject and its truth* which defines the principal concern of

Foucault's various researches. Rather than a concern with rationalisation as a totalising phenomenon across western societies, Foucault's studies map out a concern with specific rationalities. The distinct fields in relation to which they develop – madness, ill-health, death, crime, sexuality, etc. – provide the principle of delimitation of such practices. This concern with the specific rationalities relating to the conduct of the subject has close affiliations to the studies of the historian and philosopher of science Georges Canguilhem of the concepts of life in the biological sciences. For Canguilhem the phenomenon of life as specified in the biological sciences was intimately related to concepts of the normativity of its cycle. It was also characterised by its specification of a veridical discourse over life,[29] practices governed by a norm which establishes the boundaries and conditions for the formulation of true propositions. This is something which is central to Foucault's preoccupation with the category of the subject, the notion that there are a range of 'truths' around which the subject lives his or her life. What separates Foucault's concern with the transformation of living individuals into subjects from Canguilhem's project is that Foucault has given considerably greater attention to the way in which such practices serve to constitute many of the foundations of the social relations we inhabit. Foucault's researches bring home forcefully how the promotion of subjectivity as a goal for individuals to seek and as an object of knowledge is central to the very formation of western modes of life. Whether one chooses to call this phenomenon power is, in the last instance, of little consequence.

Foucault's researches have profound implications also for the understanding of that phenomenon so dear to political theorists and sociologists – the state. It is of course true that Foucault has not provided us with a new theory of the state. But what has been missed by those who have eagerly seized on the absence of that key word in his writings is the fruitful new direction which has been opened up. The term *governmentality*[30] may serve to identify this new field of investigation. Emerging in the sixteenth century the art of government was linked to the development of the administrative apparatus of the great territorial monarchies. Viewed as a general form of management, government had the advantage of penetrating to the level of the daily activities of the citizen, whilst at the same time linking these to a perfection and intensification of the condition of the population. The question of how to govern oneself came to be linked to the question of how to govern others. Through the emergence of an art of government a new series of objectives was to be constructed for the management of states. The power of the ruler was to address itself to two related phenomena. Firstly, with each individual, their conduct and their aspirations. Secondly, with the population taken as a whole. The regulation of the conduct of the individual was to become linked in this manner to the objective of improving the condition of the population taken as a whole. This concern with practices and conceptions of government was something Foucault was to formulate only towards the end of his tragically foreshortened life. But it was linked closely to a theme he had identified earlier in examining the emergence of a 'politics of health' in the eighteenth century.[31] And it was linked also to the notion of bio-power he had formulated in the early part of his analysis of sexuality.[32] The 'calculated management of life' is the most succinct way of expressing this concern with the optimisation of the functioning of the individual as a condition for optimising the condition of the population as a whole.

The limited objective of this study is to examine the interrelation between notions of power and subjectivity. By a discussion of what I argue are two distinct traditions, I try to show how this distinctiveness hinges on a difference of approach to the concept of subjectivity. The discussion does not aspire to comprehensiveness in its coverage of the writings of critical theory or of Foucault. There are many other texts which fulfil this role very well. Its concern is more limited. Broadly speaking, I argue that the critical theory of Horkheimer, Marcuse and Habermas is restricted in its analysis of domination by an *a priori* commitment to the notion of subjectivity. I examine the writings of these three in turn, with a view to identifying the different notions of subjectivity which underlie their analyses of domination.

I argue that Horkheimer installs at the heart of the original project of critical theory a philosophical concern with the notion of subjectivity. Critical theory is thus defined from the outset not just as an analysis of cultural controls, construed within an historical materialist framework. These controls are viewed as bearing specifically on the subjectivity of the individual. Subjectivity is posited as an *a priori*, and the analysis which unfolds is of the domination of this subjectivity. The reverse of this is that liberation is depicted as the release of subjectivity.

Marcuse starts from a similar position, although he seeks a resolution of the binary dilemma of domination/liberation of subjectivity by means of a 'dialectical' solution derived from

Hegel. My argument is that this resolves nothing, and that Marcuse further compounds the problem by depicting the domination of the individual's subjectivity as total.

The writings of Habermas mark something of a new departure in the explanatory framework of critical theory. Specifically, they seek to introduce a 'linguistic turn' to critical theory. The focus of Habermas's work is not an isolated individual subjectivity, but *inter*subjectivity established through communication. This appears a promising formulation at first, but the content Habermas provides it with undercuts its potential for resolving the difficulties of the *a priori* of subjectivity as a basis for analysing mechanisms of domination. Habermas proposes a *universal* foundation for the communicative bases of social life, and this centres on the rational properties of individual subjects. Intersubjectivity is based on the realisation of the rational properties of individual subjects, which also provides for the possibility of cutting through systematic distortions of communication. The linguistic turn of critical theory is not as radical as might be assumed, and does not resolve the problems of earlier formulations of critical theory.

The works of Foucault provide an entirely different framework for understanding the notion of subjectivity and its position within analyses of power. This is one which is at odds with that of critical theory. Foucault's writings provide an epistemologically informed history, covering a wide range of bodies of knowledge and institutions. The notion of the subject is central to all these bodies of knowledge. Specified within them as principal object and as that of which knowledge is to be provided, the subject is caught within their operation. The subject is actively promoted within them as well, a 'liberation' which is also an entrapment. I argue that Foucault's writings provide a more fruitful account of the interrelation between power and subjectivity than those of critical theory. I illustrate my argument by a discussion firstly of *Histoire de la Folie*. I use the French edition for this rather than the drastically abridged English version since many misunderstandings have arisen on the basis of the latter. Madness appears in that work as one of the key mechanisms through which a society provides for itself a knowledge of those subjects who exist outside the boundaries of contractual relations. Rendered visible within the walls of the *Hôpital Général*, and later the asylum, as well as in 'the community', madness is both 'liberated' and ensnared by psychiatric knowledge. An external mode of access to the truth of the subjectivity of the individual locks us into an interminable project of seeking out who we are. Provided with an institutional site in the form of the asylum, a juridical guarantee and a rapidly developing conceptual structure, psychiatry developed in the nineteenth and twentieth centuries as a knowledge of the subjectivity of the individual, and as a means of promoting, directing and regulating this subjectivity.

In *The Birth of the Clinic* Foucault analyses what he refers to as a shift in the medical 'gaze', a transformation of the conceptual knowledge of medicine, its institutional sites of exercise, and the political conditions in relation to which medicine as a liberal profession developed. The knowledge of the individual in this work is viewed as intimately related to a 'politics of health', an emergent concern to know and to act on the health of the nation as a whole. To seek to obtain a knowledge of the individual is both a matter of deriving conceptual principles which address the individual as such, and of attributing to such knowledge a significance for the management of the resources of the nation as a whole.

In *The Order of Things* Foucault adopts an entirely different procedure, concerning himself exclusively with discourses – those which centre on life, labour and language. This restricted concern with discourses, and with the structural similarities between those discourses which centre on the human subject, marks it off from the other studies discussed here. In its concern with knowledges of the human subject *The Order of Things* is viewed, however, as a crucial element in the project of investigating the formation of a conceptual and practical ensemble, a *dispositif*, which has as its central concern to produce a knowledge of the individual subject.

Much of my concern in this book with Foucault's writings is with those which appeared before 1970. After that date his writings explicitly identify the issues of subjectivity and power as interlinked phenomena. *Discipline and Punish* and the three volumes of *The History of Sexuality* are all centrally concerned with bodies of knowledge and institutional sites for constructing, regulating and knowing the subjectivity of the individual. What emerges most strongly from these writings is that the subject is not simply dominated or repressed within such *dispositifs*. The subject appears rather as an entity which is created within and through the conceptual-practical operation of the prison or of the multitude of interventions directed toward the sexuality of the individual. Modes of punishment are as much concerned with discovering who the individual *is*, as are the various devices for exploring, knowing and regulating the sexuality of the individual.

Once again these studies illustrate clearly that at issue is not simply the domination of subjectivity, but the entrapment which derives from that conceptual, institutional and political project of producing and knowing the individual subject. Those studies of Foucault's discussed here provocatively alert us to the conceptual, institutional and political conditions of our culture which have resulted in subjectivity providing the ultimate datum of our existence as individuals.

The focus of this study on the writings of Horkheimer, Marcuse and Habermas on the one hand, and Foucault on the other, entails excluding much that is worthy of consideration. I do not propose to apologise for those I have left out. One has to choose, and the choice I have made seems to go some way toward meeting the limited objectives I have set myself here. I would have liked to have included much that I have left out. For example to broaden the coverage of critical theory. Also, to include not only Foucault's own writings but those of others who have utilised and developed his insights, whilst themselves contributing to the definition and elaboration of the project he was engaged on. This would have led me to a discussion of the writings of Robert Castel,[33] Jacques Donzelot,[34] Giovanna Procacci,[35] Pasquale Pasquino,[36] and many others. I have undertaken some aspects of this wider task elsewhere.[37] Perhaps a more urgent task, however, is to develop and utilise the new field of exploration which Foucault opened up. To identify this task I suggest we dispense with the term power and begin to talk instead of regulatory practices of the self. These concerns cannot be encapsulated within the notion of ideology. They are quite simply practices. And neither can they be said to deny the existence of the state. The emergence of practices for the regulation of the self can only be fully understood in relation to the emergence and transformation of the practices of management of the state. The perfection of each is the crucial condition for their joint development. As an object of study it suggests ways in which we might begin to understand the practices through which the state maintains a relationship with the selves of those individuals over which it has jurisdiction. This is not to deny that domination and force are inconsequential. It is to suggest simply that such factors do not cover the entirety of those practices which have produced our present. There are a number of other dimensions still relatively unexplored.

PART 1

CRITICAL THEORY

•

CHAPTER 1

MAX HORKHEIMER AND CULTURAL CRITIQUE

•

A classic statement of the initial project of critical theory is provided by Max Horkheimer in his article 'Traditional and critical theory' which appeared in the *Zeitschrift für Sozialforschung* in 1937.[1] This paper provides a useful point of departure here through the relation it identifies between the Cartesian and Kantian categories of ego and subjectivity, and the domination of individuals which it posits as the defining characteristic of twentieth century capitalism. With this starting point Horkheimer inscribes the issue of subjectivity at the heart of critical theory's concern with domination.

Traditional theory, Horkheimer argues, is represented in different ways by the works of Kant and Descartes. Kant's philosophy is held to mirror a society whose 'senseless wretchedness' appears as 'an unchangeable force of nature, a fate beyond man's control'.[2] Conversely, the philosophy of Descartes is depicted as 'ideology in the strict sense, for in it the limited freedom of the bourgeois individual puts on the illusory form of perfect freedom and autonomy.'[3]

Against both Kant and Descartes, Horkheimer argues that critical theory requires a philosophical account of subjectivity which is both materialist as well as 'critical'. Traditional theory, he suggests, is based on a form of scientific activity carried on within the division of labour at an advanced stage of development. It 'speaks not of what theory means in human life, but only of what it means in the isolated sphere in which for historical reasons it comes into existence.'[4] Critical theory, however, directs itself not at the scientist in an attempt to better equip him to carry out his task. Instead it addresses 'the knowing individual as such'.[5]

But it is not simply the epistemological conception of the subject in traditional philosophy which Horkheimer considers to be at fault. More importantly what is held to be required is a restructuring of the bifurcation in which the individual is considered to exist *vis-à-vis* bourgeois society. Society, Horkheimer argues, is an 'active subject', although as an unconscious one it is a subject only in an improper sense. In relation to society the 'individual sees himself as passive and dependent'.[6] Horkheimer attributes this difference in the existence of man and society to 'the cleavage which has up to now affected the historical forms of social life.'[7] Society, he argues, has never been the result of 'conscious spontaneity on the part of free individuals'.[8] However this separation between the individual and society is not absolute. Bourgeois society is seen to be characterised by the blindness of its activity, whereas that of individuals is held to possess a conscious and purposive element. But to the extent that social action entails knowledge and its application, Horkheimer argues that one must admit the existence of a restricted rationality, even in bourgeois society. Subject and object, man and nature cannot be regarded as entirely separate. The 'world of objects' does not confront the individual as entirely alien, but is 'in large measure produced by an activity that is itself determined by the very ideas which help the individual to recognise that world and to grasp it conceptually'.[9]

This distinction between an individual and a supra-individual level of social existence, Horkheimer argues, is expressed in an idealist form in Kant's separation of passive sensation and active understanding. This distinction is held to give rise to Kant's question of 'whence the understanding derives its assured expectation that the manifold given in sensation will always obey the rules of the understanding'.[10] Kant's reply, witnessing for Horkheimer both his idealism and the depth and honesty of his thinking, is to posit a 'supra-individual activity, of which the individual is unaware', but to do so 'in the idealist form of a consciousness-in-itself, that is a purely intellectual source'.[11] It is the 'theoretical vision available in his day' that is held to have prevented Kant from comprehending the real nature of the relation between the actions of individuals and the existence of society. Horkheimer argues that the limits imposed by idealism prevented Kant from grasping the process through which, in bourgeois society, the product of man's activity is separated from him. But Kant's philosophy is none the less held to contain a 'kernel of truth' in the contradictions which it establishes. Horkheimer argues that these mirror the contradictions of bourgeois society: 'The unresolved problem of the relation between activity and passivity, *a priori* and sense data, philosophy and psychology, is therefore not due to purely subjective insufficiency but is objectively necessary.'[12] The objectivity of bourgeois society and its 'reflection' in Kant's philosophy is seen to make the latter more than an ideology.

Central to Horkheimer's critical theory is a concern to provide a 'materialist' formulation to this question of the separation of the individual and society. The aim of his critical theory is to 'relativise' this separation, to relate the societal context in which men live to its origin in human action. This is held to give rise to the possibility of subjecting human action to 'planful decision and rational determination of goals'.[13]

The opposition of critical theory to traditional theory proposed by Horkheimer derives 'from a difference not so much of objects as of subjects'.[14] Critical thought starts from the assumption that the 'objective realities given in perception . . . should be under human control and, in the future at least, will in fact come under it'.[15] Horkheimer posits here the notion of a 'tension' which he argues is central to life in bourgeois society, a tension between 'the individual's purposefulness, spontaneity, and rationality, and those work-process relationships on which society is built'.[16] Critical theory entails 'a concept of man as in conflict with himself until this opposition is removed.'[17] To the extent that activity governed by reason is held to be proper to man, bourgeois society, for Horkheimer, is the negation of man's humanity.

Horkheimer's critical theory thus places a philosophy of the subject, albeit a putatively materialist one, at its heart. But the subject of critical theory is not the isolated autonomous individual. It is rather 'a definite individual in his real relation to other individuals and groups, in his conflict with a particular class, and, finally, in the resultant web of relationships with the social totality and with nature'.[18] The subject of critical thought is embedded in a 'concrete historical' process. And the unity of subject and object to which critical thinking aspires is located in the future. It is dependent on a transformation of the social structure itself. The 'subject' of critical theory is thus also the subject of this historical transformation. In Horkheimer's words, the activity of the subject 'is the construction of the social present'.[19]

Horkheimer's 1937 essay not only locates critical theory in relation to the Kantian and Cartesian notions of subjectivity. Avowedly Marxist at this point, although not perhaps to the extent that his explicit statements might suggest,[20] Horkheimer seeks to link this concern with subjectivity with the historical materialist principle of exchange value. In itself this general mechanism is not seen to be adequate as an account of contemporary capitalism. It is considered to provide simply a starting point for critical theory, from which it 'moves further, using all knowledge available and taking suitable material from the research of others as well as from specialized research'.[21]

The introduction of Marxist economic categories does not, however, indicate a separate set of concerns to those of the loss of the individual's subjectivity. They are seen rather as necessarily linked in that an economy dominated by exchange value is one in which the self-determination of the individual is denied. The fundamentally historical nature of Marx's analysis is taken as demonstration that this situation is not an eternal condition. But for the transition to a rational society actually to be achieved what is required is that mankind be capable of positing itself as a purposive subject. Such a shift, Horkheimer argues, requires 'an exercise of will power, in the knowing subject'.[22] Critical theory is directed toward the future, but this future can be installed only by the activity of a subject whose emergence is self-generating.

Critical theory is further differentiated from traditional theory by Horkheimer through the notion of 'necessity'. Critical theory, he suggests, begins with the postulate that the present era is dominated by the exchange relationship, and that this 'must necessarily lead to a heightening of those social tensions which in the present historical era lead in turn to wars and revolutions'.[23] But the concept of necessity as a part of critical theory must, Horkheimer argues, be distinguished from the notion of necessity within traditional theory. The latter refers, he argues, to the question of logical necessity alone, the deduction of real relations from universal concepts, a notion of necessity shared by critical and traditional theory.

There is, however, 'a decisive difference when it comes to the relation of subject and object and therefore to the necessity of the event being judged.'[24] For the scientific specialist, Horkheimer argues, either everything is necessary or nothing is necessary. The object of science, he suggests, is entirely separate from both the observer and his theory: 'The objective occurrence is independent of the theory, and this independence is part of its necessity: the observer as such can effect no change in the object.'[25] Critical theory, however, is itself an important component in the transformation of society, in the transformation of the object of critical theory. To understand the course of history as following necessarily from a particular economic mechanism is, Horkheimer argues, to imply a critique of that process. The critique is generated by that social order against which it is directed:

A consciously critical attitude, however, is part of the development

> of society: the construing of the course of history as the necessary product of an economic mechanism simultaneously contains both a protest against this order of things, a protest generated by the order itself, and the idea of self-determination for the human race, that is the idea of a state of affairs in which man's actions no longer flow from a mechanism but from his own decision. The judgement passed on the necessity inherent in the previous course of events implies here a struggle to change it from a blind to a meaningful necessity. If we think of the object of the theory in separation from the theory, we falsify it and fall into quietism or confirmism. Every part of the theory presupposes the critique of the existing order and the struggle against it along lines determined by the theory itself.[26]

Horkheimer's usage of the notion of necessity here is confusing. It refers to the emergence of critical theory itself at a particular historical moment. It refers also to the injunction which critical theory contains for mankind to become 'a conscious subject and actively determine its own way of life'.[27] The concept of necessity in critical theory is, Horkheimer argues, 'itself a critical concept; it presupposes freedom, even if a not yet existent freedom.'[28] Cartesian dualism is seen to be unable to encapsulate such a concept of necessity. For the dualist, Horkheimer argues, necessity refers 'only to events which he anticipates as probable'.[29] The 'idea of a theory which becomes a genuine force [is] beyond the grasp of a mentality typified by such a dualism.'[30] The traditional concept of necessity is fundamentally limited in that it is unable to take account of 'the unity of theory and practice',[31] the notion that there is a form of causality which is dependent on the subjectivity of mankind. It is, ultimately, to this subjectivity that critical theory addresses itself.

It may be useful to distinguish at this point the notion of subjectivity on which Horkheimer's project of critical theory is based from the principle embodied in Lukács' notion of a class-subject,[32] and from Lenin's adherence to the notion of a vanguard party as bearer of a new social order.[33] Horkheimer appeals to a subjectivity, immanent, yet susceptible to the activity of the critical intellectual. The subjectivity which is to bring about this new social order does not emerge from the dialectic of history itself (Lukács), or from a scientific perception (Lenin) which endows an elite with the right to direct the course of history. The goal of critical intellectual activity is the creation of new relations of production which are viewed as the embodiment of a rational organisation of human activity. It is this rational organisation, and the potential for it which resides in mankind, which for Horkheimer is capable of both releasing and realising mankind's potentialities.

Horkheimer's 1937 essay is thus both a critique of certain economic relations and an avowedly philosophical enterprise. Critical theory, Horkheimer argues 'has continued to be a philosophical discipline even when it engages in a critique of the economy.'[34] Whilst addressing itself primarily to the economy as 'the first cause of wretchedness' it refuses to 'judge the future forms of society solely according to their economy'.[35] It is toward the sphere of 'culture' just as much as 'the economy' that critical theory is to look in the search for a rational and humane society. And 'culture' here is an intrinsically philosophical domain, to the extent that its production is obstructed without the requisite subjective attributes existing within mankind.

SUBJECTIVE AND OBJECTIVE REASON

Horkheimer's *Eclipse of Reason* was published in America in 1947. It is common to take this work, along with *Dialectic of the Enlightenment* which was published in the same year, as evidence of the shift within critical theory brought about by the previous decade spent in the United States.[36] For my concerns here, however, it is the continuity which it witnesses with Horkheimer's earlier concerns which is of interest.

In *Eclipse of Reason* Horkheimer employs a distinction between objective and subjective reason as the basis for a specification of what is both possible and desirable. Subjective reason, Horkheimer argues, is 'essentially concerned with means and ends, with the adequacy of procedures for purposes more or less taken for granted and supposedly self-explanatory. It attaches little importance to the question whether the purposes as such are reasonable.'[37] Against this, objective reason asserts 'the existence of reason as a force not only in the individual mind but also in the objective world – in relations among human beings and between social classes, in social institutions.'[38] Necessity and freedom are again, as in the 1937 article,[39] firmly connected in the tension held to be produced under specific social relations. The classical philosophical origins of such a project are openly proclaimed in its affinities with Plato's *Republic* which attempted 'to prove that he who lives in the light of objective reason also lives a successful and happy life.'[40] Objective reason turns one's attention to a focus on 'the idea of the greatest good, on the problem of human destiny, and on the way of realisation of ultimate goals'.[41]

Again, the dissatisfaction with a particular philosophical principle is due not merely to its lack of internal coherence or adequacy. Rather, the increasing technical control held to be exerted over both nature and man is seen to result in the dominance of subjective reason over objective reason. The theme of such a critique is the not unfamiliar one of the irrationality of contemporary reason. Reason in the present is seen to renounce 'even the task of passing judgements on man's action and way of life'.[42] Echoing in many respects, and despite the evident differences, not only the Lukácsian theme of reification,[43] but also the comments of those such as Weber,[44] Scheler,[45] and possibly even Oakeshott,[46] Horkheimer castigates the 'subjectivization and formalization of reason'.[47] Through such a process Horkheimer argues, thought is reduced to the level of industrial production, epitomised in the attempt by pragmatism to develop this condition into a philosophical system. This has led, Horkheimer argues, to a substitution of 'the logic of probability for that of truth'.[48] In subjecting everything to the law of calculation of the chain of means and effects, pragmatist philosophy is viewed by Horkheimer as the counterpart to modern industrialism. It leads ultimately 'to a system of prohibition of thinking . . . that must end finally in subjective stupidity'.[49]

The significance of this distinction between subjective and objective reason for Horkheimer's conception of the capacities of mankind as constitutive subject is that the reduction of reason to mere coordinating activity is seen to have had its effects at this level also. The transformation of 'each and every realm of being into a field of means leads to the liquidation of the subject who is supposed to use them'.[50] The subjectivisation of reason is paralleled by a denial of the specifically human capacity for rational action:

> The human being, in the process of his emancipation, shares the fate of the rest of the world. Domination of nature involves domination of man. Each subject not only has to take part in the subjugation of external nature, human and non-human, but in order to do so must subjugate nature in himself.[51]

The diversity of available means operates in such a manner as to prevent any correlate possibility of selection of ends. The increasing independence of the individual which this plethora of options produces leads paradoxically to a 'parallel increase of passivity'. The end product is the individual who has now 'become witless' and who 'reacts automatically, according to general patterns of adaptation'.[52] This process is held to extend even to that most 'private' of spheres – sexuality. Industrialism, Horkheimer argues, 'tends more and more to subject sex relations to social domination.'[53] The sphere of the erotic is confined in the present to the realm of marriage by those same powerful agencies that control the administration and marketing of industrial products.

The 'inversion of reason' which Horkheimer takes as the defining characteristic of industrial society is not posed exclusively in terms of the subversion of use value as abstract structuring principle of the economy. It is rather the inversion of reason as instrument of the self which is central. The irrationality of contemporary reason has made the individual the instrument of that irrational rationality, thereby depriving him of that which essentially defines his status as individual – his subjectivity and latent capacity for autonomous thought:

> When we speak of the individual as a historical entity, we mean not merely the space-time and the sense existence of a particular member of the human race, but, in addition, his awareness of his own individuality as a conscious human being.[54]

Horkheimer reaffirms his opposition to the 'abstract' individual of 'bourgeois' philosophy as a philosophical first principle stated in his 1937 article. But this is not an outright opposition to the *a priori* specification of the capacities of subjectivity. Instead what is proposed is a materialist inflection to the category of subjectivity which Horkheimer identifies in Socratic as well as Kantian and Cartesian philosophy.

Horkheimer suggests that the Socratic notion of the individual, for whom conscious choice is a 'prerequisite of the ethical way of life' elevates the individual to 'the highest of all ideas'.[55] But it fails, he argues, adequately to account for the individual's inseparability from the community. Rejecting the notion of the absolutely isolated individual as an illusion, the categories of freedom and justice which Horkheimer seeks to retain are viewed as 'social as well as individual virtues'.[56] The freedom of the individual is conceivable only in the context of a rationally ordered society.

The atomisation of society which Horkheimer argues is distinctive of the present is held to reach its peak in the phenomenon of mass culture. The question which this poses Horkheimer is whether this has produced a 'liquidation of the individual'.[57] Horkheimer is equivocal on this point, yet still declares his hope that the individual will be able to 'transcend his actual position in reality'.[58] But whereas previously it was the individual as member of a group which Horkheimer focussed on,[59] here the question of resistance is posed in terms of the isolated individual.

> There are still some forces of resistance left within man. It is evidence against social pessimism that despite the continuous assault of collective patterns, the spirit of humanity is still alive, if not in the individual as a member of social groups, at least in the individual as far as he is left alone.[60]

On this basis Horkheimer affirms his hope in 'a new era in which individuality may re-emerge as an element in a less ideological and more humane form of existence.'[61] This is not, however, a return to the Cartesian absolute ego or to the Socratic individual. Horkheimer's attempt to avoid falling into a philosophical dualism can be seen by examining his account of the relation between spirit and nature.

Rejecting what he terms the 'formalistic method' which entails either an ultimate dualism or a monism, Horkheimer regards as impermissible any ontological 'First' decision:

> The real difficulty in the problem of the relation between spirit and nature is that hypostatizing the polarity of these two entities is as impermissible as reducing one of them to the other.[62]

The solution, Horkheimer suggests, resides in 'the separateness and the interrelatedness of the two concepts'.[63] To elevate one to the status of absolute is to fail to grasp that 'their duality too must be largely understood as a product.'[64] It is within these terms that Horkheimer argues the distinction between objective and subjective reason must be viewed. The relation between spirit and nature, subject and object, and subjective and objective reason, are commensurable in that they all entail a fundamental opposition subsisting within an overall unity. Neither of these poles can eliminate the other, yet their antagonism establishes the possibility of the realisation of a genuine reason as a concrete social reality. The present is marked by the triumph of subjective reason in the form of a universalised means-end calculability which has as its correlate the suppression of those properties of the subject which define the very principle of subjectivity. Neither an absolute 'passivity' of the individual nor an absolute 'autonomy'. Instead Horkheimer postulates a 'dialectical' tension between passivity and constitutivity which makes the latter an historical possibility.

But it is difficult to see how the Marxian dialectic[65] can achieve the supersession of the formal separation of subject and object of 'bourgeois' philosophical discourse. The omnipresence of subjective reason entails that its effects can be evaluated only in terms of the absence of objective reason or the 'passivity' of the individual subject. And the transformation toward which Horkheimer's critical theory is directed can be understood only in terms of an individual subjectivity which announces itself and at the same time heralds the implementation of a truly rational social order, the inauguration of the time of objective reason. That Horkheimer adheres to the dictates of his argument can be seen in his specification of the two necessary aspects of a 'self-critique of reason'.

First, he argues that it is necessary 'that the antagonism of reason and nature is in an acute and catastrophic phase'.[66] Second, that it presupposes 'that at this stage of complete alienation the idea of truth is still accessible.'[67] A direct inverse relation is posited between the extent to which individuality is an existent force within society, and the extent of the oppression produced by industrialism. Indeed it is precisely through this relation of opposition that the possibility of change derives. It is 'the decline of the idea of the individual under the impact of the all-embracing machinery of mass culture which creates the prerequisites of the emancipation of reason.'[68] It is out of the suppression of individuality that develops the subjectivity of mankind as a force capable of transcending the present domination:

> At all times, the good has shown the traces of the oppression in which it originated. Thus the idea of the dignity of man is born from the experience of barbarian forms of domination.[69]

The contribution which critical theory can make in this situation is that of a 'denunciation of everything that mutilates mankind and impedes its free development'.[70] That which is negated in the present serves both as measure and instrument of its implementation. The role of critical theory is one of postulating that 'the notion of the dignity of the individual is one of the ideas defining a humane organization of society.'[71] The function of critical theory is to serve as 'reminder', or mild stimulus, to those that still have the capacity to 'see through' current forms of domination.

By 1957, in an essay entitled 'The concept of man'[72] Horkheimer was expressing a view similar to that which Marcuse would voice a decade later:

> The factors in the contemporary situation – population growth, a technology that is becoming fully automated, the centralization of economic and therefore political power, the increased rationality of the individual as a result of his work in industry – are inflicting upon life a degree of organization and manipulation that leaves the individual only enough spontaneity to launch himself onto the path prescribed for him.[73]

This had profound consequences for the very concept of man appropriate to such an era:

> The word 'man' no longer expresses the power of the subject who can resist the status quo, however heavily it may weigh upon him.[74]

Horkheimer develops this argument into a wholesale critique of industrial society. The intelligence of man who invented the machine is, he argues, becoming like the machines themselves in its constant adaptation to precisely prescribed tasks. The effect of this is passivity, an increasing powerlessness of individuals in relation to society and themselves. In the essay 'Threats to Freedom'[75] Horkheimer develops this theme of the diminishment of the freedom of the individual. In the areas of the economy, the family, education, politics and other spheres of daily life, this has occurred. What is decisive, he argues, is 'the shift of subjectivity from the individual to the collectivity: the clique, the professional caste, the party, the nation.'[76] The individual has, in all these areas, been deprived of subjectivity.

SUBJECTIVITY AND DOMINATION

Now the point in identifying this interrelation between the categories of subjectivity and domination in Horkheimer's work has not been merely to repeat a charge of essentialism or humanism. Such a 'verdict' on critical theory clarifies little with regard to its overall project. It fails also to distinguish those elements which may have proved to have been more of a hindrance than a productive strand of an overtly 'critical' project. My concern here is rather with Horkheimer's general attempt to provide a philosophical account of the question of domination in twentieth century capitalism. In this respect what is interesting are the difficulties which one encounters when issues as diverse as the organisation of the work process and sexual relations are posed in terms of a philosophy of the subject.

The problems entailed in specifying the field of effects of domination in this manner are, I suggest, twofold. Firstly, subjectivity acts both as measure of the extent of existing repression, as well as the basis for a break with the present. It is precisely its absence which requires that it function as measure. And it is this absence which dictates also the need for its intervention. Horkheimer attempts to turn this circularity to his advantage in the notion of the 'tension' which he posits between the present and the possible. Yet it is only its 'absence' which permits Horkheimer to invoke subjectivity as measure of the irrationality of the present. Manifestations of the 'tension' Horkheimer posits are not easy to identify. Despite his attempt to provide a 'dialectical' account of subjectivity, Horkheimer's account remains governed by a binary principle of either presence or absence, realisation or repression.

This binary opposition of presence/absence is connected with the second important difficulty which I suggest Horkheimer's account gives rise to, namely the totalising and societal manner in which domination is seen to operate. Horkheimer's critique of domination is more a diagnosis of an entire society than a careful sifting of its components, a demonstration of their connections and interdependencies. I suggest that this is not simply a consequence of the level of generality of Horkheimer's account. In so far as the analysis of particular institutions is carried out in terms of the social totality, and the absence or presence of constitutive subjectivity, then the analysis of domination becomes a matter of identifying the repression of the defining attributes of such a subjectivity. Domination produces nothing other than a series of negative effects located at the level of a certain realm of philosophically conceived capacities of subjectivity. Substantive analysis can be read off from the societal diagnosis and the philosophical premise.

This interdependence between the concepts of subjectivity and domination, and its effects at the level of the analysis of particular agencies within the overall web of domination, can be usefully examined by looking at Horkheimer's contribution to the collective work *Studien über Autorität und Familie* (1936).[77]

The problem of authority and the family occupies an important place in Horkheimer's account of domination. It is, he argues, central to 'the overall role of particular cultural spheres and their changing structural interrelationships in the maintenance or dissolution of given forms of society.[78] Such an account cannot be lightly dismissed as Therborn would wish under the convenient rubric of 'idealism'.[79] Indeed Horkheimer's analysis here might rather be viewed as a genuine materialism, at least in aspiration, in according to the 'cultural' sphere a decisive weight *vis-à-vis* the economy:

> To regard the economic process as a determining ground of events means that one considers all other spheres of life in their changing relationships to it and that one conceives this process itself not in its isolated mechanical form but in connection with the specific capabilities and dispositions of men, which have, of course, been developed by the economic process itself.[80]

A notion of culture as either the 'cement' which holds society together, or as a contributory factor in the dissolution of the society, is erected against both an economism and against any reduction of the reproduction of society to the force of naked coercion as exercised by the state:

> The materialist view, then, maintains that cultural arrangements and processes, in all areas of life, in so far as they influence the character and behaviour of men at all, are conservative or disruptive factors in the dynamism of society. Either they provide the mortar of the building under construction, the cement which artificially holds together the parts that tend towards independence, or they are part of the forces which will destroy the society.[81]

Also rejected is any proposal that the cultural apparatus 'serves in large measure only to interiorize or at least rationalize and supplement physical coercion.'[82] What Horkheimer terms the 'psychic apparatus' is formed by 'mediating institutions' such as the family, school and church, and has, he argues 'its own laws'.[83] As such it cannot be regarded as simply an extension of state power.

Wary of providing a general definition of authority which is empty of content Horkheimer attempts to clarify the terms according to which an account of authority relations within the family are to be examined. Authority, he argues, is 'a central category for history'.[84] It is through authority that 'men's drives and passions, their characteristic dispositions and reaction-patterns are stamped by the power-relationships under which the social life-process unfolds at any time.'[85] The presence of authority is indicated, much as it is for Weber, in those 'internal and external behaviours in which men submit to an external source of command'.[86] Authority is 'accepted dependence', and may 'imply a relationship which fosters progress, is in the interests of all parties, and favors the development of human powers.'[87] But perhaps more importantly for the project of critical theory 'it can also sum up in one word all those social relationships and ideas which have long since lost their validity, are now artificially maintained, and are contrary to the true interests of the majority.'[88]

However this general characterisation of authority cannot, Horkheimer argues, substitute for 'an analysis of the social situation in its totality'.[89] Its significance, he suggests, can be appreciated only in the precise historical context in which it operates. Under advanced capitalism what this entails is an account in terms of 'the camouflaging of authority as it actually operates for the worker.'[90] Horkheimer's attempt to produce not simply a materialist, but more precisely an historical materialist account of authority is evident here. Authority is to be understood in relation to the concepts of mode of production and social classes:

> Even the apparently independent vocational and private relationships of men are determined by the dependence which is grounded in the mode of production and finds expression in the existence of social classes.[91]

The product of this dependence is presented in terms of the familiar figure of the individual who considers himself to be free yet accepts the parameters within which he pursues his own interests as given. Individuals, Horkheimer argues, 'think they are acting freely, whereas in fact the basic traits of the social order remain uninfluenced by such isolated beings'.[92] This means that men 'continue to accept and confirm where they might be shapers'.[93] And the crucial area in which they might be 'shapers' is that which concerns the direction and regulation of the work process. To be 'shapers' in this sphere would allow men to design 'human relations generally in a reasonable way, that is, according to a unified plan in the interests of the generality'.[94] Such work would still be 'disciplined', yet according to the limitations of 'nature' rather than those of opposed class interests:

> In disciplined work men will take their place under an authority, but

> the authority will only be carrying out the plans that men have made and decided to implement. The plans themselves will no longer be the result of divergent class interests, for the latter will have lost their foundation and been converted into communal effort.[95]

It is within the context of authority relations established *vis-à-vis* the work process that Horkheimer locates the role of the family. It is, Horkheimer argues, one of the most important formative agencies for a specific type of authority-oriented conduct on which the bourgeois order depends. The family is a crucial functional element for those relations of dependence constituted outside it in the work-place.

Yet at the same time as denoting the family as a sphere separate from the work process, Horkheimer seems unwilling to accord it a mode of regulation of behaviours and an effectivity specific to it. The domination which takes place within the family remains secondary with respect to the domination characteristic of the economy. The domain of 'family life' is thus doubly barred from an effectivity proper to it. On the one hand through the primacy of the economy. On the other hand through the specification of relations of authority as bearing on and repressing a realm of philosophically conceived capacities of subjectivity.

But if this were all that one could say of Horkheimer's work in this respect there would be little point in following through the manner in which he confronts these questions. What makes Horkheimer's study of authority in the family of interest here is its attempt to pose the question of domination in a manner which both utilises and partially breaks with an historical materialist theoretical framework. In so doing the issue of authority as a substantive aspect of social life is raised as at least a possible field of enquiry and explanation in its own right. It is this possibility which concerns me here, although I argue that it is ultimately subverted through the terms in which it is posed.

The relation of individuals to authority is, Horkheimer argues, 'determined by the special character of the work process in modern times'.[96] This in turn is held to give rise to 'a lasting collaboration of social institutions in producing and consolidating the character types which correspond to the relationship.'[97] Domination in the present era has the appearance of an eternal and self-reproducing feature of social life. Within this network the family, Horkheimer suggests, has a 'very special place'. It is a crucial functional component of the different relations through which is produced the appropriate authority-oriented behaviour for twentieth century capitalism:

> The family, as one of the most important formative agencies, sees to it that the kind of human character emerges which social life requires, and gives this human being in great measure the indispensable adaptability for a specific authority-oriented conduct on which the existence of the bourgeois order largely depends.[98]

This is witnessed most acutely, Horkheimer suggests, in the periods of the Reformation and absolutism where obedience is increasingly valued for its own sake, and not as a means of reaching beatitude. The aim here is that of breaking the self-will of the child and ensuring that 'the innate desire for the free development of his drives and potentialities is to be replaced by an internalized compulsion towards the unconditional fulfillment of duty.'[99] The family is defined in such a period through its conscious goal of ensuring submission to authority.

Horkheimer argues that demand for immediate obedience to authority is replaced in the 'liberalist' period by the introduction of the principle of reason: 'No longer is it obedience that is immediately demanded, but, on the contrary, the application of reason.'[100] Anticipated in the Protestant conception of the family the father's superior physical strength becomes a moral fact to be respected. *De facto* strength is the basis for the *de jure* authority of the father. To be respected through the application of one's reason to the prevailing conditions of life. In this familial situation Horkheimer argues that 'we find anticipated in large measure the structure of authority as it existed outside the family.'[101] The child's respect for the father through the application of reason is 'his first training for the bourgeois authority relationship'.[102]

Yet Horkheimer acknowledges also that the family has amply demonstrated its inability effectively to carry out those functions he attributes to it. It is, he suggests, increasingly inadequate in the face of the contradictions and crises of the society in which it exists. But whilst conceding this he fiercely rebuts any suggestion that the family could be fundamentally modified within the existing cultural structure. As a functional component within bourgeois society it 'cannot be changed without change in the total social framework'.[103] Attempts to improve the whole beginning with the parts are 'parochial' and 'utopian' and simply distract attention away from more important tasks. The family, despite its 'relative autonomy and capacity for resistance' is itself in a subordinate position *vis-à-vis* 'society as a whole'.[104] It is not strictly a 'component' of the social totality understood as an organic whole, but rather a sphere separate from, or additional to that totality. Power and domination in 'public life' are not only supported by the family, but are also 'reflected in a more tolerable discipline within the home'.[105] To yield to paternal power within the family is both 'rational' and equivalent to accepting as given those property relationships dominant in the wider society. Growing up within the restrictive sphere of the family is merely preparation for those authority-relations which the child will confront in later life.

The family does, however, provide some specific characteristics which are central to 'the authority-oriented character'. Instead of helping to explain individual failure in terms of wider social causes, the family plays a positive role, through the authority of the father, in maintaining the explanation of failure at the level of the individual. The outcome of 'such paternal education is men who without ado seek the fault in themselves'.[106] The family is active in obstructing the development of an image of an alternative form of society which would not require the 'compulsive sense of guilt' characteristic of the present. Horkheimer quotes Nietzsche approvingly: 'You think you're looking for the "truth"?' says Nietzsche. 'You're looking for a leader and prefer to be given orders!'[107] This 'impulse of submission' is not an eternal force but rather, Horkheimer argues, 'a phenomenon emerging essentially from the limited bourgeois family'.[108] As long as there is no fundamental restructuring of social life 'the family will continue to exercise its indispensable function of producing specific, authority-oriented types of character.'[109] The family has a 'fundamental role' as actual 'creator' of the form of authority-oriented conduct necessary to the bourgeois order.

But the family, Horkheimer suggests, is related also to the other elements in the cultural complex in an antagonistic manner. If it is a functional complement to the authority of the work process Horkheimer is unwilling to view it as a smoothly functioning and homogeneous entity. The dream of a perfect instrument of domination is far from realised in the modern family, and even in the 'golden age' of the bourgeois period the individual could find sanctuary from the market relationships of the economy. Within the family 'the individual always had the possibility there of living not as a mere function but as a human being.'[110] The family not only produces 'authority-oriented' conduct, but 'also cultivates the dream of a better condition for mankind'.[111]

Hegel distinguished 'womanliness' as the principle of love for the whole person from 'manliness' as the principle of civic subordination.[112] To this Horkheimer adds the Engelsian theme of the overthrow of mother right as 'the world historical defeat of the female sex'.[113] And from this he suggests that it is the maternal presence within the family which is largely responsible for the preservation of genuinely human relations:

> Because it still fosters human relations which are determined by the woman, the present-day family is a source of strength to resist the total dehumanization of the world and contains an element of anti-authoritarianism.[114]

But the dependent situation of woman within the family and in society as a whole ensures that the 'humanising' role of women can never realise itself as a structuring principle either of the family or of the social whole. Indeed the role of women within the family operates to strengthen the authority of the male, which in turn provides support for authority-oriented conduct. It is not only the concern of the male for the status quo which leads to accommodation to existing authority relationships. Equally important is 'the constant spoken or tacit urging of his wife'.[115]

Contradictory and antagonistic the functioning of the family may well be. None the less Horkheimer's account of the role of the family in producing authority-oriented behaviours takes these antagonistic elements as subverted through the position of the family *vis-à-vis* the wider social field. Avowedly opposed to any suggestion that the family is a 'single and uniform reality' Horkheimer is, however, unable to incorporate this contradictory functioning within the general account of domination he seeks to provide. The 'authority-promoting function of the family'[116] is still conceived in his account as a generalised societal process which implicates the family by extension only. The family may be an important aspect in the production of a particular type of authority-oriented conduct. But those relations which it helps to support are always located in Horkheimer's account at the level of the 'cultural totality'. The general question of authority is in principle a societal issue which operates 'essentially at the particular, concrete level of the family'.[117] But that which occurs at the level of the family is always limited to the promotion of a form of authority which is constitutive of the bourgeois social order itself. The family is not successfully incorporated within such an account as a wholly 'social' sphere, productive of its own specific effects. It is located only in relation to a form of authority which is used to identify an entire historical epoch in all its manifestations.

It has been suggested above that 'authority' in Horkheimer's account, despite the bold sweep of his field of enquiry, returns ultimately to a notion of the repression of a realm of philosophically conceived subjective attributes, albeit located at a number of different levels of the cultural whole. I suggest that this theme of the repression of subjective attributes is closely linked with the notion of authority relations which operate in the family as only bearing on the level of the 'cultural totality'. If, as I suggest, domination ultimately serves merely to inhibit or prevent the emergence of a subjectivity which would be constitutive of new and different social relations, then the family can do no more than function as one element within such a societal process. The family as producer of authority-oriented conduct is necessarily restricted within such a framework to reinforcing and producing those behaviours required at the level of the cultural whole. For Horkheimer to propose in Hegelian terms that what emerges from this is a 'dialectical totality of universality, particularity, and individuality'[118] is not entirely accurate. The 'unity of antagonistic forces' which Horkheimer hopes to encapsulate in such a formulation cannot be achieved successfully since no basis is provided for the 'antagonisms' to operate within. They either succeed in securing a certain form of societal authority relations or they fail. But they cannot produce a mode of 'successful' functioning which is itself contradictory. This for Horkheimer would perhaps be a 'utopian' suggestion which failed to capture the role of the family as 'reflecting' authority relations in public life. The only 'contradiction' possible in Horkheimer's account is that which he identifies between a repressed and a liberated subjectivity. As I suggested above the 'tension' which he posits between these two states is only asserted and never demonstrated. Despite his attention to the family as a sphere of social life central to the maintenance of existing authority relations, these latter are not endowed with an effectivity which enables them to be understood other than in terms of the notion of constitutive subjectivity.

CHAPTER 2

HERBERT MARCUSE AND SUBJECTIVITY AS NEGATION

•

Marcuse's writings attained a greater popularity outside German-speaking countries than those of other critical theorists, particularly in the 1960s and 1970s. Aside from his better known texts such as *One-dimensional Man* he contributed much to the attempt to elaborate a philosophical foundation for critical theory. In this chapter I examine Marcuse's proposals for a 'dialectical' account of subjectivity. Marcuse installs, as does Horkheimer, the issue of subjectivity at the heart of his proposals for a critical theory. These owe much to a 'materialist' reading of Hegel. I discuss also Marcuse's account of domination in Western industrial societies. I argue that Marcuse is unsuccessful in his attempt to avoid what he regards as an idealist category of subjectivity. I suggest that the separation of subject and object, regarded by Horkeimer and Marcuse as one of the defining features of 'bourgeois' philosophy, is retained by Marcuse in his notion of subjectivity. The notion of subjectivity remains in Marcuse's writings as a set of *a priori* attributes, a capacity for originary action, which can only emerge through an act of self-affirmation. I argue that Marcuse's account of domination and his proposals for a dialectical notion of subjectivity are interdependent. Domination for Marcuse is the repression of subjectivity, liberation its release. I suggest that Marcuse's account of domination is limited by its dependence on a notion of the repression of subjectivity. This has effects also, I argue, for the process of liberation to which critical theory is addressed.

Before examining Marcuse's account of the notion of subjectivity it may be useful to sketch the outlines of the arena of philosophical debate into which he regards critical theory as entering. As with Horkheimer, Marcuse identifies Kant's transcendental philosophy, and the associated belief that individuals could become rational and free within the established order, as the principal philosophical opponent. Marcuse identifies this position as coterminous with 'bourgeois' philosophy, and as mirroring the society in which it arises.

This theme emerges clearly in an early discussion of Marcuse's of the notion of essence.[1] The concept of essence, Marcuse argues, whilst a perennial feature of philosophy, is subject to a historical development. At the inception of the bourgeois era, he argues, the concept of essence is located at the level of the critical autonomy of rational subjectivity whose role is to 'establish and justify the ultimate essential truths on which all theoretical and practical truth depends.'[2] At the close of this era, however, 'knowledge of essence has primarily the function of binding the critical freedom of the individual to pregiven, unconditionally valid necessities.'[3] The concept of essence, Marcuse argues, has 'followed a course leading from autonomy to heteronomy, from the proclamation of the free, rational individual to his surrender to the powers of the authoritarian state'.[4]

Prior to Descartes and the advent of 'modern philosophy', in the thought of Plato, the idea or *eidos* is seen to have provided a criterion by means of which existence could be compared to essence, to what existence *could* be. It possessed, that is, an 'ethical' dimension which ensured its retention of a fundamentally critical relation with the present. But with Descartes, Marcuse argues, the self-certainty of the *ego cogitans* and the assertion of the sovereignty of individuals against the relations of dependence in which they exist announces the reduction of the concept of essence to one of logic and epistemology. The 'thoroughly contradictory' nature of Cartesian philosophy is held to be contained in its affirmation of absolute freedom in the face of economic relations of dependence which are established 'behind the backs' of individuals.[5]

Rather than simply admonish the 'abstractness' of the Cartesian *ego cogito*, Marcuse takes this abstractness as indicative of 'the historical veracity of Cartesian philosophy'.[6] That freedom for Descartes is freedom of thought only is necessarily the case in an epoch where 'reason must disregard not only the given form of spatio-temporal existence, but even the concrete content of thought at any time, and retain only thought as such, the pure form of all *cogitationes*.'[7] Cartesian philosophy, unwittingly perhaps, is for Marcuse the truth of the bourgeois world.

Horkheimer had stressed the shift which can be detected when one passes from Descartes to Kant.[8] Foucault also identifies a similar distance between these two co-ordinates of Western philosophy, although for quite different reasons.[9] For Marcuse the transition of the concept of essence from autonomy to heteronomy achieves its most developed form in the work of Kant. With Kant, reason is confined to the understanding and can never be realised in experience. Two separate domains are established such that freedom 'can exercise its causality on the empirical world only insofar as the world has no effect whatsoever on it'.[10] The causality of reason cuts off the possibility of the empirical world affecting the intelligible essence of men. With this development the subjective idealism of the bourgeois era is held to resign its critical intent and contribute to the ideology of domination. In this situation, Marcuse argues, philosophy 'necessarily surrenders its rationally critical character and becomes heteronomous'.[11]

It is against such a fate that Marcuse proposes a materialist and critical theory. Its point of departure is the requirement to develop a dialectical account of the relationship between essence and appearance. Central here is the discussion of Hegel in *Reason and Revolution*. Although Hegel's theory of essence is seen as ultimately transcendental, it is held to contain also the elements for a dynamic and historical theory of essence which places at the centre of the analysis a tension between potentiality and actuality. Crucial to the task of developing such an account is the question of 'the essence of man. Concern with man moves to the center of theory; man must be freed from real need and real misery to achieve the liberation of becoming himself.'[12]

The critical theory which Marcuse advocates imposes a double injunction with regard to its attempted break with 'bourgeois philosophy'. Firstly, there is dictated 'a complete change in its subject, which is no longer the isolated, abstract individual at the basis of idealist philosophy.'[13] Its concepts are not to be those of a transcendental philosophy but rather 'are generated by the consciousness of specific groups and individuals who are part of the fight for a more rational organisation of society'.[14] An overtly 'historical' project which focusses on the conditions under which particular groups emerge. Secondly, the relation between potentiality and actuality, the mode in which the realisation of subjectivity is to be achieved, is to be thought of as a *dialectical* relationship. Hence 'Materialist theory takes up the concept of essence where philosophy last treated it as a dialectical concept – in Hegel's *Logic*.'[15] An overtly 'philosophical' project then also. Or rather a project in which the philosophical component is to be located in determinate historical conditions.

REASON, REVOLUTION AND SUBJECTIVITY

It is principally in *Reason and Revolution* (1941) that Marcuse seeks to locate in the work of Hegel the emergent outlines of a 'dialectical' account of subjectivity. Against the isolated ego of 'bourgeois philosophy' Hegel's writings, from his early theological works to the *Science of Logic*,[16] are seen as providing the basis for a materialist account of subjectivity which fuses the autonomy of the subject with the practical task of installing a social order governed by reason. Reason and revolution are two aspects of a single project to which the critical theorist addresses himself.

Central to the departure which Hegel's philosophy is held to represent *vis-à-vis* previous dualist philosophical systems is his formulation of the concept of reason. Marcuse argues that Hegel's notion of reason opens onto 'the material strivings for a free and rational order of life'.[17] Derived from it is a structure of concepts – freedom, subject, mind, notion. Through their interdependence Marcuse suggests they point towards the possibility of according man the potential to 'organise reality according to the demands of his free rational thinking instead of simply accommodating his thoughts to the existing order and the prevailing values.'[18] Hegel's philosophy is seen to depart from a metaphysical concept of reason to the extent that 'Reason presupposes freedom, the power to act in accordance with knowledge of the truth, the power to shape reality in line with its potentialities.'[19] But it is only through the ability of man 'to recognise his own potentialities and those of his world'[20] that the possibility of realising the unification of freedom and reason arises. The stone and the plant are excluded from the category of true subjects. Man is the only being endowed with the attribute of self-sufficiency:

> Man alone has the power of self-realisation, the power to be a self-determining subject in all processes of becoming, for he alone has an understanding of potentialities and a knowledge of 'notions'.[21]

The materialist aspect of Hegel's philosophy, and its distinguishing feature with regard to the Kantian division of phenomenal and noumenal worlds, with freedom confined to the latter, is held to centre on the insistence that freedom 'exists only through its realisation, the process of its being made real'.[22] Hegel's philosophy is regarded as offering a potential bridge between the two orders of thought and being, subject and object, which Kantian philosophy erects. This takes the form of a category of being which denotes the essential interrelatedness and processual nature of the world. Objective and subjective worlds are seen as united through the structure of movement which pervades the world. And this movement can be accorded a self-sufficient centre in the form of man. It is through man that the realisation of reason as freedom derives.

The critical edge to the materialist injunction which Marcuse detects in Hegel's philosophy is supplied by the category of 'Notion . . . [which] tells us what the thing is in itself.'[23] The notion reveals the potentiality of an object and allows one to see that these potentialities 'are limited by the determinate conditions in which the things exist. Things attain their truth only if they negate their determinate conditions.'[24] As with the categories of freedom and reason the category of notion is accorded a crucial relevance to the human world. The difference between the existent and its notion is, argues Marcuse, 'overcome only in the case of the thinking subject, which is capable of realising its notion in its existence.'[25] All immediate forms of existence are designated as 'bad' to the extent that they diverge from their 'true' being which is given in their notion. 'True' existence is that moment when beings attain the status of subjects and seek to transform their present state into its potentiality. And it is only mankind that possesses this self-determining capacity to realise itself as genuine subject:

> To grasp the world in its veritable being we must grasp it with the categories of freedom, which are to be found only in the realm of the thinking subject.[26]

It is through historical struggle that 'The objective world comes to its true form in the world of the free subject'.[27] This struggle is seen to be epitomised in the famous example of the master-slave relation depicted in Hegel's *Phenomenology*.[28] However, the struggle engendered by this relation must, states Marcuse, be understood not in terms of the individual ego but through its potential realisation of self-consciousness in the form of the universal. Through a 'life and death struggle . . . [the] self-conscious subject attains his freedom not in the form of the "I" but of the We'.[29]

This is no longer a question of the 'abstract' individual of bourgeois philosophy. Instead what is at issue is an historically determinate subject which emerges through struggle with a dominant 'Other'. This reading enables Marcuse to locate the *Phenom-*

enology as the necessary precursor to the Marxian theme of reification, the latter depicting a world in which essentially 'human' relations have been transformed into relations between things. The central theme of the opening sections of the *Phenomenology* is held to identify this state of affairs and posit man as the only subject capable of realising itself and hence the 'truth' of this world. For Hegel:

> This world is an estranged and untrue world so long as man does not destroy its dead objectivity and recognize himself and his own life 'behind' the fixed form of things and laws. When he finally wins this self-consciousness, he is on his way not only to the truth of himself but also of his world.[30]

Marcuse extends this reading of Hegel's *Phenomenology* in terms of the categories of subjectivity and self-consciousness as attributes specific to man right into the heart of Hegel's mature system. Despite equivocations at certain points, the *Science of Logic* is seen as directed, not simply at the inherent negativity of all things, but more importantly at the potentialities located within man, potentialities which can only be realised through the self-consciousness of his own freedom. Man, Marcuse argues, is not simply an example of the process of dialectical construction of the universal, precisely because man is the only existent capable of affirming its nature *qua* constitutive subject. Hegel's analysis of determinate negation through which things *are* only in so far as they arise and pass away is seen as inappropriate by Marcuse if it is taken to refer to all categories of being: 'Hegel applies to the objective world categories that find their verification only in the life of the subject.'[31]

It is not simply the processual and 'negative' character of reality which characterises the becoming of man, but rather that 'his state of existence is not reasonable and that it is man's task to make it so.'[32] This contradiction, Marcuse argues, is specific to man and 'has the force of an "Ought" (*Sollen*) that impels him to realise that which does not as yet exist.'[33]

Marcuse's reading of Hegel leads him to interpret Hegel's categories of being and finite as uniquely applicable to man. Hegel had declared that:

> When we say of things that they are finite, we mean thereby . . . that Not-Being constitutes their nature and their Being. Finite things are; but their relation to themselves is that they are related to

> themselves and something negative, and in this self-relation send themselves on beyond themselves and their Being. They are, but the truth of this Being is in their end.[34]

On this basis Marcuse argues that for Hegel being is a process of continuous becoming, that every state of existence has to be surpassed. The 'materialist' aspect of such a proposition resides, Marcuse argues, in its opposition to religious and theological influences in eighteenth-century thought. Marcuse argues that 'The current idealistic interpretation of reality in that day still held the view that the world was a finite one because it was a created world and that its negativity referred to its sinfulness.'[35] Against such moral or religious views Hegel is seen to have proposed a 'purely philosophical' concept of finitude which 'becomes a critical and almost materialistic principle with him'.[36]

The 'critical' aspect of this concept of finitude resides, Marcuse suggests, in its connection with the concept of the infinite. Marcuse argues that the process whereby a finite thing perishes, and through perishing becomes another finite thing, indicates that 'The incessant perishing of things is thus an equally continuous negation of their finitude. It is infinity.'[37] The infinite, he argues, 'is precisely the inner dynamic of the finite, comprehended in its real meaning'.[38]

Hegel had used such arguments to establish the basic principle of idealism:

> If the being of things consists in their transformation rather than in their state of existence, the manifold states they have, whatever their form and content may be, are but moments of a comprehensive process and exist only within the totality of this process. Thus, they are of an 'ideal' nature and their philosophical interpretation must be idealism.[39]

Or in Hegel's words: 'The proposition that the finite is of ideal nature constitutes idealism.'[40] But it is from this proposition also, Marcuse argues, that one can appreciate the 'materialist' aspect of Hegel's philosophy. The principle of the negation of the finite becomes, he proposes, a critical concept entailing a concept of 'ought'. Thus Marcuse suggests that 'The negation of finitude is at the same time the negation of the infinite Beyond; it involves the demand that the "ought" be fulfilled in this world.'[41] And when this principle is located alongside a proposition concerning the distinctiveness of the human as opposed to the natural world, the 'critical' aspect of Hegel's philosophy is held to reside in its injunction to 'conscious beings' to 'fulfill their potentialities through their own free, conscious acts'.[42]

Hegel's philosophy is thus held to install a 'critical' and 'materialist' distinction between man and nature, expressed in the following passage from the *Encyclopaedia of the Philosophical Sciences*:

> Man, it may be said, is distinguished from the animal world, and in that way from nature altogether, by knowing himself as 'I': which amounts to saying that natural things never attain a free Being-for-self, but as limited to Being-there-and-then, are always and only Being for an other.[43]

It is on this basis, Marcuse argues, that one can denounce the present situation in which men live as a denial of that which defines them as 'conscious beings'.

What Marcuse regards as the critical import of Hegel's thought can be located also in relation to the concept of reflection. Marcuse argues that, for Hegel, reflection 'denotes an objective as well as subjective movement. Reflection is not primarily the process of thinking but the process of being itself.'[44] The laws of reflection designate that process through which the essential negativity of things unfolds. This converges in part with Lenin's attempt in the *Philosophical Notebooks* to produce a dialectical account of the notion of being-as-such,[45] which he considers to be epitomised in Hegel's famous statement that 'All things are contradictory in themselves.'[46] This declaration that reality is itself 'contradictory', that it is characterised essentially by a process of self-movement, Marcuse identifies in Hegel also. Marcuse argues that it signals 'the point at which dialectical thinking can be seen to shatter the framework of the idealist philosophy that uses it.'[47] Hegel's nascent materialism is held to reside in the possibility of extending the proposition that every existence is essentially marked by the unfolding of its contradictions, to the point at which it reveals its historical implications:

> If the essence of things is the result of such process, the essence itself is the product of a concrete development, 'something which has become (*ein Gewordenes*)'. And the impact of this historical interpretation shakes the foundations of idealism.[48]

When the determinations of reflection are applied to historical entities we are, Marcuse argues, 'driven almost of necessity to the critical theory that historical materialism developed'.[49] For Marxism the possibility of crisis and collapse witnesses the essential nature of the capitalist mode of production. Marcuse views this as representing the historical intent within Hegel's principle of negativity, transformed from an ontological to a historical process.

As with Horkheimer[50] we have here a similar claim that what is achieved thereby is a fusing of the categories of freedom and necessity. The realisation of the essential potentiality of things, conceived as a dialectical principle, 'does away with the traditional opposition between contingency, possibility, and necessity, and integrates them all as moments of one comprehensive process.'[51] This process, Marcuse argues, is governed by *necessity* since it follows its own laws, whilst at the same time 'this necessity is *freedom* because the process is not determined from outside, by external forces, but, in a strict sense, is a self-development.'[52]

DIALECTICAL SUBJECTIVITY AND MAN

There is an important difference which Marcuse fails to remark upon between the account of the transition from one mode of production to another within historical materialism, and the passage to actuality[53] within his account of Hegel. To the extent that Marcuse seeks to derive a 'materialist' Hegel this difference is relevant, and highlights what I suggest is a central difficulty with Marcuse's notion of subjectivity.

Risking superficiality one can say that within historical materialism the transition from one mode of production to another results from the contradictory play of a variety of social relations through which certain of these relations attain a position of dominance.[54] Aside from Lukácsian interpretations,[55] transition is not the outcome of a 'subject' of history. For Marcuse, however, despite his insistence at certain points that negativity characterises Being-as-such and is not the prerogative of man, history is essentially the work of an active and self-sufficient subject. The final unity of being represented by actuality can, he argues, be attained only through the medium of self-consciousness and cognition: 'only a being that has the faculty of knowing its own possibilities and those of its world can transform every given state of existence into a condition for its self-realisation.'[56] Actuality as the perfect end-state can only be understood as 'the realisation of a knowing *subject*. Hegel's analysis of actuality thus leads to the idea of the subject as the truly actual in all reality.'[57]

Now it is true that Marcuse argues that the category subject here does not denote any particular form of subjectivity, such as man, but rather 'a general structure that might best be characterised by the concept "mind".'[58] But if we follow through Marcuse's argument on this point it can be seen that the category of subject in his account can in fact refer *only* to man. And if this is the case it will seriously weaken Marcuse's claim to have discovered in Hegel the basis for a materialist account of the formation of a historically determinate subjectivity. What I suggest emerges instead is a reiteration of the *a priori* capacities of constitutive subjectivity as attributes specific to man, and as originary in respect of the action they produce.

The concept of subject, Marcuse points out, is not the last stage of Hegel's analysis. Indeed the subject can only be understood in so far as it is notion. Its freedom consists in its ability to comprehend what is. It 'derives its content from the knowledge of the truth'.[59] That is, it derives its content from the notion. In other words, freedom is 'not an attribute of the thinking subject as such, but of the truth that this subject holds and wields.'[60] Freedom is an attribute of the notion.

This attempt to shift the 'dialectical' account of subjectivity away from a straightforward identification of ego and subject is not entirely convincing. It is not simply that Marcuse argues that 'The notion "exists", however, only in the thinking subject.'[61] This could be taken to indicate that the subject is merely a vehicle for the unfolding of the notion and plays no constitutive role within it. It is rather that for Marcuse there is only one subject that is characterised by freedom and the possibility of exercising its autonomy. It is only through the constitutive work of the thinking subject as originary point that can be installed actuality as self-identity. The 'essential unity' of the subject of this process 'is not determinate but determining being'.[62]

The 'dialectical' nature of subjectivity which Marcuse had hoped could provide a materialist philosophical basis for critical theory still has to depend on a notion of the self-sufficient autonomy of the individual subject. In attempting to overcome the dualism of subject and object identified as coterminous with 'bourgeois' philosophy Marcuse returns to an appeal to the apparent self-evidence of that very distinction:

> The essential difference between the object's mode of existence and

> that of a conscious being results in limiting the term 'finite' to things that do not exist for themselves and do not have the power, therefore, to fulfill their potentialities *through their own free, conscious acts*.[63]

Whilst there may well be a possible materialist appropriation of Hegel's notion of dialectical process as an unfolding of contradictory relations, a process which has no recourse to an originary subjective moment constitutive of a qualitatively different unity,[64] Marcuse refuses such a possibility. The 'ought' held to be implied in the negation of the finite is an imperative which can be directed only at man. The fusing of necessity and freedom which Marcuse argued was crucial is provided with no determinate conditions of possibility.

Marcuse is unsuccessful, I suggest, in his attempt to provide the notion of necessity with any substance beyond that of an invocation of the need for an era of genuine rationality. What is lacking in his account in particular is a demonstration of the specific conditions which would help to bring about the transformation he seeks to ground. In what ways would these link up with the activities and experiences of those social groups to which his notion of change was directed? This is not to reiterate the common criticism of the divorce of the Frankfurt theorists from either the working class or indeed any of those groups to whom they appealed.[65] Rather it is to suggest that *in principle* the demand for autonomy and subjectivity necessarily separates itself from any utilisation or 'implementation'. I shall return to this point again later in this study. For the present what I suggest is decisive is the absence of an historical dimension to Marcuse's philosophical task. The 'necessity' for the realisation of a realm of freedom has no reference to any particular social conditions other than through a generalised and a historical principle of the 'dialectical' interrelation of subject and object, of liberation and repression. No conceptual tools are provided with which one can demonstrate the applicability of such a schema to determinate historical periods. Marcuse does not demonstrate how the subjectivity considered essential for such a transformation is produced, or under what conditions it might emerge.

Marcuse argues that one of the merits of Hegel's system is its destruction of the notion of timelessness. The *Philosophy of History* contains, he suggests, an historical component which enables reason to be understood in terms of the content of history. Marcuse identifies what appears *prima facie* to be a contradiction in this work of Hegel's. The proposition established in the *Logic* that 'the true being is reason, manifest in nature and come to realisation in man'[66] makes mind the subject and driving force of history. As a part of nature man may play a role in this process, but his existence as an individual is always 'confined to particular conditions'.[67] Yet as a thinking subject man is also related to the universal as the 'true subject of history'.[68]

Marcuse argues that this apparent contradiction is resolved by Hegel through recognising the dual nature of the dialectical process. On the one hand 'the needs and interests of individuals are the levers of all historical action'.[69] In history the individual achieves realisation and fulfilment. On the other hand it is historical reason that asserts itself. Thus in promoting the process of mind individuals perform a task that advances freedom. The 'universal principle . . . latent in the particular aims of individuals' could make it appear 'as if mind uses individuals for its unwitting tool.'[70] However, since the process of reason as it works itself out through individuals has neither a natural nor unilinear course, it is only through the 'efforts of a self-conscious mankind' that can be achieved an 'advance to a higher plane of history'.[71]

But it must be asked whether this formulation achieves the resolution of the dichotomy subject/object which Marcuse seeks. Matter, argues Marcuse, in so far as it is held to have unchangeable laws that express its movement 'is nowhere the subject of its processes, nor has it any power over them.'[72] Against this, a being 'that is the active and conscious subject of its existence stands under quite different laws.'[73] As a self-conscious being man is related to the universal principle of history to the extent that its laws 'are taken into the subject's will and influence his acts.'[74] History is process, yet as process a necessary part of it is that moment of self-consciousness which can be supplied only by man. Historical tendencies only come into operation if man comprehends them and acts on them.

I argue that this formulation is unsatisfactory in terms of Marcuse's attempt to avoid the abstract self-positing ego of 'bourgeois' philosophy. If historical tendencies only operate through an act of self-consciousness, then it is hard to see how they can be accorded a materiality separate from that self-consciousness. When one combines this with what I have argued is Marcuse's failure to incorporate within such processes their historical conditions of possibility, it is difficult to see how Marcuse can escape from the notion that historical laws actually *originate* in and through the activity of man. Their existence is dependent on a self-consciousness of them. Marcuse himself acknowledges this difficulty in places:

> Historical laws, in other words, originate and are actual only in man's conscious practice, so that if, for instance, there is a law of progress to ever higher forms of freedom, it ceases to operate if man fails to recognise and execute it.[75]

Hegel's philosophy may have entailed a 'determinism', but to the extent that the determining factor is freedom Marcuse bestows approval. Such approval is limited, however, in so far as for Hegel the final subject of history is not man but the world mind (*Weltgeist*). History for Hegel ultimately operates behind the backs and over the heads of individuals. History is not the conscious activity of man, but rather the necessary result of objective historical forces.

Marcuse suggests that in fact Hegel only glimpsed that the history of man is also the history of man's alienation (*Entfremdung*). It was, he argues, only with Marx's critique of capitalism that the origin and significance of man's estrangement could be grasped. And only then could it be seen that what this process demanded was that man elevate himself above the status of the particular and make himself the constitutive subject of history. With this step the installation of reason could be achieved.

Marcuse ends up discarding the last vestiges of a 'dialectical' and materialist account of the realisation of freedom. Whilst insisting on the radically historical nature of Marx's analyses, Marcuse affirms that man's *actual* history can only be introduced 'by an autonomous act on the part of men, that will cancel the whole of the existing state.'[76] The new era introduced through such an act demonstrates the *truth* of the old, but such truth can only be realised through an act of self-affirmation. Man's subjectivity is the truth of the world. And that subjectivity is necessarily self-sufficient. Marcuse returns, I suggest, to a simple demand that man realise his essential subjectivity, and thereby install an era of genuine rationality purely through an act of self-affirmation. Without an account of the determinate conditions under which this capacity may emerge, the only content which this notion of subjectivity has is that supplied by philosophical discourse. The 'contradiction' Marcuse posits, between the present era and a future one governed by rationality, has no demonstrable existence. All that Marcuse can offer is a notion of subjectivity characterised by a binary division of presence or absence, liberation or repression.

DOMINATION, REPRESSION AND RATIONALITY

Marcuse's project to establish a 'dialectical' notion of subjectivity exerts a significant influence over his account of domination. Scattered throughout his entire work the analysis of domination animates the critique of Sartrean existentialism,[77] the discussion of the concepts of industrialism and capitalism in the works of Max Weber,[78] and the influential text *One-Dimensional Man*. It is with the latter that I shall be chiefly concerned here.

The analysis of domination is regarded by Marcuse himself as directly related to the philosophical account of the critical subject developed in *Reason and Revolution*. In the preface which he added to later editions of that work he argues that the category of negation central to 'dialectical' thought starts 'with the experience that the world is unfree'.[79] It was with the hope of contributing to the revival of the power of 'negative thinking' that *Reason and Revolution* was written. *Reason and Revolution* can thus be located as something of a precursor to *One-Dimensional Man* and the notion of the 'Great Refusal' which Marcuse was to propose in the latter. Negation in *Reason and Revolution* was seen to consist in an 'effort to contradict a reality in which all logic and all speech are false to the extent that they are part of a mutilated whole'.[80] It is a negation of an entire society which is proposed, a refusal in the face of a totalised domination. It is this theme which Marcuse develops in *One-Dimensional Man*.

One-Dimensional Man opens with a characterisation of advanced industrial civilisation in terms of the 'comfortable, smooth, reasonable, democratic unfreedom'[81] it is held to promote. Independent thought and political opposition are, Marcuse suggests, 'being deprived of their basic critical function in a society which seems increasingly capable of satisfying the needs of the individuals through the way in which it is organized'.[82] Against this he asserts the possibility of a society in which the 'very structure of human existence would be altered; the individual would be liberated from the work world's imposing upon him alien needs and alien possibilities. The individual would be free to exert autonomy over a life that would be his own.'[83]

But advanced industrial societies, Marcuse suggests, are tending towards a form of totalitarian domination which 'precludes the emergence of an effective opposition against the whole'.[84] Advanced industrial societies, Marcuse argues, are characterised by the 'false needs' which are 'superimposed upon the individual by particular social interests in his repression: the needs which perpetuate toil, aggressiveness, misery, and injustice.'[85] Love and hate, the need to relax and have fun, all belong to this category of 'false needs'. Such needs, Marcuse argues, are not eternal. Rather, they are historical, they have a societal content and function; and at present they are the 'products of a society whose dominant interest demands repression'.[86]

'False needs' are of course counterposed to 'true needs'. This opposition raises the question of who is to distinguish between true and false needs. In the 'last analysis' this question can, Marcuse argues, be answered only by the individuals themselves. But the problem this creates is that this can only be achieved 'if and when they are free to give their own answer.' To the extent that individuals are 'indoctrinated and manipulated . . . their answer to this question cannot be taken as their own'.[87]

Advanced industrial society and its attendant mass production and mass distribution have, Marcuse argues, claimed 'the *entire* individual. The result is not adjustment but *mimesis*: an immediate identification of the individual with *his* society and, through it, with the society as a whole.'[88] This, Marcuse argues, is the world of one-dimensional thought. In it those 'ideas, aspirations, and objectives that, by their content, transcend the established universe of discourse and action are either repelled or reduced in terms of this universe.'[89] Opposition in a one-dimensional society is 'redefined by the rationality of the given system and of its quantitative extension'.[90]

Just as individuals in advanced industrial societies are held to have been subordinated to the logic of domination, so too are the various political parties. The British Labour Party, the West German Social Democratic Party, and the various national communist parties have, Marcuse argues, all become a part of the inability to provide effective opposition to a 'one-dimensional' reality. They have themselves become one element in the multiplicity of available options which lack that qualitative difference required to make them genuine alternatives. And the gradual dissolution of the working class as a viable political force means that it 'no longer appears to be the living contradiction to the established society'.[91]

Domination has, Marcuse argues, become transfigured into administration through the bureaucratisation of the production process. Inequality is concealed beneath the 'technological veil' which perpetuates unfreedom in the name of 'rationality'. The Lukácsian theme of reification[92] is seen to encapsulate this condition where man exists 'as an instrument, as a thing'. But 'as reification tends to become totalitarian by virtue of its technological form'[93] even the administrators become dependent on the machinery they administer. The Hegelian dialectical relationship between Master and Servant is no longer applicable in this 'vicious circle which encloses both the Master and the Servant.'[94]

Marcuse argues that there exist 'centrifugal tendencies' within this increasingly repressive logic. Automation is one such tendency in so far as 'automation to the limits of technical possibility is incompatible with a society based on the private exploitation of human labour power in the process of production'.[95] Automation is, he suggests, a potentially explosive catalyst in advanced industrial society. But such centrifugal forces are, Marcuse argues, manageable within the present framework. Even the welfare state is held to be a part of such a process in so far as it is capable only of raising the standard of '*administered* living'.[96] The welfare state, Marcuse argues, is 'a historical freak between organized capitalism and socialism, servitude and freedom, totalitarianism and happiness'.[97] Marcuse is not prepared to condemn the welfare State entirely, on behalf of 'abstract ideas of freedom'. The 'rule of law', he argues, 'no matter how restricted, is still infinitely safer than rule above or without law'.[98] But none the less the welfare state is, Marcuse argues, the counterpart to a democracy which 'would appear to be the most efficient system of domination.'[99]

This extension of one-dimensionality to the political sphere is held to have its correlate in the realm of 'higher culture'. Today we are witnessing, Marcuse argues, 'not the deterioration of higher culture into mass culture but the refutation of this culture by the reality'.[100] 'Higher culture', Marcuse suggests, was 'always in contradiction with social reality, and only a privileged minority enjoyed its blessings and represented its ideals'.[101] But what is novel in the present era is the flattening out of this antagonism between culture and social reality. This is achieved, he suggests, through 'the obliteration of the oppositional, alien, and transcendent elements in the higher culture by virtue of which it constituted *another dimension* of reality.'[102] The *two-dimensional* nature of culture is being erased through the incorporation of 'higher culture' into the established order, through its reproduction, diffusion and display on a massive scale. The themes of joy and sorrow, individuality and freedom are held to 'contradict the society which sells them'.[103] But this does not count, Marcuse argues. Or rather it is precisely this 'contradiction' which defines contemporary culture. For in it the ideal is 'brought down from the sublimated realm of the soul or the spirit or the inner man, and translated into operational terms and problems'.[104] 'Higher culture' thus becomes a part of the 'material culture' and in this transformation 'it loses the greater part of its truth.'[105]

What Marcuse argues has changed in the realm of culture in advanced industrial society is the relation between 'higher culture' and popular culture. The 'absorbent power of society depletes the artistic dimension by animating its antagonistic contents.'[106] Previously, Marcuse asserts, literature and art preserved the contradiction between the actual and the possible. They constituted 'a rational, cognitive force, revealing a dimension of man and nature which was repressed and repelled in reality.'[107] Art is held to preserve this negation throughout the nineteenth and into the twentieth century. But 'this essential gap between the arts and the order of the day, kept open in the artistic alienation, is progressively closed by the advancing technological society.'[108] And with the closing of this gap the possibility of the 'Great Refusal' is, Marcuse argues, itself denied. The 'other dimension' witnessed by art is absorbed into the prevailing state of affairs. Domination comes to acquire its own, democratic aesthetics.

Artistic alienation, Marcuse argues, is sublimation. But the imagery which it produces, when incorporated into the kitchen, the office and the shop, is, he suggests 'desublimation'. Immediate gratification replaces mediated gratification. And this desublimation is practised 'from a "position of strength" on the part of society, which can afford to grant more than before because its interests have become the innermost drives of its citizens, and because the joys which it grants promote social cohesion and contentment.'[109] There are, he suggests, 'repressive modes of desublimation, compared with which the sublimated drives and objectives contain more deviation, more freedom, and more refusal to heed the social taboos.'[110]

Repressive desublimation, Marcuse argues, is operative also in the 'sexual sphere'. Here, as in the desublimation of higher culture, 'it operates as the by-product of the social controls of technological reality, which extend liberty while intensifying domination.'[111] Advanced industrial society, he argues, has de-eroticised 'a whole dimension of human activity and passivity'.[112] And at the same time it has effected a reduction of the erotic to sexual experience. Citing what he regards as a fundamental contrast between love-making in a meadow and in a car, Marcuse argues that in the former 'the environment partakes of and invites libidinal cathexis and tends to be eroticized. Libido transcends beyond the immediate erotogenic zones – a process of nonrepressive sublimation.'[113]

It is not to suggest a tinge of absurdity in his account that I cite Marcuse on this point. It is important to his argument. For what it highlights is his notion that 'technological reality', in diminishing the erotic and intensifying sexual energy '*limits the scope of sublimation*. It also reduces the *need* for sublimation.'[114] And this limiting is not restricted to the sexual sphere. It is held to be characteristic of a technological rationality which generates submission through offering immediate satisfaction. Advanced industrial society has, Marcuse argues, achieved a state in which there exists a 'pre-established harmony between individual needs and socially-required desires, goals, and aspirations'.[115] There is nothing unique to the sexual sphere, for in it what occurs is merely the same as that which takes place across the whole of contemporary society. In Marcuse's words:

> This society turns everything it touches into a potential source of progress *and* of exploitation, of drudgery *and* satisfaction, of freedom *and* of oppression. Sexuality is no exception.[116]

REPRESSION AND LIBERATION: THE BINARY OPPOSITION

The prognosis of *One-Dimensional Man* is bleak. Prospects for a transformation of 'technological rationality' are seen to be extremely limited, even if they are not completely ruled out. Indeed it is difficult to see how it could be otherwise given the ubiquity of the mechanisms by which one-dimensional thought is considered to operate. But I argue that Marcuse does not arrive at such a position by virtue of the unsophisticated nature of his conceptual tools. Rather, I argue that one can more fruitfully examine Marcuse's position in terms of the notion of subjectivity discussed above. It is, I suggest, through establishing an opposition of repression and liberation in terms of a philosophy of the subject that Marcuse has more or less to renounce the hope of a transformation of the current technological rationality.

I argued above that Marcuse is unable to formulate an account of the notion of subjectivity which demonstrates its determinate conditions of formation. In so far as the present era is identified through the absence of autonomous, critical subjectivity, I argue that Marcuse is confined either to refusing the possibility of change, or to appealing to a notion of subjectivity which arises from *outside* the domination he identifies as characteristic of advanced industrial society.

In *One-Dimensional Man* Marcuse poses the question as to how 'the people who have been the object of effective and productive domination by themselves create the conditions of freedom.'[117] The difficulty which this question raises for Marcuse's account is that 'liberation depends on the *consciousness* of servitude, and the emergence of this consciousness is always hampered by the predominance of needs and satisfactions which, to a great extent, have become the individual's own.'[118] This 'consciousness' can never develop *within* the various practices and institutions through which individuals' needs and desires are repressed, precisely because these institutions and practices are defined entirely through their repression of individuals' 'true' needs. One is either dominated by 'false needs' or capable of critically asserting the need for a society based on 'real needs'.

This image of repression as an effectively realised process must be understood in terms of that object upon which Marcuse regards it as operating. This object is that subjectivity whose liberation represents the possibility of realising the latent potentiality held to reside in man. To the extent that repression is seen by Marcuse to operate uniquely on such an object, then liberation can only be conceived as the obverse of the present era. And in so far as society is understood by Marcuse as an aggregate of individuals, this polarity is absolute since repression is considered to be a phenomenon which defines a *society*.

Critical theory, in particular Marcuse's formulation, might appear an elitist philosophy. The role of enunciating 'true' needs that it reserves for the philosopher-statesman is considerable. I argue, however, that this is not due to an *ad hoc* propensity for 'elitism'.[119] What is important is that the critical intellectual, not unlike Mannheim's *freischwebende* intellectual, is located *outside* these processes of domination, in an important sense *outside society as such*. It is only thus that the critical theorist can be held to be free from the logic of repression characteristic of advanced industrial society.

To break with this dichotomy of repression and liberation would seriously weaken any proposal couched in terms of a one-dimensional *society*. It would become necessary then to specify the differing extents and modes in which domination operated in discrete social practices. That this is not provided within the framework of *One-Dimensional Man* results, I suggest, not from any 'excess' which it allows itself in its stress on the ubiquity of domination, but rather from the inverse relation which it posits between repression and subjectivity. Repression for Marcuse operates entirely at the level of a subjectivity which, to the extent that it constitutes itself *as* subjectivity, would institute a break with that repression:

> The attainment of autonomy demands conditions in which the repressed dimensions of experience can come to live again; *their liberation demands repression of the heteronomous needs and satisfactions which organise life in this society.*[120]

That this does not obtain is a *sine qua non* of the analysis in *One-Dimensional Man*. Repression is societal and fully realised. But Marcuse still wishes to retain some prospects, however limited, for that subjectivity which is the necessary precursor to any liberation.

It is here, I suggest, that Marcuse's analysis encounters its greatest difficulty. It is precisely this transition which Marcuse's account is unable to provide. As I argued was the case with the formulation in *Reason and Revolution*, in *One-Dimensional Man* subjectivity is characterised precisely by its self-sufficiency and its ability to operate without any conditions of formation. The difficulty here resides in the mode of effectivity of existing systems of domination:

> The power and efficiency of this system, the thorough assimilation of mind with fact, of thought with required behaviour, of aspirations with reality, militate against the emergence of a new Subject.[121]

Since domination as repression of subjectivity operates as a uniform and non-contradictory process there cannot develop points of resistance within certain institutions or populations. That 'subject' upon which liberation depends for Marcuse cannot be *produced* within the practice and development of resistance precisely because it is 'a necessary *a priori* of liberation'.[122] Autonomy of thought and its practical effectuation is required in exactly that situation identified by its repression and denial.

Marcuse is not unaware of the consequences of this means of conceptualising domination. In response to the 'pure form of domination' he proposes as its opposite 'the pure form of negation'. But this has the effect that any content that might have resided in a negation directed at a historically specific practice is 'reduced to the one abstract demand for the end of domination'.[123] Again Marcuse acknowledges the effect of such a formulation. The negation which this produces, he argues, appears 'in the politically impotent form of the "absolute refusal" '.[124]

The pessimism which pervades *One-Dimensional Man* and the faint glimmer of hope which is attached to certain social groups can now be appreciated. On the one hand, as suggested above, the pessimism is inseparable from the conception of domination as a totalised and societal repression of *subjectivity*. On the other hand, those groups to which Marcuse appeals are identified precisely by virtue of their *exclusion* from that society. Their position is defined in a similar manner to that of the philosopher-statesman. The societal scale of repression means that a subjectivity cannot be *produced* since it must exist as an *a priori* of that process of liberation. It is only from an 'outside' that any force can emerge, as a *deus ex machina*. The groups to whom Marcuse gestures are thus 'the outcasts and the outsiders, the exploited and persecuted of other races and other colors, the unemployed and the unemployable'.[125] Whilst Marcuse argues that it is the intolerable conditions under which such groups live that engender the possibility of their revolt, I suggest that this is not the most important reason for his appealing to them. What is more significant when viewed in relation to the image of repression which *One-Dimensional Man* erects is that they are *excluded* from the societal logic of domination which defines 'advanced industrial societies'. Like the philosopher-statesman their ability to express the truth of the world is conditional on their not being implicated in that logic which is held to define its present.

It is not central to my concerns here to assess whether those 'outsiders' to whom Marcuse refers may be considered potentially revolutionary. In any case, Marcuse clearly holds out little hope that they will be effective in instigating the process of the 'Great Refusal'. More important for my purposes is the lacuna which it betokens in Marcuse's critical theory, a lacuna which I argue is directly related to the subjectivity/repression interrelation and the appeal to an *a priori* subjectivity as the condition for removal of domination. The absolute distinction which this produces between repression and liberation creates serious problems for one of the central questions for a critical theory, namely how to conceive the transition from the present to the future. Marcuse openly declares this absence in his critical theory:

> The critical theory of society possesses no concepts which could bridge the gap between the present and its future; holding no promise, and showing no success, it remains negative.[126]

Since resistance, and hence liberation, appeals necessarily to an *a priori* capacity, there can be no account of its conditions of formation. In an earlier article a notion of 'phantasy' is invoked to fill that place in the transition from the present to the possible which Marcuse's scenario leaves empty:

> The abyss between rational and present reality cannot be bridged by conceptual thought. In order to retain what is not yet present as a goal in the present, phantasy is required.[127]

Perhaps one might wish to suggest that the claims of *phantasy* have suffered at the hands of a particular 'rationalist' determination of what is judged to be desirable. But in Marcuse's account the notion of phantasy serves only to indicate the space which his conceptual schema leaves empty, and which is not filled in *One-Dimensional Man*. One could legitimately request an historical account of the antagonisms between different social groups, and how they may be regarded as constitutive of that tension which justifies the hope for an era of genuine Reason. But at this point one finds only a generalised denunciation of 'every form of production that dominates man instead of being dominated by him'.[128] A noble project perhaps, but one which I argue is vitiated through the terms in which it is formulated.

Frequently these questions are regarded as evidence of Marcuse's 'technological determinism',[129] or of his separation from 'practical', that is, working-class, struggles.[130] I have suggested above that my focus here is more restricted. It concerns the philosophical foundations of Marcuse's diagnosis of advanced industrial society.

There is a further difficulty in Marcuse's analysis. It was argued above that critical theory for Marcuse, as indeed for the other Frankfurt theorists, was a project which had both philosophical and historical dimensions. At issue here was a critique both of a certain epistemology and the determinate societal form it was seen to mirror. The solution was held by Marcuse to reside in a break with the abstract *a priori* positing of philosophical principles. In its place was to be substituted a 'dialectical' and historical account of the conditions of formation of a concrete subjectivity firmly located in that world which it was destined to destroy. But what is noticeable in its absence from Marcuse's description of contemporary societies is just that historical dimension which would represent a condition for the success of such a project. The timelessness of Marcuse's notion of repression finds its counterpart in the *a priori* of subjectivity which is the only alternative he offers.

CHAPTER 3

JURGEN HABERMAS: HUMAN INTERESTS, COMMUNICATION AND LEGITIMATION

•

Delineations of critical theory into 'stages' generally entail a separation of the works of Habermas from those of other critical theorists.[1] Habermas's studies, especially the more recent ones, are considered to represent either a separate moment in the project of critical theory, or the inauguration of a distinct set of concerns. My arguments in this chapter are at odds with such an interpretation in so far as I concentrate on the continuity between those aspects of Marcuse's and Horkheimer's work discussed in the previous two chapters, and certain concepts central to Habermas's arguments.

This continuity is held to reside firstly at the level of the attempt to produce a philosophical account of subjectivity as the basis for a critical theory. Secondly, it is argued that this provides the foundation for a critique of domination, which is conceived as bearing specifically on a realm of subjectivity. Domination, it is argued, comes to be seen as operating through the repression of a certain realm of subjective attributes. Liberation is conceived as the reappropriation by the subject of those attributes which define its status *qua* subject. This interconnection between the notion of subjectivity and the account of domination is considered to limit the latter, as I argued was the case with Horkheimer and Marcuse. The elucidation of the various mechanisms through which is secured a certain cultural apparatus takes second place to a philosophy of domination.

Emphasising the continuity between Habermas's approach and that of Horkheimer and Marcuse runs the danger however of obliterating the distinctiveness of their concerns. This distinctiveness needs to be identified particularly with respect to the philosophical project of establishing a notion of subjectivity at the heart of critical theory. Habermas's approach to this question is quite distinct from that of Horkheimer and Marcuse. Rather than continuing the search for a 'dialectical' notion of subjectivity, Habermas attempts to elaborate a concept of *inter*subjectivity. This is evident both in his early writings as well as in his more recent. It is this notion of intersubjectivity which is my principal concern in this chapter. I attempt to bring out the different aspects and stages of Habermas's work, from his concern with the notion of 'human interests', through the model of linguistic intersubjectivity which grounds the concept of universal pragmatics, the proposals for a notion of legitimation crisis and an analysis of domination, to his synthetic project of attempting to link together his various concerns in a theory of reason and rationality as social phenomena. Despite the evident shifts in Habermas's perspective across the years, the notion of intersubjectivity as a foundation for critical theory is viewed as a common concern throughout his writings. It is on this basis that I argue his project has fundamental limitations for grounding a critical theory.

This chapter is divided into four sections. In the first I examine Habermas's attempt to develop the notion of intersubjectivity on the basis of categories derived from Hegel's Jena lectures.[2] The tripartite division of 'human interests', and more particularly the notion of emancipatory interest is central here. I examine Habermas's attempt to develop a notion of self-reflection which depends neither on a transcendental concept of subjectivity, nor on an image of the self-positing capacities of the ego. I argue that Habermas is unsuccessful in such a project, that an *a priori* notion of the subject remains as the ultimate foundation of the notion of intersubjectivity. Emancipation for Habermas, I argue, is conceived as the realisation of this *a priori* notion of subjectivity. The 'political intent' of Habermas's critical theory is considered to suffer as a consequence.

In the second section I examine Habermas's project for a universal pragmatics and the attempt to elaborate the concept of intersubjectivity according to a model of linguistic communication. An ideal notion of intersubjectivity is understood as the foundation of communication. The notion of an 'ideal speech situation' in which 'mutual understanding' can obtain is examined and assessed. I argue that Habermas does not succeed in substantiating his position. Despite Habermas's arguments to the contrary, I suggest that a notion of rational subjectivity as the transcendental basis of speech underlies his notion of communication. To the extent that this notion of rational subjectivity is not demonstrated by Habermas to be operative in speech I argue that Habermas fails to avoid an *a priori* concept of subjectivity. The notion of a universal pragmatics as indicating a 'linguistic turn' in critical theory is also questioned to the extent that Habermas accords no effectivity to language at the level of intersubjectivity.

In the third section I discuss Habermas's account of legitimation crises and its dependence on the model of the 'ideal speech situation' and the notion of 'generalisable interests'. Habermas argues that one can talk of a legitimation crisis to the extent that legitimation is secured through norms that 'admit of truth'. The account of legitimation crises thus depends on a notion of intersubjectivity governed by the norms of 'rational speech'. The notion of rational subjectivity which supports the proposals for a universal pragmatics underlies this attempt by Habermas to produce a theory of legitimation crises. I argue that as a result Habermas is unable to support his claim to have avoided a transcendental foundation for critical theory. Moreover, I argue that the concepts Habermas does produce are of little assistance in developing the project of a critical theory. The notion of 'generalisable interests', and the suggestion that it is the task of critical intellectuals to identify such interests, offers little more than a denunciation of the present in terms of a notion of the possibility of realising the model of rational subjectivity. Once again, the 'political intent' of Habermas's critical theory is held to be vitiated.

In the fourth section I discuss some criticisms of Habermas's work, the replies he has given to these criticisms, and the recent developments of his arguments in *The Theory of Communicative Action* as they bear on the concerns of this study. Whilst Habermas may have modified the details of his conceptual framework, I suggest that the revisions have not been sufficient to overcome the difficulties which I argue are central to his undertaking.

HUMAN INTERESTS, INTERSUBJECTIVITY AND SELF-REFLECTION

Habermas's early attempt to produce a philosophical foundation for the critique of domination can be seen in the essays gathered together in *Knowledge and Human Interests*[3] and *Theory and Practice*.[4] In those books the project of critical theory was based on the categories of self-reflection and reason. The latter was to be realised through the former. The challenging of repressive forms of social organisation was held to take place through a change in the consciousness of human subjects, with emancipation conceived as the realisation of a specifically human capacity for autonomous constitutive activity. It implied 'the anticipation of an emancipated society and actualised adult autonomy for all human beings'.[5]

Habermas conceived such a project as 'a theory of society conceived with a practical intention'.[6] Such a theory combined a reflection on its origins by which it is made possible with a specification of those to whom it is addressed. The latter were to be informed of their emancipatory role in the process of history. Habermas attempted to provide this theory with a set of philosophical categories which would distinguish it from those idealist philosophies of the abstract and self-positing subject. In so doing he followed Horkheimer and Marcuse's attempts to avoid both the Kantian transcendental subject and the Fichtean postulate of the world-constituting ego.

The Kantian separation of man into phenomenal and noumenal spheres was a key issue here. Habermas raised the question of how it is that men, the potential authors of history, have as yet failed to constitute themselves as its subject; why it is that they remain on the one hand causally determined as a species of nature, and on the other hand morally free. As with Horkheimer and Marcuse, Kant's transcendental philosophy and its distinction between empirical/sensual motives and the realm of morality as pure reason is considered by Habermas to generate serious problems for a formulation of the category of freedom of the will. Since freedom for Kant is defined as independence from empirical motives, to talk in terms of realising these motives would imply situating them within the sensual/empirical sphere. But this would then mean that the domain of moral, and hence free action had been departed from. Habermas argues that this fundamental problem entails that the Kantian transcendental framework cannot cope with the question of the realisation of pure reason through the activity of human subjects, that it cannot provide support for the notion of an 'interest of reason'. For Kant there cannot exist a drive inherent within reason to realise itself in the world of practical human activity.[7]

Habermas argues that Fichte took the step necessary to break with this separation of pure and practical reason. With Fichte the act of reason is conceived as a 'reflected action that returns into itself, and makes the primacy of practical reason itself into a principle'.[8] In this formulation reason is rendered immediately practical through the capacity of the ego to raise itself to the level of a constitutive subject. The organisation of reason is 'subordinate to the practical intentions of a subject that posits itself'.[9] The break with dogmatism is understood here through an original act of self-reflection by which the ego becomes transparent to itself in its self-production.

But whilst Kant may have proved unable to demonstrate the possibility of realising the principles of morality, Habermas is equally unwilling to adopt the Fichtean 'idealist standpoint of autonomy and responsibility'.[10] Hence he argues that:

> Fichte reduces the interests that intervene in the defense of philosophical systems to the fundamental antithesis between those who let themselves be moved by the interest of reason in emancipation and the self-subsistence of the ego and those who stay caught in their empirical inclinations and interests and thus remain dependent on nature.[11]

Fichte, in declaring the identity of theoretical and practical reason, attributes autonomy to the self-positing subject to the extent that the ego apprehends itself in intellectual intuition. The interest in actions of free will precedes self-reflection and realises itself through it. This elevation of the interest of reason in self-reflection and autonomy to a position of primacy leads to the notion of a species-subject constituting itself in an absolute movement of reflection. Habermas refuses such a formulation because 'the conditions under which the human species constitutes itself are not just those posited by reflection.'[12]

Habermas rejects the connection of reason and emancipation in the self-reflection of an absolute ego that produces itself and the world through the very act of intuition. In its stead he proposes a notion of intersubjectivity:

> Hegel's dialectic of self-consciousness passes over the relation of solitary reflection in favour of the complementary relationship between individuals who know each other. The experience of self-consciousness is no longer considered the original one. Rather, for Hegel it results from the experience of interaction.[13]

Hegel's theory of spirit, Habermas argues, is based on the notion of a medium within which one ego *communicates* with another and from which the two mutually form each other as subjects. Consciousness is the middle ground on which subjects encounter each other. This is held to provide the basis for avoiding the idealist notion of autonomy of the will and the subject conceived as a self-contained entity. The development of morality can now be understood in the context of communication between subjects who are constituted 'on the always precarious basis of mutual recognition'.[14] The constitution of the 'I' is now understood not in terms of the reflection of the solitary 'I' on itself. It takes place instead through a range of formative processes in which primacy is accorded to the *intersubjective* medium within which the individual ego is formed.[15]

It is on the basis of this notion of intersubjectivity that Habermas attempts to establish the project of a critical social science. The emancipatory goal of such a project is conceived by Habermas as one dimension of a broader framework of knowledge-constitutive interests. Habermas distinguishes between the 'empirical-analytic' sciences which '*grasp reality with regard to technical control*'[16] and the 'hermeneutic sciences' which '*grasp interpretations of reality with regard to possible intersubjectivity of action-orienting mutual understanding*'.[17] To these correspond respectively the notions of a technical and a practical knowledge-constitutive interest. These are derived by Habermas from a further set of categories, the notions of instrumental action and symbolic interaction, the former corresponding to a technical interest, and the latter to a practical interest. Such interests are held to be 'rooted in specific fundamental conditions of the possible reproduction and self-constitution of the human species, namely *work and interaction*.'[18] Interests, Habermas argues, are neither 'merely' empirical nor wholly transcendental. Knowledge-constitutive interests 'mediate the natural history of the human species with the logic of its self-formative process'.[19]

In addition to the notions of technical and practical interests Habermas posits that of an 'emancipatory interest'. To this corresponds the project of a critical social science which is grounded in the concept of 'self-reflection'. The pursuit of reflection, Habermas argues, 'knows itself as a movement of emancipation'.[20] An emancipatory cognitive interest 'aims at the pursuit of reflection'. It offers the possibility of combating repressive social conditions by bringing to consciousness the determinates of the self-formative process of the species. Human beings are considered to have the ability to reflect on their own development and to act with autonomy by virtue of this emancipatory interest.

The notion of an emancipatory human interest depends particularly on Habermas's assertion that the three knowledge-constitutive interests 'derive both from nature and *from the cultural break* with nature'.[21] Central here is the question of language. For 'What raises us out of nature is the only thing whose nature we can know: *language*. Through its structure, autonomy and responsibility are posited for us.'[22] We can detect here the basis on which Habermas attempts, in his more recent works, to develop the notion of a universal pragmatics. Thus he argues that 'Our first sentence expresses unequivocally the intention of universal and unconstrained consensus.'[23] Taken together, 'autonomy and responsibility constitute the only Idea that we possess a priori in the sense of the philosophical tradition.'[24]

Habermas does not attempt in *Knowledge and Human Interests* to develop the notion of self-reflection explicitly in terms of a philosophy of language. His account of the possibility of autonomy remains in that book at the level of the notions of emancipatory interest and self-reflection. I shall return shortly to what I consider to be the difficulties of these concepts. For the present it is instructive to turn briefly to Habermas's attempt to develop the notions of emancipation and self-reflection via the model of the psychoanalytic encounter.

Psychoanalysis, Habermas argues, is oriented not toward an understanding of symbolic structures in general. Instead 'the act of understanding to which it leads is self-reflection.'[25] The starting point for psychoanalytic theory is taken to be the experience of resistance, the force that stands in the way of the 'free and public communication of repressed contents'.[26] The analytic process is regarded in terms of its attempt to enable the development of a mature ego, to reinstate a model of pure communicative action. This is in opposition to the process of splitting-off and suppression of certain actions connected with excluded symbols, processes which are 'the result of suppression by social institutions'.[27] The aim of analysis is to achieve the formation of a unitary ego since 'what has become unconscious is transformed into consciousness and re-appropriated by the ego, repressed impulses are detected and criticised, the divided self can no longer bring about synthesis, etc. . .'.[28]

The psychoanalytic process in this account is conceived according to the model of the constitutive ego reappropriating that which was temporarily lost to consciousness:

> The experience of reflection induced by enlightenment is precisely the act through which the subject frees itself from a state in which it had become an object for itself. This specific activity *must be accomplished by the subject itself*.[29]

Rather than challenge this account of the practice of psychoanalysis,[30] its relevance for this present study is that the acquisition by the ego of a constitutive status is situated at the level of an *intersubjective* relation between doctor and patient. Self-reflection is not the result of an isolated act. It can be understood only 'at the level of an intersubjectivity that must be created between the subject as ego and the subject as id. This occurs as physician and patient together reflectively break through the barrier to communication.'[31] The psychoanalytic process 'has its telos in the self-consciousness of a reflectively appropriated life history'.[32] This self-consciousness is attained only when the 'subject remembers its identifications and alienations',[33] when it is fully transparent and present to itself.

The value of Freud's work is held to consist in its provision of a framework within which to think the category of reflective knowledge. But Habermas argues that it also enables one to comprehend the category of *distorted* communicative action.[34] It is seen to allow the possibility of 'the conceptualisation of the origins of institutions and the role and function of illusions, that is of power and ideology.'[35] The account of communicative intersubjectivity hence becomes the basis for an account of domination, understood as a situation in which 'genuine' intersubjectivity fails to obtain. The sphere of the 'cultural' is designated as that of a collective unconscious which diverts the path of genuine communication into 'channels of substitute gratification'.[36] Whereas for Marx, Habermas argues, men distinguished themselves from animals by their production of the means of subsistence, Freud 'clearly set out the direction of the history of the species, determined simultaneously by a process of self-production under categories of work and a self-formative process under conditions of distorted communication.'[37]

Habermas's account of psychoanalysis provides him with a notion of distorted communication and repression which is seen to have its effects at the level of the individual subject. It supplies also the model of the intersubjective context in which the subject regains its autonomous status through self-reflection. The former serves as a basis for an image of society's repressive effects on the individual; the latter provides the basis for a notion of emancipation held to operate through the regaining of the attributes of subjectivity by the individual.

Let us turn now to examine some of the difficulties which I argue are contained in Habermas's account of the notions of intersubjectivity and self-reflection. Habermas attempts in *Knowledge and Human Interests* to displace both the transcendental subject of Kant, and Fichte's autonomous ego through the notion of intersubjective self-reflection. Self-reflection, Habermas argues, is one of the capacities of human beings. It is located at the level of one of the 'interests' of the human species, yet it must be realised in the context of intersubjectivity. Autonomy is a capacity possessed by subjects, yet it can only be realised at the level of an intersubjective relation. The psychoanalytic dialogue is considered to provide an appropriate model of intersubjectivity. It is through such a relation that the subject reappropriates itself *qua* constitutive subject.

The question I wish to raise is how successful Habermas is in grounding self-reflection in a human interest which is neither merely empirical nor entirely transcendental. My argument is that far from laying the foundations for a decisive break with the Kantian theme of the transcendental subject these early works rely on a philosophy of the subject without which the concept of emancipation in Habermas's work could not be sustained. The emancipatory interest which Habermas argues derives from an 'actual life structure' can, I suggest, be conceived only in connection with an *a priori* conception of the subject as a rational constitutive being capable of realising itself in a suitable context. The importance of the notion of self-reflection in Habermas's schema is not that it enables an account to be given of those processes through which a subject is actually *formed* as constitutive *via* the intersubjective medium of communication. Rather, it depends on the reappropriation by the subject itself of its defining features which are considered to have been repressed and distorted by a certain form of social organisation. The category of intersubjectivity in Habermas's account possesses no effectivity of its own *vis-à-vis* the process of self-reflection.

In a later paper Habermas reflects on the categories outlined in *Knowledge and Human Interests*.[38] The notion of a rational subject on which the postulate of an emancipatory interest depends is explicitly acknowledged.[39] Thus Habermas refers to 'subjects capable of speech and action',[40] over whom an 'object domain' has, he argues, gained dominance. Against such domination Habermas proposes the model of a dialogue in which 'the understanding subject must invest a part of his subjectivity . . . in order to be able to meet confronting subjects at all on the intersubjective level which makes understanding possible.'[41] Habermas warns against 'overburdening the concepts of the philosophy of reflection'[42] and suggests that the notion of subject should remain a designation 'for something that can only be arrived at intersubjectively, in the consultation or the cooperation of individuals living together'.[43]

I argue, however, that the notion of intersubjectivity Habermas develops does not indicate that he has heeded his own warnings. The difficulty resides, I suggest, not simply in that Habermas fails to separate clearly the notion of self-reflection from that of emancipation,[44] thereby implying that self-reflection is co-extensive with freedom. Nor is it that the notion of emancipation is separated from the question of its organisational context. Rather, it is the concept of rational subjectivity on which the category of emancipatory interests depends which to my mind produces the greatest difficulties.[45] Such a model operates according to a simple binary model of a subjectivity which is seen to be either repressed and distorted or released and unfettered. As with Horkheimer and Marcuse, I suggest that this model does not allow one to conceptualise the shift from repressed to liberated subjectivity, something which has damaging consequences for the 'political' role of critical theory in so far as this is conceived in terms of a concept of liberated subjectivity.

Habermas argues that it is through intersubjectivity that the subject establishes itself as autonomous. But the realm of intersubjectivity supplies nothing more than the context in which the attributes of subjectivity are considered to emerge. It is still the individual subject as constitutive being which is required to assert its character *qua* subject. Intersubjectivity has no effectivity in terms of the *production* of the subject. This notion of emancipation conceived in terms of the image of a self-positing subjectivity is, I argue, in continuity with the formulations of Horkheimer and Marcuse. In those early writings I suggest that Habermas does not progress beyond the either/or model of the liberation of subjectivity which I argued characterised the works of both Horkheimer and Marcuse.

The 'political intent' of Habermas's critical theory sufffers, I argue, from its dependence on the binary distinction of presence and absence of subjectivity which Habermas employs to characterise the act of emancipation. Habermas conceives emancipation in terms of a notion of political enlightenment which is dependent on a moment of subjective recognition on the part of the repressed masses. Critical theory, he argues, 'serves primarily to enlighten those to whom it is addressed about the position they occupy in an antagonistic social system and about the interests of which they must become conscious in this situation as being objectively theirs.'[46] It is only when such enlightenment is actually accepted that 'the analytically proposed interpretations actually become consciousness'.[47] The 'autonomy of theory and enlightenment',[48] Habermas argues, is required. But it is implemented by means of subjects recognising in themselves the repressed capacities for autonomous action. And having recognised their situation they must, Habermas argues 'form a common will discursively'.[49]

Habermas has at this point begun to introduce the elements of a more explicitly 'communicative' notion of intersubjectivity. But the role of critical theory in political enlightenment remains, as was the case with Horkheimer and Marcuse, tied to a notion of the awakening of subjectivity and consciousness. The present situation is held to be one in which subjects have not recognised their position and the extent of their repression. The goal of critical theory in such a situation is to instigate the process of enlightenment. This is to be achieved by awakening the specifically human capacities for autonomous action.

Habermas is clearly unhappy with the situation into which this leads his account of the role of the critical intellectual. He does not wish to side entirely with a notion of intellectuals directing the process of enlightenment. But he is unable to argue that without it this emancipation will occur. The awakening of subjectivity still requires 'theory', albeit a *critical* theory. Thus he asserts on the one hand that 'the vindicating superiority of those who do the enlightening over those who are to be enlightened is theoretically unavoidable.'[50] Alongside this he adds weakly that this assumption is 'fictive and requires self-correction: in a process of enlightenment there can only be participants.'[51] Put crudely, enlightenment should ultimately be democratic, but the citizens need to be informed of their roles. This is a difficult position to sustain, unless one conceives enlightenment as a simple act of affirmation rather than a process of active self-enlightenment by the participants. It is the former which I suggest Habermas adopts. Political enlightenment is dependent on the notion of a subject affirming itself. Habermas's critical theory, I argue, offers little more than a proposal for awakening those capacities which define subjectivity. It remains, I suggest, tied to an *a priori* model of subjectivity which prevents it from conceptualising the *production* of that subjectivity on which emancipation is held to depend.

UNIVERSAL PRAGMATICS: THE 'LINGUISTIC TURN' IN CRITICAL THEORY

Habermas had already identified in *Knowledge and Human Interests* the role which a theory of communication might play in establishing the notion of a genuine consensus as a basis for critical theory. At that stage, however, he had not developed this idea. Habermas's proposals for a universal pragmatics represent a more explicitly 'linguistic turn' in critical theory.[52] The notion of universal pragmatics is relevant to my concerns in two respects. Firstly, it is used by Habermas in an attempt to develop the notion of intersubjectivity beyond that discussed in the previous section. Secondly, it provides the basis for an account of processes of legitimation and the production of 'systematically distorted communication'. The question of legitimation is dealt with in the next section of this chapter. In this section I concentrate on the proposals for a universal pragmatics, and the manner in which Habermas defines these in terms of a notion of intersubjectivity. I argue that the project of a universal pragmatics does not succeed in freeing itself from a philosophy of the subject which I suggested characterises Habermas's earlier proposals. The potentially innovatory role of the 'linguistic turn' in critical theory, I argue, is reduced as a result of the particular notion of communication which Habermas develops.

Central to Habermas's proposals is the need to develop a philosophical position which combines the 'universal' and the 'pragmatic' dimensions of speech, the transcendental and the empirical. This is in continuity with his proposals for a theory of knowledge-constitutive interests. The shift in his work is the attempt to take speech as the focus for avoiding a fully transcendental notion of subjectivity. Habermas argues that 'the problem of language has replaced the traditional problem of consciousness.'[53] A linguistic model of intersubjectivity is to provide the basis for avoiding the isolated ego as the foundation of a philosophy.

The notion of a universal pragmatics is developed by Habermas in relation to the philosophy of language of Austin[54] and Searle,[55] and in opposition to both Chomsky's concept of generative grammar[56] and sociolinguistics.[57] As distinct from sociolinguistics, a universal pragmatics is held to be directed at an examination of the meaning of linguistic expressions 'only insofar as it is determined by formal properties of speech situations in general, and not by particular situations of use'.[58] Against Chomsky, Habermas argues that speech competence does not consist merely in the mastery of an abstract system of linguistic rules, that it cannot be viewed simply as the application of linguistic competence. Rather, it must be understood in terms of a 'structure of intersubjectivity which is in turn linguistic'.[59] This structure of intersubjectivity is held to derive neither from a system of linguistic rules nor from the extra-linguistic conditions under which they operate.

Habermas argues that it is possible to subject the pragmatic dimension of language, namely speech, to a formal analysis. The production of a grammatical sentence can, he argues, be distinguished from an *utterance*, the integration of a grammatical sentence in an *intersubjective* context of *possible understanding*. It is toward utterances that a universal pragmatics is directed:

> I would defend the thesis that not only language but speech too – that is the employment of sentences in utterances – is accessible to formal analysis. Like the elementary units of language (sentence), the elementary units of speech (utterances) can be analysed in the methodological attitude of a reconstructive science.[60]

The task of a universal pragmatics as opposed to an empirical pragmatics or a formal linguistic analysis is 'to identify and reconstruct universal conditions of possible understanding'.[61] The ability to employ sentences in speech acts has 'just as universal a core as linguistic competence'.[62] Habermas argues that it is possible to elicit *from everyday speech* by means of a second-level process 'the generative structure underlying the production of symbolic formations'.[63] This procedure of reconstruction is held to be possible by virtue of those 'universal capabilities' possessed by 'competent subjects'. It is these capacities which provide the ontological foundation for the production of the surface structures of speech. Chomsky's grammatical theory is regarded as unable to 'reconstruct the competence that directly underlies speaking and understanding a language.'[64] This competence is the orientation toward mutual understanding which Habermas postulates as the essential feature of communication.

This orientation toward mutual understanding is defined by Habermas through the notion of the 'ideal speech situation'. This entails the supposition of a realm of 'discourse' in which are suspended all motives except a willingness to come to an understanding; it requires also a willingness to eliminate judgments as to the rightness of certain values. In such conditions Habermas argues that one can guarantee that a consensus can be arrived at which will be the result of the 'force of the better argument', rather than of constraints on discussion. Such a situation can, he argues, only obtain when all participants have an effective equality of chances to engage in the discussion.

This definition of communication in terms of an orientation

toward mutual understanding is connected with a notion of 'truth', posed by Habermas in terms of 'universal validity claims' held to be raised in speech. Speech, Habermas argues, entails that anyone acting communicatively must raise 'universal validity claims' and suppose that they can be vindicated. Aside from the necessity that a speaker must choose a comprehensible (*verständlich*) expression it is argued that three other validity claims are raised in all speech. The speaker must firstly have the intention of communicating a true (*wahr*) proposition; second, the speaker must want to express his intentions truthfully (*wahrhaftig*); third, the speaker must choose an utterance that is right (*richtig*) with respect to a recognised normative background. Habermas argues that every instance of communication requires that the system of all validity claims comes into play, that they are all raised simultaneously.

Corresponding to these validity claims of truth, truthfulness and rightness, Habermas identifies three modes of language use, namely the cognitive, expressive and interactive. He suggests that most types of speech action correlate with one of these modes of language use. Whilst all three validity claims are simultaneously raised in speech the speaker is considered to have the additional possibility of thematising one of them in a certain type of speech action. Table 3.1 demonstrates the schematic model Habermas erects for the correlation between modes of communication, types of speech action, and thematic validity claims:

Table 3.1 Habermas's typology of modes of communication

Mode of communication	Type of speech action	Theme	Thematic validity claim
Cognitive	Constatives	Propositional content	Truth
Interactive	Regulatives	Interpersonal relation	Rightness, appropriateness
Expressive	Avowals	Speaker's intention	Truthfulness

The 'truthfulness' with which a speaker utters his intentions is, Habermas argues, especially emphasised in the 'expressive' use of language. Paradigms of such a usage are first-person sentences in which wishes, intentions, and feelings are disclosed. But except for situations in which the speaker's truthfulness is not taken for granted,[65] the 'truthfulness' of intentions does not need to be thematised. 'Truthfulness', Habermas argues, is a 'universal implication of speech, as long as the presuppositions of communicative action are not altogether suspended'.[66] Expressive speech acts are not the central concern of a universal pragmatics.

It is with the *double structure* of speech that a universal pragmatics is principally concerned. On the one hand with 'the *level of intersubjectivity* on which speaker and hearer, through illocutionary acts, establish the relations that permit them to come to an understanding with one another.'[67] On the other hand, with the *level of propositional content* which is communicated. Communication is not merely the transmission of content, but entails also a relational aspect. Habermas argues that participants in a dialogue communicate on both levels simultaneously. The task of a universal pragmatics, he proposes, is the 'rational reconstruction of the double structure of speech'.[68]

Yet whilst a universal pragmatics directs itself toward the 'double structure' of speech, one of these elements, namely the illocutionary, is clearly prioritised in Habermas's account. Thus Habermas argues that although there are other modes of language use, 'the illocutionary use seems to be the foundation on which even these other kinds of employment rest.'[69] The content of an utterance is only held to acquire a specifically *communicative* function when the conditions for the occurrence of an interpersonal relation are fulfilled. In Habermas's words, for a theory of communicative competence 'the third aspect of utterances, namely the establishment of interpersonal relations, is central.'[70] Propositional content refers to 'the objectivating attitude of observers who correctly report their experience in propositions.'[71] Illocutionary meanings, however, are acquired 'in connection with communicative experiences that we have in entering upon the level of intersubjectivity and establishing interpersonal relations'.[72] Propositional content is a necessary condition of all speech acts, but *communication* is defined in terms of the attempt to bring about *intersubjective* agreement.

Habermas argues that the *success* of a speech act consists in its ability to bring about an interpersonal relation between speaker and hearer. It is, he proposes, only when the hearer actually enters into the relationship intended by the speaker that the speech act can be deemed to have succeeded. The notion of 'illocutionary force' refers to this 'generative power' of speech acts. Habermas takes this 'generative power' of speech acts as a basis for arguing that the conditions of acceptability of a speech act reside 'within the *institutionally unbound* speech act itself'.[73] The condition that the speaker must 'engage' himself must, Habermas argues, always be fulfilled when it is a case of communicative action oriented to reaching understanding. The performance of an illocutionary act requires that the speaker guarantee that he will fulfill certain conditions as a consequence of his utterance. For instance, a speaker must consider a question settled when an adequate answer has been provided, drop an assertion when it proves false, and so on.[74]

Since Habermas is referring here to 'institutionally unbound' speech acts, illocutionary force cannot be traced back to any particular institutional or normative context. Habermas argues that '*the illocutionary force of an acceptable speech act consists in the fact that it can move a hearer to rely on the speech-act-typical commitments of the speaker.*'[75] And these 'speech-act-typical commitments', Habermas argues, are '*connected with cognitively testable validity claims*'.[76] That is, the reciprocal bonds into which the speaker enters in the performance of an illocutionary act have a 'rational basis'. They depend on 'the ability of a subject to have cognitions' and on the 'ability of a subject to assume responsibility'.[77]

Habermas's proposals for a universal pragmatics, it will be recalled, were advanced with a view to securing a non-transcendental basis for a critical theory. In this respect I argue that his account runs into serious difficulties. Illocutionary force, in Habermas's account, is considered to be secured to the extent that it has a 'rational foundation'. And this rational foundation derives from the attributes Habermas ascribes to communicating subjects. Illocutionary force depends on a notion of the essential capacities of subjects which provide the conditions of possibility of communication. Without these attributes illocutionary force, and indeed communication itself, would not be able to function. It is, I argue, this attempt to elaborate the notion of intersubjectivity through the concept of illocutionary force which undercuts Habermas's attempt to produce a universal pragmatics. To the extent that illocutionary force is conceived as separate from normative and institutional conditions of possibility, the 'pragmatic' dimension of speech is, I suggest, thereby excluded from a universal pragmatics. The 'universal' dimension of speech, which in turn depends on an *a priori* conception of the attributes of subjects as rational beings, becomes the absolute basis of intersubjectivity. In this way intersubjectivity is reinstated as a transcendental foundation for critical theory.

Habermas provides us with a tour through a variety of positions within the philosophy of language in an attempt to establish the concepts for a universal pragmatics. I have only alluded to some of these alternative positions above,[78] and I have only included those details of Habermas's argument of direct relevance to my concerns. But it is, I argue, to the *a priori* capacities of the speaking subject that we are returned. It is ultimately with a notion of the rational properties of the subject that Habermas is concerned, for it is on this basis that the possibility of communication depends. I suggest that in this respect Habermas does not progress to any significant extent beyond the proposals examined in previous chapters. The notion of a universal pragmatics is in part an attempt to connect more explicitly the question of emancipation with everyday processes of communication. An unfettered subjectivity is considered by Habermas to be a counterfactual assumption on which all speech, and indeed all social action[79] depends. Yet the priority Habermas accords in his account to the notion of illocutionary force, and the extent to which this notion is dependent on a concept of rational subjectivity, prevents him from establishing the connection between emancipation and intersubjective communication. Habermas argues that the normative context of communication is secondary in relation to rational subjectivity as the universal basis of communication. This, however, is little more than an assertion. Habermas explicitly renounces the attempt to trace illocutionary force back to a specific normative context; instead he derives it from a notion of the rational properties of a subject conceived as anterior to all empirical situations of language use. The notion of emancipation remains, I argue, fundamentally divorced as a result from empirical processes of communication.

Habermas seeks to avoid such a criticism by arguing that whereas the Kantian transcendental analysis implied a set of *a priori* conditions of possibility of experience, the term transcendental in his account denotes 'the conceptual structure recurring in all coherent experiences'.[80] This weaker version entails, he argues, an attempt to discard the claim that this structure can be demonstrated *a priori*. In place of the Kantian transcendental subject is substituted an investigation of 'the conditions for argumentatively redeeming validity claims that are at least implicitly related to discursive vindication'.[81] But elsewhere he states that a universal pragmatics aims to elucidate the '*a priori* concepts of utterances in general – that is, the basic concepts of situations of possible understanding, the conceptual structures that enable us to employ sentences in correct utterances'.[82] This apparent confusion can be clarified by noting that for Habermas the break with transcendental philosophy resides in that a universal pragmatics investigates the general structures of speech as primarily oriented to the goal of *reaching an understanding* and not in terms of *the objects of possible experience*.

But I suggest that this is not sufficient to enable Habermas to avoid a transcendental notion of subjectivity. For Habermas still retains an *a priori* notion of the capacities of subjects to 'reach an understanding'. The transcendental element is retained in the form of the notion of the rational properties of the subject that engages in communication. Indeed without such a postulate Habermas's notion of the orientation of communication towards 'reaching an understanding' could not be maintained.

This notion that communication is oriented toward 'reaching an understanding' means in Habermas's account that 'the *design* of an ideal speech situation is necessarily implied in the structure of potential speech, since all speech, even of intentional deception is oriented toward the idea of truth.'[83] As noted above, this notion of an 'ideal speech situation' entails the 'guarantee that intersubjective recognition can be brought about under suitable conditions'.[84] Now it is true that Habermas presents this as a counterfactual assumption. Moreover it would be wrong to object to it simply by offering an alternative *a priori* notion of what communication is. But in so far as Habermas wishes to argue that such a model is the foundation on which all speech takes place, one can object that Habermas produces no grounds for assuming that 'genuine intersubjectivity' is the *a priori* of communication, and no grounds for prioritising it in his account.

Habermas asserts that communication is founded on a model of the ideal speech situation, which in turn depends on an image of genuine intersubjective agreement. He then proceeds to erect a complex conceptual structure around this assertion. But he fails to produce grounds for his initial assumption. This is, of course, not to deny that the attempt to 'bring about agreement' may be an important part of communication. But this is not what Habermas is concerned to establish. He seeks rather to demonstrate that *all* speech is founded on such a possibility. Further, he does so in terms of a philosophical model of agreement between rational subjects. It is this progression from empirical speech, to a notion of communication conceived in terms of the orientation toward 'reaching an understanding', to an image of the latter as established *via* the capacities of rational subjects which I argue can be disputed. I argue that by virtue of this progression Habermas cannot claim to have incorporated the empirical dimension of speech within a universal pragmatics. And it is for this reason that I argue Habermas's proposals for a universal pragmatics fail to advance beyond a philosophy of the subject as a foundation for critical theory. Whilst a theory of intersubjectivity is Habermas's expressed intention, this is grounded in a philosophical *a priori* of the capacities of subjects.

To summarise this discussion of Habermas's proposals for a universal pragmatics two points can be made. Firstly, I have argued that the notion of illocutionary force becomes something of a philosophical 'first principle' for the project of a universal pragmatics. To the extent that illocutionary force is separated from the context of particular norms and institutions under which communication takes place, intersubjectivity is provided with no substantive conditions of existence. I have argued that intersubjectivity can only be understood as the realisation of the *a priori* attributes of subjects, primarily the rational properties required for 'reaching an understanding'. I suggest that this leaves Habermas's project for a universal pragmatics fully on the terrain of a philosophy of the subject. Despite the concern to move beyond a philosophy of the subject to an empirically grounded concept of intersubjectivity, I argue Habermas's arguments are in continuity with the concerns of Horkheimer and Marcuse discussed in the previous two chapters.

Secondly, the notion that Habermas's work represents a 'linguistic turn' in critical theory must, I suggest, be considerably weakened. Language is not incorporated in Habermas's account as something with its own effectivity, it has no effects proper to it with regard to the formation of intersubjectivity. Again, I argue that Habermas fails to break with the earlier concerns of critical theory. This non-effectivity of language is, I suggest, interwoven with Habermas's inability to incorporate the 'pragmatic' dimension of speech within his proposals for a universal pragmatics. Despite the complex and apparently innovative nature of Habermas's excursions into the philosophy of language, I argue that he fails to break with the problems of conceptualising subjectivity which beset Horkheimer and Marcuse's project for critical theory.

LEGITIMATION CRISES AND THE COMMUNICATION-COMMUNITY

The notion of a universal pragmatics connects with the concepts of legitimation and domination which Habermas develops in *Legitimation Crisis*.[85] I am not concerned here to follow through all he details of Habermas's systems model of crisis tendencies.[86] I shall confine myself to examining Habermas's attempt to establish the concepts of legitimation and legitimation crisis in terms of the model of the 'ideal speech situation' discussed in the previous section of this chapter. From this I suggest that one can demonstrate serious difficulties with Habermas's account of legitimation. I argue that these derive largely from Habermas's attempt to base a universal pragmatics on a notion of communication which is dependent on a model of rational subjectivity.

It may help to begin by providing definitions of Habermas's notion of crisis, and of the concepts of 'system integration' and 'social integration' on which the theory of crisis tendencies depends. A crisis, Habermas argues, cannot be defined entirely in terms of an 'objective process viewed from the outside'. A notion of crisis requires also that one include 'the viewpoint of the one who is undergoing it'.[87] Thus the 'objectivity of illness' entails that the patient 'is a subject condemned to passivity and temporarily deprived of the possibility of being a subject in full possession of his powers.'[88] Likewise, a social-scientific notion of crisis requires 'the idea of an objective force that deprives a subject of some part of his normal sovereignty.'[89] To speak of a crisis, Habermas argues, is to invoke an implicitly normative meaning. This normative aspect resides at the level of the subject who is involved; the resolution of the crisis 'effects a liberation of the subject caught up in it'.[90]

Having defined the concept of crisis in these terms, Habermas rejects an exclusively systems-based notion of crisis.[91] It is necessary, he argues, that one provide a concept of crisis which includes as one important aspect the dimension of the subject involved in the crisis. But he proposes that this be achieved without discarding entirely a systems framework. Thus he offers a distinction between 'system integration' and 'social integration'. 'System integration' refers to the 'specific steering performances of a self-regulated system,'[92] in terms of its capacities for boundary maintenance and ability to master the environment. 'Social integration' refers to 'the systems of institutions in which speaking and acting subjects are socially related (*vergesellschaftet*)'.[93] Social systems are viewed here as symbolically structured *life-worlds*. Crises derive their 'objectivity' from unresolved steering problems at the system level, which in turn generate problems which affect the consciousness of subjects in such a manner 'as to endanger social integration'.[94]

Habermas argues that a theory of crisis tendencies must attempt to resolve the question of the interconnection between life-world and system. Crisis occurrences, Habermas argues, 'owe their objectivity to the fact that they issue from unresolved steering problems'.[95] Whilst 'subjects are not generally conscious' of these steering problems, they are nevertheless held to be affected by them in such a manner as to endanger 'social integration'.[96] And it is when social integration is threatened that we can, Habermas argues, speak of crises. That is, we can speak of crises 'when members of a society experience structural alterations as critical for continued existence and feel their social identity threatened.'[97] Crisis states exist 'when the consensual foundations of normative structures are so much impaired that the society becomes anomic.'[98]

With this starting point Habermas seeks to develop an account of those crisis tendencies he considers specific to advanced capitalism. The aim of such an enterprise is to locate the possibility of a 'post-modern' society, that is, 'a historically new principle of organization and not a different name for the surprising vigor of an aged capitalism'.[99] The account of legitimation crises Habermas prosposes is thus in continuity with the concerns of Horkheimer and Marcuse in that it attempts to provide the basis for an analysis of the present with a view to demonstrating the possibility of a future society no longer based on class divisions and the imposition of false needs.

My concern here is principally with the terms in which Habermas elaborates the notion of legitimation crisis. I do not propose to discuss Habermas's stunningly formalistic delineation of the 'universal properties' of social systems, neither shall I dwell on the distinctions between the notions of economic crisis, rationality crisis, legitimation crisis and motivation crisis. Habermas attempts to develop a concept of legitimation in accordance with the principles of a universal pragmatics. He also attempts to reformulate the notion of the 'end of the individual' discussed in chapters 1 and 2. That is, Habermas raises the question as to whether communication today still occurs under conditions which 'admit of truth', and hence whether there is any foundation for a project of critique.

The central question for Habermas's notion of legitimation problems is whether 'justifiable norms can be distinguished from norms that merely stabilize relations of force'.[100] If this can be achieved, and Habermas maintains that it can, then one is able, he suggests, to broach the question of legitimation problems in contemporary society. The question here is whether existing norms are capable of justification in terms of the model of the 'ideal speech situation', whether existing norms 'admit of truth'. Without this obtaining, legitimation problems would cease and legitimation would be a question simply of responding to steering imperatives of the social system;[101] I shall come to this question shortly. For the moment let us recap on the notion of the 'ideal speech situation', and how Habermas uses this model for the task of examining the notion of legitimation problems.

Belief in legitimacy can, Habermas argues, be considered in terms of an 'immanent relation to truth'.[102] The grounds on which a legitimacy claim is established 'contain a rational validity claim that can be tested and criticized independently of the psychological effect of these grounds'.[103] This, of course, is to reaffirm the claim of a universal pragmatics that recourse can be had to 'the fundamental norms of rational speech, which we presuppose in every discourse'.[104] If this 'capacity of practical questions for truth'[105] could be disputed, Habermas notes that his position would be untenable. He thus seeks to establish firstly 'the *possibility* of justifying (*begrunden*) normative-validity claims, that is, of providing rational grounds (*rational motivieren*) for their recognition.'[106] Secondly, and equally important, he raises the question of 'whether the acceptance of binding decisions without grounds has today become routine, or whether functionally requisite motivations are still produced through internalisation of norms that need justification.'[107]

The latter question entails a discussion of the postulate of the 'end of the individual'. I return to this below. With regard to the former, the *possibility* of justifying normative-validity claims, Habermas maintains that the binding character of norms could not be explained if only empirical motives were underpinning the agreement. He proposes a distinction between 'obeying concrete commands' and following 'inter-subjectively recognised norms', with the latter based on the model of the communication-community held to operate according to the 'fundamental laws of rational speech'. Consensus in such a situation can, he argues, only be achieved 'with reasons'; the binding character of norms established in this context is held to reside in the possibility that they may be questioned at any time. The conditions which are required in order to enable this discursive-testing of validity claims are:

> That the bracketed validity claims of assertions, recommendations, or warnings are the exclusive object of discussion; that participants,

> themes and contributions are not restricted except with reference to the goal of testing the validity claims in question; that no force except that of the better argument is exercised; and that, as a result, all motives except that of the cooperative search for truth are excluded.[108]

If a consensus is arrived at under such circumstances then Habermas argues that this can be considered to express a 'rational will' which can arise 'only through appropriately interpreted, *generalizable* interests, by which I mean needs that can be *communicatively* shared'.[109] It is the possibility of realising this state of affairs which Habermas considers avoids both the difficulty of separating generalisable interests from those that remain particular, as well as the abstract positing of a pure reason which can never be actualised. It entails the 'introduction of a "moral principle" that obliges each participant in a practical discourse to transfer his subjective desires into generalizable desires.'[110] And this 'moral principle' does not, Habermas argues, entail the Kantian separation of the sphere of morality from the empirical spheres. It is achieved rather through the telos of mutual understanding toward which all speech aspires:

> In taking up a practical discourse, we unavoidably suppose an ideal speech situation that, on the strength of its formal properties, allows consensus only through *generalisable* interests. A cognitivist linguistic ethics (*Sprachethik*) has no need of principles. It is based only on fundamental norms of rational speech that we must always presuppose if we discourse at all.[111]

On this basis the notion of the 'suppression of generalisable interests' is employed to distinguish norms based on a 'rational consensus' from those norms that merely 'stabilize relations of force'.[112] Ideological legitimations can be identified, Habermas argues, in that they seek to demonstrate the legitimacy of the validity claims of existing norms whilst at the same time avoiding the testing of discursive-validity claims. Against this critical theory 'starts from the *model of the suppression of generalizable interests* and compares normative structures existing at a given time with the hypothetical state of a system of norms formed, *ceteris paribus*, discursively.'[113] A 'counterfactual reconstruction' is proposed which seeks to answer the question of how the members of a given social system would have intersubjectively developed social relations 'if they could and would have decided on organisation of social intercourse through discursive will-formation, with adequate knowledge of the limiting conditions and functional imperatives of their society?'[114] The role of critical theory in such a situation is that of identifying generalisable yet suppressed interests 'by counterfactually imagining (*fingieren*) the limit case of a conflict between the involved parties in which they would be forced to consciously perceive their interests and strategically assert them'.[115]

Habermas attempts to establish the very possibility of a critical theory of legitimation through its ability to identify an 'ideological consensus'. I argue, however, that this project founders precisely on those difficulties which I have suggested the model of intersubjectivity itself encounters. It was argued above that the notion that speech fundamentally implies an orientation toward a condition of genuine understanding has only been asserted by Habermas. A critique of domination mounted on such a basis can, I argue, be no more than a denunciation of existing norms in terms of an *a priori* image of the good life and of the attributes of subjectivity required to realise it. The Kantian separation of the sphere of morality from that of sensuous human activity is, I argue, reproduced in so far as discourse is understood as 'that form of communication that is removed from contexts of experience and action'.[116] Habermas's cognitivist linguistic ethics is considered to merely reaffirm a *prima philosophia* from which I argue the critical theory of Horkheimer and Marcuse unsuccessfully attempted to separate itself. Moreover, when one asks how the principle of the 'suppression of generalisable interests' might be usefully applied a number of problems arise.

An initial difficulty is that since the notion of 'rational reconstruction' is a second-level construct, and since in a process of communication there can only ever be participants, there is no explanation of how one is to translate the knowledge of the observers into the practical activity of the participants. The only model available to Habermas is that which I discussed critically in the first section of this chapter. That is, a vacillation between a notion of theory as enlightenment, as the awakening of consciousness; and on the other hand a 'popular' demand that participants remain the arbiters. I suggest that Habermas is restricted to either vacillation or incoherence, by virtue of his failure to confront adequately the connection he posits between the model of the communication-community and the 'everyday knowledge' of the participants in communication.

More important perhaps is the problem which arises when one

asks how the conditions necessary for the discursive testing of validity claims might be secured. Habermas specifies a range of conditions which refer on the one hand to the empirical setting in which such a process occurs – for example, whether there is free movement into and out of the group, or whether one person is in a position of power over others. On the other hand they refer to the capacities of the subjects participating in such a process – that they be motivated by no other force than that of the better argument, and that they be capable of subjecting norms to a rational questioning. The difficulty here is that Habermas provides no indication as to how one would demonstrate that both these conditions are operative and that a genuine understanding as opposed to an ideological consensus is secured.

This attempt to demonstrate that the conditions have been supplied in which can obtain a situation of mutual understanding may be conceded in respect of the appropriate empirical conditions which Habermas specifies in advance – that there be free movement in and out of the group, that no one person be in a position of power over others, and so on. But it does not suffice for the question of how the participants, as dialogue-constitutive subjects, are to *rid themselves* of those ideological contaminations which hitherto have obstructed the development of a genuine consensus. To pose this question is to return to the problems identified in the previous section. Habermas offers no grounds for assuming speech to be ultimately grounded in the possibility of genuine consensus.

Habermas develops, I argue, an account which depends on a binary model of the repression and liberation of the attributes of rational subjectivity; and it is formulated in such a manner as to separate the notion of subjectivity from that of its empirical conditions of existence. The latter, for Habermas, provide only the context and have no effectivity at the level of the constitution of that subjectivity on which depends the model of mutual understanding. To this extent Habermas provides no basis for conceptualising the process by which an ideological consensus gives way to a genuine consensus based on rational subjectivity. An 'ideological consensus' may be one in which rational subjectivity cannot operate in such a fashion as effectively to realise mutual understanding. But Habermas does not provide the concepts which would enable one to think through the transition from an ideological consensus to a situation of mutual understanding. This deficiency can, I suggest, be seen to derive from the *a priori* notion of rational subjectivity on which Habermas's proposals for a universal pragmatics depend. The attributes of rational subjects on which speech is held to operate in Habermas's account are not *produced* under determinate conditions of existence. Habermas does not demonstrate how such capacities might emerge in communication. They remain, I argue, only a counterfactual *assumption*.

We can now take up the question of the 'end of the individual'. This illustrates the difficulties entailed in Habermas's conception of critical theory at the level of its 'practical intent'. Habermas argues that it is an 'open question whether in complex societies motive formation is *actually* still tied to norms that require justification, or whether norm systems have lost their relation to truth.'[117] Thus it is possible, he states, that 'the steering imperatives of highly complex societies could necessitate disconnecting the formation of motives from norms capable of justification.'[118] In this case legitimation problems, he argues, would no longer exist.

Habermas is at his most interesting when he states that 'until now no one has succeeded in extracting the thesis of the end of the individual from the domain of the malaise and self-experience of intellectuals and made it accessible to empirical test.'[119] Unfortunately, however, he declares himself unable to provide the 'empirical test' necessary to answer such a question. Referring to the notion of the 'end of the individual' Habermas states that 'I cannot see how this question can be decided empirically.'[120] Unable to settle the question empirically Habermas attempts to deal with it obliquely, by examining Luhmann's arguments on the matter.

Luhmann's work provides some support for the criticisms I have advanced against Habermas.[121] He argues that:

> Habermas sees the subject, just as the intersubjectivity which precedes it, primarily as a potential for foundations admitting of truth. The subjectivity of man consists for him in the possibility of specifying rational grounds in intersubjective communication, or of being able to accommodate oneself to such grounds or to the refutation of one's own grounds. He thereby captures, however, only a derivative aspect – and, moreover, one which seems to me to be historically conditioned and long antiquated – of a much more deeply seated concept of the subject.[122]

Luhmann suggests that it is through a notion of subjectivity that Habermas seeks to ground the thesis of intersubjective communication as founded on 'truth'. Habermas takes issue with Luhmann, but only to turn the argument round and attack Luhmann's systems model of power. Habermas argues that Luhmann's 'problem of world complexity requires an essentialistic and exclusive application of the concept of system'.[123] Because the problem of 'world complexity' assumes priority in Luhmann's account 'the problem of a rational organization of society in conjunction with formation of motives through norms that admit of truth has lost its object.'[124]

Luhmann, Habermas argues, has prejudged the question of the 'end of the individual' by the 'choice of his methodological approach'.[125] But Habermas, by his own admission, cannot decide the matter empirically. He is in fact able to muster only one argument in favour of his own proposal that a situation in which motive formation is no longer tied to 'truth' may not yet have been reached. He argues that 'While critical social theory can founder on a changed reality, universal functionalism must suppose – that is, prejudge at the analytical level – that this change in the mode of socialization and the "end of the individual" have already come to pass.'[126]

Habermas appears unable to accept the extent to which he himself has settled the question in advance. An empirical demonstration of whether the 'end of the individual' has come to pass is, according to Habermas, not possible. Yet Habermas cannot accept Luhmann's diagnosis of the 'end of the individual' because to do so would dissolve the project of a universal pragmatics and the possibility of a critical theory founded on it. Habermas's theory of legitimation requires that rational subjectivity not only be a counterfactual assumption, but also a possible genuine force in society. A communications-based notion of critical theory could not function if legitimation were to operate through norms that do not 'admit of truth'. And it is, by Habermas's own admission, not possible empirically to settle the question as to whether or not this has occurred. Habermas's critical theory thus can only *assume* that the 'end of the individual' has not come to pass. And what this means in terms of the notion of rational subjectivity which I have discussed in the previous section is that it has to remain an *a priori* in Habermas's account. Without this priority accorded to a philosophy of the subject Habermas would, I argue, not be able to sustain his account of the notion of legitimation.

A THEORY OF COMMUNICATIVE ACTION

Habermas's writings have always managed to provoke widespread debate. This is no less true of his recent work than of his earlier involvements in political argument. Critics have taken the very concept of critical theory to task,[127] as well as the recent attempt by Habermas to found such a project on a concept of language as representing a rational principle which turns out not to be found in language as such.[128] This latter criticism is of the notion of an *a priori* ideal which is similar to my arguments above. To view language as a medium of free dialogue is to invoke a notion of rationality as intersubjective recognition which is not identical with language and is not found in all acts of speech. The utilisation of the Kantian model of transcendental reflection for understanding linguistic communication cannot be assumed to be appropriate.

The project of a universal pragmatics has also had directed at it some forceful criticism. Habermas's arguments concerning the presupposition of an ideal speech situation have been considered problematic. The actual operation of speech situations which would exclude external constraints as well as eliminate internal constraints has been questioned.[129] There is no guarantee that a formally symmetrical distribution of opportunities to select and employ speech acts will result in anything more than an expression of the *status quo*. Habermas's model neglects also the fact that social life is constrained not only by access to speech acts, but by access to other more material factors such as wealth or weapons.

Habermas has replied briefly, although not entirely convincingly, to some of the criticisms raised against his approach. He has also 'replied' in a vastly expanded form in his two volume *Theorie des kommunikativen Handelns*, volume one of which is now translated into English as *The Theory of Communicative Action*.[130] This represents an attempt to synthesise and elaborate the concepts developed in his theory of communicative action and rationality. The book provides assessments of the major theoretical traditions which have influenced him, particularly Weber. It provides also a range of conceptual adjustments to his communicative basis for a theory of reason and rationality. The argument that rationality and communication are intrinsically related remains central, providing a basis for an opposition to relativism. The concept of communicative action, which emphasises interaction between two or more subjects in an attempt to arrive at an understanding, continues to provide the basis for avoiding a notion of action as the pursuit of an agent's intentions. The work of Weber is representative of the latter interpretation. Habermas is preoccupied also with maintaining the role of critique, but shifting its target from the instrumental reason attacked by Horkheimer and Marcuse to functionalist reason.

Habermas reiterates his attempt to go beyond the works of Austin and others on the theory of speech acts. Austin's limitation is considered to be his focus on the requirements for the performance of particular speech acts. Habermas's concern is with the general presuppositions entailed in speech acts. The 'validity claims' raised by speech acts depend in general on there being reasons and grounds for their acceptance. A 'rational motivation' is at work, Habermas argues, in the process of communication.

The attempt to provide an account of the reason fundamental to speech is more closely connected to the attempt to delineate the role of reason in social development than in his earlier writings. The ambition underlying Habermas's project in *The Theory of Communicative Action* might be identified as the locating of speech more firmly in *social* interaction than in counterfactually proposed images of institutionally unbound discourse. Habermas seeks to locate the basis of communicative action not in transcendental postulates of ideal speech, or the quasi-transcendental of a knowledge-constitutive interest. It is the 'competencies' of social actors which is central. The postulate of intersubjective recognition based on the notion of validity claims raised in speech (truth, rightness, sincerity and comprehensibility) is retained. The 'rational motivation' underlying speech is retained also as a fundamental premise. Habermas attempts, however, to avoid the more pronounced transcendental features of his notion of an ideal speech situation. The notion that this represents the anticipation of an actual form of social life is replaced by a view of a wholly rational society as only an illusion. Such an image is to be judged by its empirical and theoretical fruitfulness for the detection of pathologies within society.

It is clearly impossible to attempt to do justice to the scope and rigour of Habermas's arguments in this recent work in the space of only a few pages. It will indeed be some while before its achievements will be fully assessed. With regard to the limited focus of my concerns in this study I can, however, identify one key reservation I have with the project. This reservation concerns the attempt to found the theory of communication on principles much the same as those of the notion of a universal pragmatics. My concern with Habermas's arguments for a theory of communication centres on his continued affirmation that orientation toward reaching an understanding is the fundamental basis of speech. Habermas retains this argument in *The Theory of Communicative Action*. But as one sympathetic yet perceptive commentator on Habermas's work has remarked, in what sense does telling a joke presuppose the truth of what is said, or collective bargaining operate according to criteria of sincerity?[131] The force of objections such as these resides not in the individual examples, but in the general problem they raise for attempting to found a theory of communication on the general postulate of orientation toward reaching an understanding.

In *The Theory of Communicative Action* Habermas retains the notion that it is the '*rationally motivated binding* (or bonding: *Bindung*) *force*' of an utterance which can motivate a hearer to accept the offer contained in a speech act.[132] Despite the distinction between social action oriented toward success and that which is oriented toward reaching understanding, it is the latter which Habermas posits as fundamental. Rational motivation in this schema remains institutionally unbound. The rational basis of a communicatively achieved agreement cannot be imposed by either party. Agreement obtained by force or violence does not count subjectively as agreement. Common convictions or the acceptance by each party are what is required for agreement in Habermas's schema.

Habermas's method remains that of an elaborate definitional web which excludes as external or irrelevant that which does not fit. This is necessary in order for him to establish his fundamental point, that 'the use of language with an orientation to reaching understanding is the *original mode* of language use, upon which indirect understanding, giving something to understand or letting something be understood, and the instrumental use of language in general, are parasitic.'[133] To achieve this end Habermas simply defines communicative action in such a manner as to render orientation toward understanding as the essence of communication: 'I count as communicative action those linguistically mediated interactions in which all participants pursue illocutionary aims, and *only* illocutionary aims, with their mediating acts of communication.'[134] The wholly circular nature of the argument is manifest when Habermas returns to explain the basis of his choice of a formal-pragmatics as opposed to an empirical pragmatics. The latter, he argues:

> would not have the conceptual instruments needed to recognize the

> rational basis of linguistic communication in the confusing complexity of the everyday scenes observed. It is only in formal-pragmatic investigations that we can secure for ourselves an idea of reaching understanding that can guide empirical analysis into particular problems – such as the linguistic representation of different levels of reality, the manifestation of communication pathologies, or the development of a decentered understanding of the world.[135]

The complexity of linguistic communication, its deviation from the principles of a formal-pragmatics as outlined by Habermas, can only be understood by positing, or asserting, that ultimately it has a rational basis. This has the additional advantage of allowing us to detect what Habermas calls 'pathologies' of communication.

Even in his recent and extensive discussion of a communicative theory of action Habermas fails, I argue, to provide grounds for his arguments. The model of the ideal dialogue, its counterfactual status, the notion of rational motivation, all these ideas to my mind have not been substantiated by Habermas. The outcome of his arguments has always been known in advance, as one persistent critic has pointed out so clearly.[136] Habermas has sought to establish and redirect the project of critical theory by elaborating a concept of reason borrowed from idealist philosophy with the aid of a theory of language. This equation of language and reason, however, has not been demonstrated to be possible. Construed in the way Habermas presents the project of critical theory, reason has no means at its disposal for becoming the instrument of critique Habermas wishes it to be. Its abstractness, its counterfactual nature, the abyss which separates it from empirical communication, leaves it devoid of substance, little more than a highly elaborate version of the negative denunciation of the present that Marcuse arrived at. Habermas's work has always been open to the criticism that his arguments are primarily assertions. This applies equally to his recent work as to his proposals for a set of quasi-transcendental interests. Unfortunately, there is little in his recent work that indicates that he has developed the argument beyond assertion. There is no doubting the systematic and rigorous manner in which he has pursued the project of a critique of rationalisation. There is little indication, however, that he has been willing to accept the extent of the revisions in his fundamental premises which would be required to overcome the reservations which have been expressed with it.

CONCLUSION

I have discussed Habermas's work in this chapter in terms of the restricted concerns of this study with the interrelation between the concepts of domination and subjectivity. I have examined Habermas's attempt to avoid a transcendental notion of subjectivity through his elaboration of the notion of intersubjectivity. The latter, Habermas argues, is the basis on which all speech, and indeed all social action takes place. Habermas's work has been considered to demonstrate a continuity of concerns in this respect, despite the shifts in emphasis which it has undergone. The communicative notion of intersubjectivity developed by Habermas in his recent writings serves as an attempt to avoid an *a priori* notion of subjectivity, and as a means of developing the concepts regarded as appropriate for a critique of domination. The latter is conceived in terms of a model of speech as fundamentally based on an orientation toward understanding. This model of speech depends, I have argued, on an *a priori* notion of the rational properties of the subject. I suggest that Habermas does not succeed in avoiding a philosophy of the subject, despite his ambitious attempt to develop an intersubjective foundation for critical theory. The project of a critical theory suffers, I argue, as a consequence.

PART 2

MICHEL FOUCAULT: GENEALOGIES OF THE SUBJECT

•

CHAPTER 4

UNREASON TO MADNESS: THE KNOWLEDGE OF SUBJECTIVITY

•

Foucault's work can usefully be read overall as a genealogy of the modern subject, as an account of the formation of the subject as object-to-be-known. *Histoire de la Folie* is central to this enterprise.[1] In it Foucault charts the diverse conditions of possibility of psychiatry and psychology as systematic investigations of the subjectivity of the individual which provide a knowledge of the individual inaccessible through the experience of the subject alone.[2] As a genealogy of the modern subject Foucault's account in *Histoire de la Folie* demonstrates what he has termed elsewhere the 'surfaces of emergence'[3] of a particular body of knowledge and series of operations directed both at madness and at the individual insane person. Madness was not, Foucault argues, separated from all the other categories of internment of the seventeenth and eighteenth century as a result of the arrival of a scientific knowledge of insanity. Rather, he suggests that the possibility of a detailed and systematic knowledge of madness must itself be related to such questions as differentiations effected within the world of internment, changes in the functioning of the legal apparatus, and a reorganisation of the sphere of assistance.

The importance of such transformations for the purposes of this study is that they demonstrate firstly the historicity of the modern subject as object of psychiatric knowledge. Foucault shows conclusively that the knowledge of madness and of the insane person which became possible with nineteenth-century psychiatry was not the culmination of a centuries-old project to decipher the manifestations of insanity. The subject of which nineteenth-century psychiatry provided the knowledge was, that is, an 'invention' of the late eighteenth and early nineteenth century. Second, Foucault argues that the knowledge of madness which developed in the nineteenth century was based on the notion that such knowledge provided access to the 'truth' of man. It was, he suggests, only through madness that the truth of man as a *subject* could become the *object* of a scientific knowledge.

This was, he suggests, an 'event' which did not consist in finally recognising what had always been there. It was, rather, a correlative formation of the subject and object of knowledge. What is decisive for my purposes here is that this object is also a subject, yet knowledge of it can only be provided to the extent that it becomes an object of scientific perception. Third, Foucault introduces into his account of the conditions of possibility of psychiatry the question of the administration and government of populations.[4] As a domain-to-be-administered Foucault demonstrates how, in the case of insanity, this was finally to be effected on the basis of a body of positive knowledge of the subject.

This attention to the question of the surfaces of emergence of psychiatric knowledge illustrates that the individualisation of madness was only in part a question of theoretical elaboration and investigation. In addition to locating the conditions of possibility of psychiatry at the level of changes in the world of internment and in the functioning of the judicial apparatus,[5] Foucault situates psychiatry also in terms of the question of assistance. Thus in the late eighteenth century Foucault argues that the connection of human labour with the production of wealth entailed a reorganisation of the relations between poverty, illness and assistance. For the first time, Foucault suggests, illness found itself isolated as a result of this reorganisation from the question of poverty.

Madness in Foucault's account achieved its singularity *vis-à-vis* the other categories of asocial behaviours through a range of diverse operations. It was not individualised as a result of the persistent and finally successful endeavours of medical men.[6] Nor was it simply delivered ready-made into the hands of a profession which was created as a response to demands by society that madness be treated. Foucault unravels rather the complex web of conditions of possibility of both madness and of psychiatry as the profession to which the insane were entrusted.

In the context of this study what is crucial in Foucault's account are the linkages which it establishes between three elements – the category of the subject, the role of a particular body of knowledge, and the question of administration. Foucault demonstrates admirably how the second of these lay claim to a knowledge of the former, at least in part through a reorganisation of the sphere of government.

There are of course numerous histories of psychiatry other than Foucault's.[7] But as I have remarked already, *Histoire de la Folie* is not a history of psychiatry, it is rather a history of the *conditions of possibility* of psychiatry. As such it is distinct in its approach from an account such as Ackerknecht's *Short History of Psychiatry*.[8] Ackerknecht begins his history of psychiatry by stating that 'The history of psychiatry, like that of scientific medicine in general, really begins with the Greeks.'[9] By chapter five we are informed that 'In the eighteenth century psychiatry at last reached the status of an independent science. Psychiatric achievements surpassed earlier efforts, at first in quantity and later also in quality.'[10] Ackerknecht's account is a sophisticated one, as indeed are his other valuable contributions to the history of medicine.[11] Yet it is still couched in terms of the progressive elaboration through history of a genuinely scientific understanding of the nature of mental illness. This does not prevent him from appealing to ethnological research[12] to assert that the nature of mental illness is determined by the culture within which it appears. 'What is psychologically normal', he argues, 'depends to a high degree on the attitudes of different societies.'[13] But despite this Ackerknecht is concerned ultimately to chart the process through which psychiatry finally provides a knowledge of that object, madness, which was awaiting its scientific revelation. The Middle Ages is simply a period in which the advances made by the Greeks are tragically lost, and in place of a nascent psychiatry was substituted a belief in possession by the devil.[14]

One could chart also the differences between Foucault's account and a study such as Zilboorg and Henry's *History of Medical Psychology*.[15] Zilboorg, in much less sophisticated terms than Ackerknecht, is concerned to show how psychiatry emerged as a rational account of mental illness in place of earlier religious and superstitious doctrines. As with all medicine it was, Zilboorg argues, a response to the demands of the sick person to be treated, a demand which stretches back uniformly to the earliest feelings of sickness:

> No matter how far back into the remote past we delve, the sick man has never doubted that he was sick. . . . Whether he sought help of his companion of the forest or the desert, or of the primitive priest, the shaman, the medicine man, whether it was magic he desired or infusions of herbs, he was making the history of medicine: his very demand for help caused the appearance of primitive doctors.[16]

This type of account of the emergence of modern medicine has been seriously challenged in recent years. It is instructive, however, in so far as it emphasises my argument that *Histoire de la Folie* is not a history of psychiatry, but rather an account of the conditions which made psychiatry possible. The importance of this for the purposes of this study is that the conditions of possibility of psychiatry are also central to the conditions of possibility of the modern subject more generally as an entity which can be known.

It is worth noting that Foucault's concern with the question of madness is not confined to *Histoire de la Folie*, the first edition of which appeared in 1961.[17] In 1954 Foucault had published *Maladie Mentale et Personnalité*, which appeared in revised form in English as *Mental Illness and Psychology*. In 1957 we encounter the lengthy article 'La recherche du psychologue'[18] which, although not concerned with madness, touches on questions concerning psychology's claims to scientific truth and its status as a research practice. And more recently (1973) Foucault has edited and contributed to the dossier on Pierre Rivière,[19] the son of a French peasant who, in 1835, violently killed his mother, his sister and his brother.

It would be inaccurate to suggest that these different enterprises demonstrate a single theme constant throughout Foucault's researches over the past thirty years. But a continuity can be identified at the level of their concern to chart the complex of shifts at theoretical, institutional, administrative and judicial levels which enabled psychiatry to emerge as a specialised sphere of competence which could operate on and produce a knowledge of the individual insane person. That psychiatry has more recently come to function without recourse to the category of madness,[20] suggests that what is perhaps decisive for psychiatry's existence is its concern to produce a knowledge of the subjectivity of the individual rather than a knowledge of madness. To a large extent this is the way in which I have approached *Histoire de la Folie* for the purposes of this study. Viewed in these terms madness becomes one of the conditions of possibility of the contemporary concern with the subjectivity of individuals.[21] Madness is only one of the means through which the modern subject appears, even if *qua* means it also has its own effectivity.

This chapter offers a partial reading of *Histoire de la Folie* in terms of these themes. I examine Foucault's account in terms of the interrelation between the category of the subject, the knowledge which both operates on and produces the truth of that subject, and the question of administration or government. The aim is to follow through what I have argued is distinctive about Foucault's 'response' to the philosophy of the subject, namely the historical account he provides of the conditions of formation of the modern subject.

There are of course a number of difficulties in such an enterprise. One of these is due to the density of Foucault's argument in places. This is not to repeat the now monotonous charge of the 'idiosyncratic and self-consciously opaque pyrotechnics of Michel Foucault. . .'.[22] It is simply to suggest that despite the length of *Histoire de la Folie* its argument is in places extremely condensed. I do not pretend, however, to have provided a résumé of the book.[23] Rather I have read it in terms of the restricted concerns of this study. That this leaves untouched a number of important issues is self-evident and inevitable.[24]

Another difficulty resides at the level of the historical detail of what follows. In places this is unavoidably dense. It is worth noting also that on the question of historical detail some commentators have argued that there are a number of empirical inaccuracies in *Histoire de la Folie*.[25] I have chosen to omit an evaluation of these criticisms. This is because to confront them adequately would require more space than I can afford in the confines of this study. It is also because I do not consider that these criticisms affect my arguments here.

A further point should be noted. In the discussion of *Histoire de la Folie* that follows I have utilised the full length French edition. The abridged English translation (based on an abridged French edition) omits over half the original text, the bibliography, the various documents quoted in an appendix, and over 900 of its notes. This is, to say the least, not unimportant in view of comments made against Foucault's attention to historical detail.[26]

THE PROJECT OF A 'HISTORY' OF UNREASON

Histoire de la Folie begins with the figure of the leper in the European Middle Ages. Foucault argues that a concept of madness did not exist then, that leprosy was the object of social exclusion and was seen to be imposed by God's grace. Rather than take up Foucault's account at this point I begin with what he terms the classical experience of madness.

Foucault locates the advent of what he terms the classical experience of madness around the middle of the seventeenth century. But this chronological point is itself dispersed, as well as located at a number of different levels – institutional, philosophical, political and economic. A passage from Descartes[27] serves as a reference point to mark this moment at which madness is located as 'other', as object to be interned. In a discussion of Descartes omitted from the English translation of the book, Foucault seeks to demonstrate in the work of Descartes an imbalance between madness on the one hand and dreams and error on the other. With Descartes the certainty of *not* being mad, Foucault argues, is held to reside within the very interior of the subject that thinks, within the *cogito*. Madness for Descartes is seen to reside at a level other than that of the subject that thinks. The impossibility of being mad is ascertained not at the level of the object of thought but at that of the thinking subject. Madness is both the 'condition of impossibility of thought'[28] as well as that which is excluded by the subject that doubts. For Descartes the possibility of madness is expelled from the exercise of Reason. Whilst *man* may become insane, *thought* as the exercise of the sovereignty of the subject cannot be insane.

This passage from Descartes plays an important role in Foucault's account throughout *Histoire de la Folie*. It serves to denote at a symbolic level that process through which he suggests the classical age was to operate a division within Reason itself, or rather a separation which established the boundary of Reason. Whereas prior to the mid-seventeenth century the mad were a part of everyday life,[29] the 'great internment' of the seventeenth century was to operate an exclusion of madness which placed it firmly beyond the limits of Reason. The beginning of this 'great internment' was marked by the founding of the *Hôpital général* in Paris in 1656.

The importance of the three pages which Foucault devotes to Descartes in *Histoire de la Folie* is disproportionate to that which a simply quantitative assessment of the book might suggest. Derrida,[30] however, has taken this passage as fundamental to Foucault's enterprise in *Histoire de la Folie*. Foucault's entire project, he suggests 'can be pinpointed in these few allusive and somewhat enigmatic pages. . .'.[31] The very 'feasibility' of Foucault's history of madness is seen to depend on the discussion of Descartes, where it is both the interpretation of Descartes which is seen to be at stake, as well as '*certain* philosophical and methodological presuppositions of this history of madness.'[32]

The 'debate'[33] which took place between Foucault and Derrida on this question is not relevant here in all its details. But it does serve a useful purpose in clarifying what I regard as the nature of Foucault's enterprise, and not only in *Histoire de la Folie*. Derrida raises a number of objections to Foucault's account. Foucault, he suggests, attempted to write a history of madness *itself*, he wanted madness to be the subject of his book rather than an entity described from within the language of reason. This Derrida terms the '*maddest* aspect of his project.'[34] Derrida argues that disengagement from that language through which madness is exiled can be achieved only by not mentioning that 'silence' to which madness is reduced, or by following the madman down the road of his exile.

Part of Foucault's reply consists in arguing that the Greek notion of *hubris* did not entail that it functioned as contrary; the Greeks, he argues, had a different and perhaps closer relation to madness. Against this Derrida argues that the notion of a moment prior to the exclusion of madness results in an attempt to write the history of that division, an enterprise which 'runs the risk of construing the division as an event or a structure subsequent to the unity of an original presence, thereby confirming metaphysics in its fundamental operation.'[35] With regard to Derrida's own work this objection has an absolutely central importance. Moreover, Foucault is held to write the history of madness, a 'false and disintegrated concept' in Derrida's eyes, as if he *knew* what 'madness' means: 'Everything transpires as if, in a continuous and underlying way, an assured and rigorous precomprehension of the *concept* of madness, or at least of its nominal *definition*, were possible and acquired.'[36] The emphasis in this last quotation I have added myself because Derrida's objections on this point take us to the heart of the matter. Derrida objects also to Foucault's history of madness as 'structuralist', he demands to know whether the 'great internment' of the seventeenth century was a symptom or a cause, whether Foucault's utilisation of philosophical notions has a privilege and how they are related to scientific concepts. These objections can, I think, all be located together with Derrida's request for a 'definition' or 'concept' of madness.

Derrida devotes considerable space to a detailed analysis of Descartes's *Meditations*, replete with references to the meaning which is lost in the translation from the Latin to the French. What Derrida seems to miss, however, is that in Foucault's account in *Histoire de la Folie* Descartes's comments on madness provide only one means of indicating a transformation in the perception and objectivation of madness. This process took place at a number of different levels, not all of them 'philosophical'. The internment alongside the insane of such groups as the poor, the unemployed, and libertines is not an event which Foucault locates primarily or causally in terms of a philosophical notion of reason or unreason.

It was not philosophy which placed the insane beyond reason. As Foucault notes, the creation of the *Hôpital général* in 1656 was essential to this division, a division which was a question of 'police', a matter of order within the city, a result of the imperative of labour, a new reaction to poverty. The *Hôpital général* was an 'administrative entity' which belonged to no medical initiative and which was directly connected to monarchical power:

> The Hôpital Général is a strange power that the King establishes between the police and the courts, at the limits of the law: a third order of repression. The insane whom Pinel would find at Bicêtre and La Salpêtrière belonged to this world.
>
> In its functioning, or in its purpose, the Hôpital Général had nothing to do with any medical concept. It was an instance of order, of the monarchical and bourgeois order being organized in France during this period. It was directly linked with the royal power which placed it under the authority of the civil government alone.[37]

Internment was also a condemnation, a form of moral punishment which both provided for the poor whilst playing a moral role. Until the end of the classical age Foucault argues that internment functioned in terms of an equivocation between assistance and repression. Above all, and before becoming the object of knowledge or pity, the interned person was treated as '*sujet moral*'.

For Derrida these 'other' events are so much dross, in relation that is to *the* question of the status of Foucault's reading of Descartes. Foucault's reply in this respect is very much to the point. He suggests that what Derrida has omitted in his attempt to capture the heart of Descartes's discussion of madness is that the categories Descartes uses are precisely *juridical*. If a reading of Descartes is to act as arbiter, then it must be noted that the 'disqualification of the subject' as a subject that thinks is not simply a question of a philosophical disqualification; it refers also to that category of people incapable of certain religious, civil and judicial acts. The Latin *amens* and *demens* used by Descartes denote the juridical disqualification which is a crucial part of that general disqualification Foucault argues the seventeenth century bestows on those interned. The 'great internment' of the mid-seventeenth century must, Foucault suggests, he examined in terms of 'the form of sensibility to madness in an epoch we are accustomed to define by the privileges of Reason'.[38] Descartes has,

Foucault notes, 'obscurely sensed this juridical connotation of the word'.[39] Indeed, Derrida remarks that 'In question is a philosophical and juridical operation.'[40] But Foucault insists that what is missed in Derrida's reading is 'that Descartes's text plays on the gap between two types of determination of madness (medical on the one hand and juridical on the other).'[41] Above all, Foucault argues, it is not a question of the 'truth of ideas'. It is rather a matter of the 'qualification of the subject'.[42] The excesses which may emerge in one's dreams do not challenge this capacity, one's qualification to continue reasoning.

Central to Foucault's history of madness is, as he expresses it, the task of 'having to analyse the modes of implication of the subject in discourses'.[43] That is, the capacity of the subject to engage in rational discourse, indeed the very existence of the subject *qua* subject is a question which entails 'replacing discursive practices in the field of transformations where they are carried out'.[44] But for Derrida it is a question of 'the reduction of discursive practices to textual traces',[45] a pedagogy 'which teaches the pupil that there is nothing outside the text, but that in it, in its gaps, its blanks and its silences, there reigns the reserve of the origin; that it is therefore unnecessary to search elsewhere. . .'.[46] As I have suggested already, it is precisely Foucault's search 'elsewhere', in the relations he identifies between philosophical, literary, juridical, administrative and finally medical practices that the novelty of his enterprise in *Histoire de la Folie* resides. It is at these different levels that I suggest Foucault's genealogy of the modern subject must be located.

MADNESS AND THE CLASSICAL AGE; THE WORLD OF INTERNMENT

If the 'great internment' of the mid-seventeenth century can be regarded a 'failure' in terms of its functional response to problems of order and the seventeenth-century economic crisis,[47] then it is not simply on such an index that Foucault locates the perception of madness. This 'failure' can be regarded also, he suggests, in terms of its contribution to a certain 'ethical' valorisation of labour. With poverty placed in a simple opposition to labour, the latter regarded 'as a general solution, an infallible panacea, a remedy to all forms of poverty',[48] the seventeenth century came to regard labour in terms of its ethical foundations. Labour was a means of avoiding a fall into the 'infernal triumph of Sloth'.[49] It is in these terms that the question of labour in the world of internment was to be formulated: 'Labour in the houses of confinement thus assumed its ethical meaning: since sloth had become the absolute form of rebellion, the idle would be forced to work, in the endless leisure of a labour without utility or profit.'[50] The *Hôpital général* was not concerned simply to provide a refuge for those unable to work, or to utilise forced labour. It was rather 'a moral institution responsible for punishing, for correcting a certain moral "abeyance" '.[51]

The novelty of the 'ethical status' of the *Hôpital général*, its character as an institution of morality, resided in that here for the first time a synthesis was established between moral obligation and civil law. The law no longer condemned, instead the seventeenth century began to intern 'in cities of pure morality, where the law that should reign in all hearts was to be applied without compromise, without concession, in the rigorous forms of physical constraint.'[52] Morality could henceforth be administered just like trade or economy.

It was not only the French houses of internment which operated in this manner, but also the German *Zuchthausern* and the English workhouses[53] which functioned as 'fortresses of moral order, in which were taught religion and whatever was necessary to the peace of the State.'[54] Internment in the seventeenth century represented, Foucault suggests, the 'myth of social happiness', a 'police'[55] which concealed both 'a metaphysics of government and a politics of religion'.[56] The houses of internment in the classical age can be located in those terms in which Delamare was to formulate the notion of 'police' in his *Traité de Police* in 1738.[57] Internment as 'policing' conceived itself 'as the civil equivalent of religion for the edification of a perfect city'.[58]

In Foucault's history of 'unreason' this generalised internment of the seventeenth century was decisive. From this moment on madness was conceived according to questions of poverty, incapacity to labour, and inability to integrate oneself within the group. Madness was to become, through the 'great internment' of the seventeenth century, an 'event' which resided not only at the level of the 'advent of a Ratio'. It concerned equally matters pertaining to the order of the city, the necessity for moral regulation of those behaviours which the act of internment placed beyond the boundaries of reason. Beyond, but inextricably linked to the dictates of reason.

But if internment operated as 'exclusion' of a range of asocial behaviours, it was also a *positive* act. Internment did not play a purely negative role of exclusion but also a positive role of *organisation*. As an 'archaeology of alienation' Foucault illustrates in *Histoire de la Folie* how the 'great internment' was actually accomplished, how it constituted through its operation 'a domain of experience which had its own unity, coherence and function. It brought together in a unitary field personages and values between which previous cultures had perceived no resemblance.'[59]

This 'reorganisation of the ethical world' Foucault locates in relation to three domains. These three 'domains of experience', Foucault suggests, 'form with madness, within the space of internment, a homogeneous world which is one in which madness assumed the meaning with which we are acquainted.'[60] Firstly, he suggests, it touches 'sexuality in its relations with the organisation of the bourgeois family'.[61] The 'therapies' applied in the treatment of those suffering from venereal diseases, the moral condemnation of both sodomy and homosexuality which during the Renaissance had been separated,[62] and the repression of prostitution can, Foucault suggests, all be regarded in terms of the moral exigencies of the familial order.[63] Internment was, for the classical age, placed by the absolute monarchy at the discretion of the bourgeois family; it was to remain so until the 1838 code finally established a new framework within which psychiatry was able to establish its position:[64]

> In a sense internment and the whole regime of police which surrounded it served to control a certain order within the familial structure which functioned as social rule and norm of reason. The family with its exigencies became one of the essential criteria of reason; and it was the family above all that demanded and secured internment.[65]

A second regrouping which took place alongside that relating to sexuality concerned all the categories of profanation. Between 1617 and 1649 Foucault notes that there were 34 executions for blasphemy.[66] After 1657 the houses of internment were gradually to become filled with such groups. Through this shift blasphemers were to receive a new status, but not through a simple relaxation or 'liberalisation' of the laws. They were to become instead a matter of 'disorder', deprived of a sacrilegious efficacy and accorded a practical equivalence at the level of unreason, the legitimate object of internment. Those who attempted suicide were likewise to be henceforth interned, annexed by the 'neutral' domain of unreason. The same is true for sorcery and magic which Foucault suggests were no longer to be judged according to the principle of profanation, but according to that of unreason.[67] It is, Foucault proposes, no longer blasphemy and profanation which are at issue with the great internment of the seventeenth century, but rather a question of 'illusions'.[68]

The final figure in relation to which Foucault suggests the practice of exclusion was to operate was that of the libertine. At issue here were the 'new relations which were being installed between free thought and the system of passions'.[69] This inclusion of the figure of the libertine within the moral constraint which operated through internment highlights a central feature of the seventeenth-century act of exclusion. This theme is central to Foucault's history of unreason, namely that internment as the imposition of moral constraint was connected with the principle of allowing those interned to return to truth. The house of internment, Foucault suggests, can be regarded as having an almost pedagogical role with respect to the creation of truth.[70]

The provision of access to truth was a crucial component of these 'domains of morality', and one which was to be utilised effectively at a later date.[71] Access to truth was to be provided through the moral constraint they exercised. Internment had as one of its defining features the project of a moral reform which would provide a closer relation to truth:

> In the repression of thought and control of expressions, internment was not only a convenient variant of customary condemnations. It had a precise meaning and played a specific role: that of effecting a return to truth by means of moral constraint. And through this it designated an experience of transgression which had to be understood above all as ethical.[72]

The libertine no longer represented free thought existing in relation to reason. Instead, from the mid-seventeenth century on the libertine was located in a 'state of servitude in which reason made itself the slave of desires and the servant of the heart'.[73] Foucault notes that Sade, the first to attempt to provide a coherent 'theory' of the libertine in the eighteenth century, was to exalt just this condition of slavery.

With the 'great internment' of the seventeenth century the same line of rejection, the same moral abandon, the same social space characterised a diverse array of characters, including blasphemers, homosexuals, libertines and alchemists. But Foucault argues that it was not through a purely negative exclusion that such a division was achieved. Rather it took place through an *ensemble* of operations within which the classical age was to identify and isolate the world of unreason, localised in such a manner as to become object of *perception*:

> In fact all these various operations which displaced the limits of morality, established new prohibitions, diminished the condemnations or lowered the thresholds of scandal, all these operations doubtless adhered to an implicit coherence; a coherence which was neither that of a law nor a science; the more secret coherence of a *perception*.[74]

Internment is not for Foucault the 'cause' of the formation of the seventeenth-century notion of unreason. Internment rather signals the process through which the world of reason was to produce that quasi-homogeneous field which became object and target of a number of techniques and interventions. Equally, though, internment is not 'symptom'. Foucault's account suggests instead that the location in a single institutional space during the classical age of a wide variety of groups previously subject to quite different practices was a central aspect. But also that this operation was possible only on the basis of an entire 'readjustment of the ethical world'. And that it was on this basis that the nineteenth century was to 'discover' the insane amongst those interned, and to operate its 'positive' and 'scientific' perception of mental illness. Psychiatry was to 'discover' the insane in the world of unreason, as object of constraint and moral condemnation.

MADNESS IN THE CLASSICAL AGE: A JURIDICAL AND SOCIAL EXPERIENCE

Foucault is careful not to reduce the classical perception of madness to a uniform phenomenon. He notes that certain institutions in the seventeenth century already concerned themselves solely with the insane,[75] and also that special quarters within the *Hôtel-Dieu* were provided for them. However limited, it is clear that in the seventeenth century in some cases madness was individualised as a phenomenon worthy of treatment. Rather than efface such examples Foucault seeks to account for this apparently contradictory 'evidence' – that the insane person was individualised, albeit to a limited extent, both as object of punishment and treatment.

Foucault takes this limited individuation of the insane person as a means of posing the question of the status of the insane in the classical age. He distinguishes firstly between what he identifies as a 'juridical' and a 'social' experience of madness. The juridical experience of madness, Foucault proposes, took the person as subject of right and sought in all the domains of the activity of the subject the polymorphous nature of madness. The recognition of madness here depended on a medical diagnosis without which the forms, limits and existence of madness could not be determined with any certainty. Referring to the *Questions médico-légales* of Zacchias[76] produced in the second quarter of the seventeenth century, Foucault notes that for juridical purposes it is only the doctor who is considered capable of deciding whether an individual is mad, and what degree of capacity his madness leaves him.

Against this juridical experience of madness, when it was a question of internment, of the 'social experience' of madness, no medical competence or judgment was employed despite formal requirements that they be provided.[77] Whereas until 1692 internment in France was generally carried out by magistrates without the intervention of medical expertise, after this date the procedure most frequently employed was that of the *lettre de cachet*.[78] And although occasionally accompanied by a medical certificate such cases were a minority. In general it was the family, the neighbours, and the parish priest who served as 'witnesses'.[79] Madness located according to the index of internment was, Foucault remarks, a question of 'social sensibility'. Alongside crime and scandal it could be judged, but according to 'the most spontaneous and primitive forms of this sensibility'.[80]

There were, then, two distinct spheres: on the one hand 'a certain experience of the person as subject of law, of which one analysed the forms and obligations'.[81] On the other hand a conception which belongs to 'a certain experience of the individual as a social being'.[82] In the one madness is analysed in terms of a system of obligations and responsibilities; in the other it is implicated in a set of moral relations which justify its exclusion. Neither is more 'advanced'; they belong rather to distinct domains. The one brings into play questions concerning the capacities of the subject of law, thereby preparing the ground for 'a psychology which would blend in an uncertain unity, a philosophical analysis of the faculties and a juridical analysis of the capacity to contract and commit oneself.'[83] The other, in bringing into play questions concerning 'the conduct of social man',[84] prepares the ground for a dualist pathology, in terms of the categories of normal and abnormal.

Instead of posing these two spheres in a relation of causality, either with each other or in relation to a third term, Foucault suggests that it was on the basis of their uneasy coexistence that nineteenth-century alienist psychiatry was to establish itself. And whereas the eighteenth century constantly attempted to bring these two themes into line, nineteenth-century psychiatry operated on the basis of a coincidence or circularity between them. The juridical disqualification of the mad was at the same time a recognition of the problem posed by madness to the social question of the regulation of behaviours. Speaking of nineteenth-century medicine Foucault comments:

> It was to admit as already established and proven that the madness of the subject of law could and must coincide with the madness of social man, in the unity of a pathological reality which was analysable in terms of the law and discernible to the most immediate forms of social sensibility.[85]

The 'success' of the nineteenth century was that it was able effectively to combine these two distinct themes, to ensure that for the first time the insane were to be recognised as both juridically incapable *and* as insane. The 'fine structures' of responsibility and capacity were at the same time to provide the basis for criteria of internment. The perception of madness as mental illness was, Foucault argues, only possible when the encounter between the social decree of internment and the judicial knowledge which discerns the capacity of the subject of right became a firmly established synthesis.

Pinel's psychiatry[86] which proposed for the first time to treat the insane as human beings was, Foucault suggests, only possible on the basis of a reconciliation of this central division within the eighteenth-century perception of madness. And if it was through this development of psychiatry that the disqualification of the subject was rendered more solid, Foucault does not suggest that this is because of the role of the law as ideology. Rather it is depicted as a result of the form of combination which was possible between the juridical instance on the one hand, and psychiatry as specialised knowledge and competence on the other.

This distinction between a juridical and a social experience of madness Foucault relates also to the image of the animality of the insane which he argues characterised the classical age. The juridical concern with madness in the seventeenth and eighteenth century, Foucault argues, sought to distinguish carefully authentic from feigned states of insanity.[87] For the world of internment, however, it mattered little as to whether madness affected the will of the subject. For internment madness was regarded as inseparable from an 'act of reason which inaugurated an ethical choice'.[88] The opposition of reason and unreason for the world of internment was seen to operate 'in the open space of choice and liberty'.[89] This social experience of madness in the classical age depended on a freely accomplished choice between reason and unreason. Reason affirms itself as a decision against the world of unreason. Internment, Foucault argues, established itself on the basis of this image of a fundamental choice as a condition of the exercise of reason.

Foucault argues that the image of animality in the seventeenth- and eighteenth-century treatment of the insane is central to this ethical perception since it bears specifically on the notion of an animal *freedom*. In its most extreme forms Foucault argues that madness for classicism is 'man in immediate relation with his animality, without reference or recourse'.[90] The animality exhibited in madness demonstrates that the insane person is not ill and hence does not require protection or treatment, indeed that the madness protects the individual from illness. Madness contained within it an animal ferocity which protected the individual from the dangers of the illness, providing an invulnerability similar to that which nature bestowed on animals.[91] It was, Foucault suggests, on this basis that madness was distinguished from the other forms of unreason in the classical age, even if in other respects it was placed alongside blasphemy, libertinism and prostitution. The animality of the insane was held to protect them from hunger and extremes of temperature as well as rendering impossible any form of treatment other than a form of training (*dressage*). In this reduction to animality 'madness found both its truth and its cure'.[92] But this 'cure' hinges on the abolition of the human being: 'madness is cured since it is alienated in something which is nothing other than its truth.'[93]

Whilst in the nineteenth century this figure of the animality of the insane was to be accorded a determinist nature, for the seventeenth and eighteenth century it was situated instead according to a principle of liberty.[94] Classicism did not locate madness on the horizon of *nature* but on the basis of an unreason which revealed a liberty which appeared in the monstrous forms of animality.[95] This, Foucault comments, is probably the main paradox of the classical experience of madness: on the one hand enveloped in an ethical experience of non-reason and subjected to internment; on the other hand located in relation to an animal unfreedom which was the absolute limit of human reason. Tied at once to a 'moral valorisation of reason' and to the animal world with its 'monstrous innocence', this social experience of insanity was distant both from juridical definitions which operated according to the principles of responsibility and determinism, and from the medical analyses of that time which sought to render madness a phenomenon of nature. A singular experience established on an ambiguity which Foucault argues nineteenth-century psychiatry, and even that of the twentieth century, has secretly inherited from these relations which classicism installed within the sphere of unreason. Modified and displaced perhaps, but still informed by 'the ethics of unreason and the scandal of animality'.[96]

MADNESS, PATHOLOGY AND CLASSIFICATION: THE EIGHTEENTH CENTURY

Foucault's account of what he terms the 'classical experience' of unreason emphasises its contradictory functioning. The identification of madness was, Foucault suggests, achieved in part according to the division between a juridical and a social experience. Central to the latter was the 'immediacy' through which the mad person was identified as mad and interned. Foucault suggests that this act of segregation took place quite separately from the attempt to insert madness into a theoretical system. From this he posits two levels at which the classical experience of madness operated: on the one hand the recognition of the insane person (*le fou*); on the other hand the identification of madness (*la folie*) in its generality.

Madness, Foucault argues, never presented itself as such in the seventeenth and eighteenth century. It appeared only through the immediacy of the insane person whose identification was not equivalent to the recognition of the general discourse of madness. There is, Foucault suggests, a certain 'absence' of madness in the classical age. The certainty through which it was possible to identify the mad rested on no theoretical account of what madness was. There was, however, a series of attempts to produce a theoretical elaboration of the concept of madness during the eighteenth century. The best known of these can be identified with the names of Jonston, Sauvages, Linnaeus (Linné) and Weickhard.[97] But this 'patient labour of classification' set out not from the question of the insane but from the space of illness in general, from 'the logical and natural domain of illness, a field of rationality'.[98] The aim here was to situate illness in terms of its observable positive characteristics. Sauvages remarked that 'The definition of an illness is the enumeration of the symptoms which allow us to know its type and species, and to distinguish it from all others.'[99]

The disappearance of the notion of morbific substances at the end of the seventeenth century[100] was central here. Henceforth illness was to be deciphered by means of 'a singular truth which resides at the level of the most visible phenomena, and from which it must be defined'.[101] Illness was to be understood during the eighteenth century in terms of a symptomatology[102] which sought 'to reconstruct illness in the exactitude of a portrait'.[103] Moreover the principle of classification of observable symptoms was based on the attempt to locate illness in terms of a botanical model. Pathology was to be understood by means of the same principle that served to classify plants.[104]

It was into this theoretical space that madness was to be inserted. The title of one of the chapters of *Histoire de la Folie*, omitted in the English translation, captures this well: 'Le fou au jardin des espèces'. Madness was to become a part of the rational ordering which extended from the ordering of plants to the ordering of illness. As such it obeyed, along with the plant kingdom, the rationality of nature.

It is perhaps surprising that madness should have been so readily incorporated into the grand classificatory schemas of the eighteenth century. What, Foucault asks, of those other levels at which the classical experience of madness can be located? Should one neglect as inconsequential the insertion of madness into the general domain of a theoretical elaboration of pathology? Rather than erase this apparent paradox Foucault takes the imbalance between the social perception of the insane person and the location of madness within a theoretical knowledge of all possible illnesses as the sign of a problem. In a footnote which is well worth quoting, Foucault likens this apparent contradiction to that between the hospitalisation and internment of the insane since the mid-seventeenth century:

> This problem seems to be the replica of another that we encountered in the first part, when it was a question of explaining how the hospitalisation of the insane coincided with their internment. This is only one of the numerous examples of structural analogies between the domain explored in terms of practices, and that which emerges across scientific and theoretical speculations. Here and there the

> experience of madness is singularly dissociated from itself and contradictory: but our task is to rediscover in the depth of the experience the foundation of its unity and dissociation.[105]

A further 'difficulty' in explaining the place of madness within the general domain of eighteenth-century pathology is that the 'patient labour of classification' evident in the works of Sauvages, Linnaeus and Weickhard was itself to be entirely displaced with the advent of the nineteenth-century classifications. The latter, Foucault argues, supposed the existence of categories such as mania, paranoia, or *dementia praecox*, 'not the existence of a logically structured domain in which illnesses were defined within the totality of the pathological'.[106]

Foucault takes this 'inefficacy' of eighteenth-century classification as the sign of a problem. The question it poses, he argues, is that of 'the obstacles with which the classificatory activity was confronted when practised on the world of madness'.[107] What was it, Foucault asks, in the experience of madness which prevented it from attaining the coherence of the nosographic plan essential to eighteenth-century medical thought? In reply Foucault identifies three levels at which the project of a classification of the observable manifestations of madness encountered obstacles.

Firstly, Foucault identifies the apparent contradiction of dividing the forms of madness according to its signs. It was, he suggests, 'as if the relation of madness to that which it was able to show of itself was neither an essential relation nor one of truth.'[108] The difficulty of a symptomatology of madness Foucault locates at the level of relating the observable manifestations of the insane person to a general category of madness. The attempt to classify insanity according to its visible signs surreptitiously returns, he argues, either to a moral denunciation or to a causal system. Pinel remarked in 1819,[109] looking back at the 'illnesses' which appeared in the eighteenth-century classifications – these included such categories as jealousy, timidity, pride and vanity – that whilst quite often they were incurable illnesses, 'their proper place was in the *Maximes* of La Rochefoucauld or the *Caractères* of La Bruyère rather than in a work on pathology.'[110]

Foucault remarks that whilst it was the morbid forms of madness which were sought, all that was discovered were the deformations of moral life. This search for the morbid forms of madness returned, Foucault argues, to the same denunciations of moral life that one encounters in the internment registers. This is despite the fact that none of the eighteenth-century nosographers had contact with the *hôpitaux généraux*.

Where it was not this 'moral experience' of unreason which erupted in the aspiration toward a scientific knowledge of madness Foucault argues that one finds instead a causal account based on corporeal mechanisms. Thus Sauvages distinguished between '*les hallucinations*', '*les bizarreries*' and '*les délires*'. But the differentiation between delirium and hallucination entailed locating the origin of the former in the brain alone rather than in the diverse organs of the nervous system. Foucault remarks that whilst the classification was faithful to a symptomatology at the general and abstract level, 'as soon as one approached the concrete forms of madness, the physical cause became the essential element in the distinctions. In its real life, madness was entirely traversed by the secret movement of causes.'[111]

The antinomy between a moral judgment and the analysis of physical causes is, Foucault argues, only apparent. The classical theory of passion[112] was to effect the synthesis between madness in general and the insane person on which the eighteenth-century experience of unreason rested. Beyond the descriptions and classifications of the eighteenth-century nosographers Foucault argues that one can detect a general theory of passion, of imagination and of delirium. This, he suggests, enabled relations to be established between madness in general and the insane person in particular. It also allowed links to be established between madness and unreason.[113] It is in this sense, Foucault argues, that one can talk of a 'transcendence of delirium', which, 'directing the classical experience of madness from on high, rendered derisory the attempts to analyse it according to its symptoms alone.'[114]

The second level at which Foucault suggests the activity of classification was obstructed is through the persistence of a number of themes formulated well before the classical age. Despite changes in name and attempts during the eighteenth century to modify them these themes persisted, Foucault argues, until the beginning of the nineteenth century. Foucault identifies them as *mania*, a delirium without fever; *melancholia*, a delirium operating on one or two particular objects; and *dementia* which was opposed to both mania and melancholia in so far as it was 'an abolition of the faculty of reason'.[115] The eighteenth-century noso logies, Foucault argues, were not to modify these three basic underlying themes.[116]

The third obstacle to the persistence of eighteenth-century classificatory systems for madness Foucault identifies through the resistances and developments of medical practice itself. At the end of the seventeenth century there occurred what Foucault refers to as an 'event'. In reinforcing the autonomy of the practices of therapy Foucault argues that this event was to provide medicine with the possibility of a new line of development. The event in question was that of the definition of the phenomenon known as 'vapours', elaborated in the eighteenth century under the name of *maladies de nerfs*.[117] This realm of vapours and *maladies de nerfs* had its own rules which did not correspond to those of the nosographies.

The originality of these concepts and what distinguished them from the existing nosography resides, Foucault argues, in that 'they were immediately linked to a practice; or rather, since their formation they were wholly impregnated with therapeutic themes.'[118] In this new world of pathology theoretical explanation finds itself for the first time combined with an attempted *cure*.[119] From this moment and throughout the eighteenth century, Foucault argues that 'a medicine developed in which the doctor-patient couple was in the process of becoming the constituent element.'[120] The pathological forms which emerged from this doctor-patient relation were, Foucault argues, increasingly unassimilable to a classificatory principle of ordering of illnesses.

MADNESS AND UNREASON: THE INITIAL SEPARATION

The classical age had, Foucault argues, barely distinguished madness and unreason. Yet in the second half of the eighteenth century Foucault identifies a decisive shift from which madness was to develop in a manner distinct from that of unreason. A central component of this shift was the medicalisation of madness. Yet this medicalisation was, Foucault proposes, to be achieved in part on the basis of the 'great fear' which erupted in the middle of the eighteenth century. This fear was based on the notion that the putrid air of the houses of internment produced fevers which endangered the health of the whole population.[121] This was a fear 'formulated in medical terms, but which was animated at heart by an entire moral myth'.[122]

Foucault identifies as decisive in the panics concerning the risk of epidemics emanating from the *hôpitaux généraux* the fact that the encounter between medicine and madness which resulted centred on the *fear* of the world of internment.[123] The medicalisation of the world of internment which this produced was not the result of a benevolent concern with the health of the inmates: 'If it was the doctor who was called upon and asked to observe, it was out of fear.'[124] And this fear was, Foucault argues, not only of disease but of a moral contagion:

> The great reform movement that developed in the second half of the eighteenth century originated in the effort to reduce contamination by destroying impurities and vapors, abating fermentations, preventing evil and disease from tainting the air and spreading their contagion in the atmosphere of the cities. The hospital, the house of correction, all the places of confinement, were to be more completely isolated, surrounded by a purer air: this period produced a whole literature concerning the airing of hospitals, which tentatively approaches the medical problem of contagion, but aims more specifically at themes of moral communication.[125]

The separation of madness from unreason in the second half of the eighteenth century took place, Foucault suggests, in the context of this fear of unreason. A central feature of this differentiation was that madness was henceforth to be accompanied by 'a certain analysis of modernity, which situates it from the start in a temporal, historical and social context'.[126] This locating of madness in a historical and social context was, Foucault notes, to provide a whole new series of concepts. The concept of '*forces pénétrantes*'[127] was central to this development which sought to locate madness in its social milieu. It was, he suggests, increasingly to lead the explanation of madness in the direction of political and economic factors. The moral origin of madness and the animality of the insane was to be replaced by a framework which sought instead to situate madness 'in that milieu where man's relation with his feelings, with time, with others, are altered; madness was possible because of everything which, in man's life and development, is a break with the immediate.'[128]

This new departure in the perception of madness was, Foucault argues, as decisive as Pinel's 'liberation' of the insane at Bicêtre. Henceforth the possibility of madness was to increase as it became related to the limitless mediations civilisation offered.[129] Madness was no longer the presence of a counter-nature, of animality. It became rather the other side of progress and achieved a crucial temporal dimension.

The concept of degeneration was, Foucault argues, central to the shift through which madness was to be separated from unreason and situated in a social and historical milieu. Rather than identify Morel as having founded the theory of degeneration in the nineteenth century,[130] Foucault suggests that Morel was in fact to start from 'the lessons which the eighteenth century transmitted to him'.[131] Tissot was central to the eighteenth century account, and although much separates his work from that of Morel there is, Foucault argues, a continuity.[132] This continuity is that for both Tissot and Morel madness 'resided not in man himself, but in his milieu'.[133] This was, Foucault suggests, to provide the essential link through which madness was connected with the attempt to provide a knowledge of the 'truth' of man. Madness as alienation[134] was, Foucault argues, the loss of man's truth; it was in the milieu in which men lived that madness resided. The human milieu was the condition of possibility of all madness.

Although rudimentary, the late eighteenth-century conception anticipated the themes central to the reflections on man which were to flourish in the nineteenth century:

> At the end of the eighteenth century one sees emerging the general lines of a new experience in which man, in his madness, does not lose truth but *his* truth; it is not the laws of the world which escape him, but he himself who escapes the laws of his own essence.[135]

Madness for the classical age had entailed the notion of an eruption of animality. At the end of the eighteenth century, however, Foucault argues the insane person was connected to his madness as that which deprived him of *his* truth.

THE SINGULARITY OF MADNESS: INTERNMENT AND ASSISTANCE

Foucault locates the shift in the perception of madness during the second half of the eighteenth century in relation to two indexes. On the one hand the movement which took place within the space of internment through which madness was distinguished from all the other categories of internees. On the other hand a movement which took place through an economic and social reflection on poverty, illness and assistance.

In the middle of the eighteenth century a number of institutions were opened reserved specifically for the insane.[136] Although this had already occurred to some extent during the seventeenth century it now became a regular occurrence and took place across the whole of Europe.[137] Preceding in chronological terms both the nineteenth-century reforms and any change in the juridical conditions of internment, madness achieved through this development a decisive autonomy in relation to the other categories of internees. This process indicates, Foucault argues, a transformation in the 'experience' of madness which can be identified prior to its seizure by a certain form of *savoir*. Distinct from the undifferentiated world of unreason madness became, through a movement within the sphere of internment, a singular object of perception. Reason no longer simply counterposed itself to unreason in a relation of exteriority; it began rather to identify multiple and varying figures of difference. The isolation of the insane in asylums designed specially for them was gradually to distance madness from the other categories of internees.[138]

Utilising the internment registers as indices of the new categories Foucault proposes that slowly one can see develop a '*perception asilaire*' of madness. He notes, for instance, the increasing number of categories identified in the registers of Saint-Lazare between 1721 and 1733.[139] This movement was, Foucault argues, both parallel to and separate from the work of theoretical classification; it established two separate domains which the nineteenth century was never to succeed in uniting – a 'medical analytic' and a '*perception asilaire*'. The imbalance between them demonstrates, he suggests, not a distinction between theory and practice, but rather a fundamental division within the experience of madness from the classical age to the present.

The transformation within the eighteenth century consciousness of madness was not, Foucault argues, the result of a humanitarian movement of reform[140] or of a 'scientific need'. It was rather, he suggests, a process which took place *within the space of internment itself*.

> No medical advance, no humanitarian approach was responsible for the fact that the mad were gradually isolated, that the monotony of insanity was divided into rudimentary types. It was the depths of confinement itself that generated the phenomenon; it is from

confinement that we must seek an account of this new awareness of madness.[141]

Together with the political critique of internment which erupted with particular force in the early nineteenth century madness was, Foucault argues, to become connected more firmly than ever to the world of internment. The increasing differentiation of the insane from the other categories of those interned during the second half of the eighteenth century meant that 'The polemic instituted by the eighteenth century against confinement certainly dealt with the enforced mingling of the mad and the sane; but it did not deal with the basic relation acknowledged between madness and confinement.'[142]

Alongside this process of differentiation the practice of internment was, Foucault argues, modified by a complex of crises affecting the whole of French society. In the early part of the eighteenth century internment served as a relay in the attempt to secure adequate numbers for the Colonies. Moreover this decanting relieved the *Hôpital général* of those which it would have been impossible to sustain indefinitely.[143] On the other hand, from the second half of the seventeenth century a disruption of the agricultural economy produced a large number of displaced agricultural labourers, thereby ensuring that unemployment was no longer an urban phenomenon.[144]

However, as the century progressed, and especially from the recession following 1770, internment came to be employed less as a means of responding to successive crises. From this moment Foucault argues that internment was recognised as an ineffective response to economic crises. This shift, he proposes, challenged the entire traditional politics of assistance. And whereas previously poverty had been regarded as a moral offence, it now came to be recognised as an economic phenomenon. The inverse relation posited between the concepts of *poverty* and *population* in the writings of the economists,[145] with population regarded as a positive element within the production of wealth, Foucault takes as indicative of this shift. With human labour now linked to the production of wealth,[146] the more numerous the population the greater was seen to be the wealth of the nation. Internment became a predominantly economic rather than a purely moral error, since in supporting the *poor* by charity a part of the productive *population* was also lost. Instead of removing the poor from the process of production they should be re-inserted into its cycle.

The reorganisation of assistance which took place was

accomplished, Foucault argues, on the basis of the principle of economic freedom and by means of a reinvigoration of the distinction between '*pauvres valides*' and '*pauvres malades*'. The difference was not one of degree but concerned the crucial point of capacity for work. The '*pauvres valides*' should work, although in full economic freedom, since their labour was the essential condition of the production of wealth. The '*pauvre malade*' on the other hand necessitated total assistance, although this was founded not on economic utility but rather on a moral principle of social obligation. Thus conceived assistance was, he suggests, not 'a state structure, but a personal bond linking man to man'.[147]

Foucault argues that with this reorganisation of assistance 'The social space in which madness was situated found itself entirely renewed.'[148] The eighteenth century fragmented the space within which poverty and illness had existed since the Middle Ages. In its stead it produced a 'structure of moral discontinuity', a variety of separate and homogeneous domains. Within this differentiation madness was still identified as that which was to be excluded from the social space; but now it was 'confronted also with all the new problems posed by assistance for the sick'.[149] It was, Foucault argues, through this labour of reorganisation of the spheres of unreason, illness and assistance that the modern notion of madness was slowly produced.

THE EMERGENCE OF PSYCHIATRY: MADNESS AND 'TRUTH'

Even before the Revolution Foucault demonstrates clearly that madness was individualised through a number of distinct processes. And yet Foucault argues this separation left madness without a precise point of insertion within the social space. This 'difficulty' provoked, he suggests, a dual reaction: on the one hand a series of long term decisions to create institutions reserved for the insane; on the other hand a series of immediate repressive measures to deal with madness. This ambiguity bears witness, Foucault argues, to the 'new forms of experience in the process of emerging'.[150]

Three structures were determinant, Foucault argues, in this process of displacement through which a 'new experience' of madness was to develop, that of nineteenth-century psychiatry. The first was that through which the old site of internment was integrated, somewhat modified, with a medical perception formed elsewhere. A second structure was that which established between madness and those designated to recognise and evaluate it, 'a new, neutralised relation, apparently purified of all complicity, and which is of the order of the objective gaze.'[151] A third figure confronted the insane with the criminal without reducing them to each other, and authorised at the same time a division of different forms of madness 'according to the new forms of morality'.[152]

For a long time medical thought and the practice of internment had remained quite separate processes. At the end of the eighteenth century a certain convergence between them took place, the result Foucault argues, of an 'obscure labour in which the old space of exclusion, homogeneous, uniform, rigorously limited, was confronted with the social space of assistance which the eighteenth century had only recently fragmented and rendered polymorphous'.[153] Foucault argues that this new space, however, was not adapted to the problem of madness. Whilst illness and poverty had only recently become, for the first time, a *private* affair, belonging to individuals and families, madness required a *public status* and a place of confinement. At the outset of the Revolution there were, Foucault argues, two series of projects: one which sought to revive internment, but to reserve it for criminals and the insane: the other which sought to define a *statut hospitalier* for madness.

Foucault identifies these two distinct strands on the one hand through the projects for ideal places of confinement such as those of Brissot and Musquinet.[154] The dream here was of a perfect moral control of those interned coupled with an economic utility obtained through their labour. On the other hand the proposals of Doublet and Colombier[155] sought actually to take those interned as worthy of *treatment*, thereby connecting madness with a concept of illness. An attempted equilibrium then between 'pure and simple exclusion of the insane and medical care given in so far as they were considered sick'.[156] However the 'essential step', Foucault argues, was taken only when Tenon and Cabanis provided internment with its own particular status which made the negative gesture of exclusion also a positive attempt at a cure:

> Of itself, and without being anything other than this isolated liberty, internment is hence an agent of cure; it is medical, not by virtue of the type of care brought to bear, but by the play of the imagination, liberty, silence, and limits, by the movement which organises them spontaneously and returns error to truth, madness to reason.[157]

The important point in this passage from house of internment to asylum is, Foucault argues, that it was achieved not through a progressive investment of medicine from an exterior site. Rather it was achieved, he suggests, through an internal restructuring of that space which the classical age had given the functions of exclusion and correction. The progressive altering of its social significations, the political critique of repression and the economic critique of assistance, the 'appropriation' of the entire field of internment by madness whilst the other figures of unreason were liberated. This is what made internment a doubly privileged site for madness, 'the site of its truth and its abolition'.[158] Madness and internment were henceforth to become inseparable. The contradictory demands of protection (for society) and cure (for the sick) were finally to be accorded a harmony. It was not, Foucault argues, the doctor who forced his way into the world of internment in order to treat madness.[159] The extension of medical control of the asylums during the nineteenth century was rather, he suggests, possible only on the basis of the increasingly therapeutic value attributed to internment.[160]

In addition to this reorganisation of the world of internment the figure of madness itself was to alter through the new status accorded to the confinement of the insane. The mad were no longer simply interned according to a binary division of reason/non-reason. Instead they were subjected to a constant observation through which the 'truth' of madness was determined by means of 'an always relative, always mobile play of liberty and its limits'.[161] The medical certificate supplied on entry no longer provided a definitive assessment of the insane person; it was now the task of internment itself to supply this. The proposal by Cabanis for an 'asylum journal'[162] is, Foucault argues, an index of this shift through which madness was to become object of a constant surveillance. The 'silence' of classical madness and the animality it exhibited was replaced by a gaze directed toward madness as an object to be known. Madness was no longer regarded as the negation of man's humanity. Rather it was to take its place 'in the positivity of things known'.[163]

Foucault argues that this step was decisive, if not irreversible, for the status of madness and the insane. Henceforth madness could be no more than an *object*[164] for the exercise of reason:

> If it was necessary to summarise in one word this entire evolution, one could say without doubt that the distinctive feature of the experience of unreason was that madness was subject of itself; but

> that in the experience that was forming towards the end of the eighteenth century, madness was alienated from itself in the status of object that it received.[165]

Des Essarts had distinguished in the notion of 'police'[166] between the magistrate and the administrator: 'The first is the man of the law; the second that of government.'[167] In 1789 he commented that the question of government was henceforth to be a matter for the ordinary citizen.[168] With this shift madness was to be situated fully in the public domain. The citizen was called upon to set the limits of order and disorder, to install the division between madness and reason.[169] Transitory phenomena such as the '*tribunaux de famille*' made the citizen both a 'man of law' and a 'man of government'.[170] Or rather the family came to occupy the place which previously the sovereign had occupied, pronouncing on the different forms of civil incapacity and madness.

Foucault suggests that other transformations witness this insertion of madness into the public domain. For Brissot[171] public scandal was the ideal punishment, immediately adequate to the offence and also a means of preventing criminal acts. Through such notions Foucault suggests that 'an entire psychology was in the process of emerging which was to change the essential significations of madness and to propose a new description of the relations of man to the hidden forms of unreason.'[172] The paradox is evident – psychology as knowledge of the interior of man was constituted through the exteriority of the scandalised public consciousness.

The reform of criminal justice was to provide a solid institutional basis for this transformation, with the jury now figuring as the representative of the public conscience within the judicial process. Criminality was, Foucault argues, to lose its unity and to be divided into two separate spheres: the one which related the offence to the penalty through the norms of public opinion; the other which related the offence to its origin. The latter was a relation of knowledge and was to focus on the *individual*.[173]

It was, Foucault argues, only in 1792, in the first attempt to submit a plea of '*cause passionnelle*' before a jury that a distinction was sought between criminal responsibility and a psychological determination.[174] The speech of the defence council Bellart exhibits, Foucault argues, the outlines of a psychology 'which no longer concerns sensibility but knowledge only, a psychology which speaks of a human nature in which the figures of truth are no longer the forms of moral validity.'[175] Witnessed here, he suggests, is the beginning of a movement which, in aspiring to pronounce on the 'truth' of man, deprives him of responsibility.[176]

This removal of responsibility effected by the introduction of psychological expertise, and the 'innocence' which went with it, should be given a precise formulation Foucault argues. It was not a question of 'a liberation of the psychological in relation to the moral, but rather a restructuring of their equilibrium. Psychological truth only renders innocent in a very precise sense.'[177] In delimiting the sphere of responsibility psychology neither fully achieved a position of neutrality nor continued the classical experience of unreason which had failed to install a precise distinction between madness and criminality.

There are, Foucault argues, two separate processes through which madness achieved its own domain. On the one hand the 'liberation' of madness, its separation from the world of unreason; on the other the formation of 'new structures of protection' in which madness was inserted. These two processes form, he argues, 'the coherent unity of a gesture through which madness is offered to knowledge within a structure which, from the start, is alienating.'[178] It was, Foucault argues, through this double movement that the 'modern experience' of madness was finally established. Table 4.1 indicates the opposition and unity of these two distinct processes.

The objectivity accorded the different forms of mental illness within the 'modern experience' of madness indicates, Foucault argues, not simply an increase in knowledge. It is rather a certain conscience of non-madness that provides a solid basis from which to know madness.[179] It is in this, Foucault proposes, that one can ascertain the distance separating the contemporary 'positivist' knowledge of madness and reason from the classical division of reason/unreason. In the classical age a double constitution of reason *vis-à-vis* unreason operated: 'an immediate and daily apprehension of difference, and a system of exclusion which confused madness with other dangers'.[180] The success of a positive psychiatry resided, Foucault argues, in its ability to connect two elements, an 'interior' knowledge of unreason and the act of confinement.[181]

Through madness, Foucault argues, man was to become an object of knowledge. At least in principle the individual was henceforth transparent to objective knowledge. It remained only for Pinel and Tuke to provide, in the shape of the asylum, the institutional framework in which this knowledge of madness and the individual was to be 'applied'.

Table 4.1 The unity of the modern experience of madness

Forms of liberation	Structures of protection
1 The suppression of a system of internment which assimilates madness to all the other forms of unreason.	1 The designation for madness of an internment which is no longer a terrain of exclusion, but rather the privileged site where it shall return to its truth.
2 The constitution of an asylum whose purpose is solely medical.	2 The capture of madness by an inescapable space which must be at once the site of its manifestation and the space of its cure.
3 The acquisition by madness of the right to express itself, to be heard, to speak in its own name.	3 The elaboration, around and over and above madness, of a sort of absolute subject which is wholly gaze, and which confers on madness a status of pure object.
4 The introduction of madness into the psychological subject as the everyday truth of passion, violence and crime.	4 The insertion of madness into a world of incoherent values and the play of unhappy conscience.
5 The recognition of madness, in its role of psychological truth, as an irresponsible determinism.	5 The division of the forms of madness according to the dichotomous demands of a moral judgment.

CONCLUSION: MADNESS, MORAL REGULATION AND THE 'TRUTH' OF MAN

As noted at the beginning of this chapter, *Histoire de la Folie* is a history of the conditions of possibility of psychiatry. It is not a history of the functioning of the 'golden age' of psychiatry.[182] Chronologically the point of culmination is the birth of psychiatry with the asylum and the moral regulation of Tuke and Pinel. Let us look briefly at how Foucault presents their contribution to the formation of psychiatry's institutional space.

The regime of Tuke's *Retreat* at York and Pinel's at Bicêtre differed considerably.[183] However, they both witnessed, Foucault argues, the existence of a domain designed to reveal the truth of madness through a form of moral regulation. That Tuke was a Quaker was not unimportant for the organisation of the *Retreat*.[184] The *Retreat* was, Foucault argues, designed to operate as an instrument of moral and religious segregation which resembled that of the Community of Quakers. Religion operated there both as nature and rule, as that which could not be alienated by madness. The insane person (*aliéné*) was placed 'within a moral environment where he will be in debate with himself and his surroundings.'[185] The principle of fear which had characterised seventeenth-century internment still operated, indeed it was essential. Yet it functioned in a quite different sense. No longer an exterior relation, it now addressed the patient directly and by means of the principle of responsibility:

> The assignation of guilt is no longer the mode of relation that obtains between the madman and the sane man in their generality; it becomes both the concrete form of coexistence of each madman with his keeper, and the form of awareness that the madman must have of his own madness.[186]

Tuke's 'liberation' of the insane was, Foucault argues, more accurately an *organisation* of madness through labour and the gaze of others, one which attempted to return the insane to reason through a consciousness of being a free and responsible subject.

Within the *Retreat* madness was, Foucault argues, organised as childhood and placed within an equivalent relation of authority. The juridical status of minor was organised through the relations between guardians and patients in an attempt to structure the *Retreat* on the model of a large family, 'The entire existence of madness, in the world now being prepared for it, was enveloped in what we may call, in anticipation, a "parental complex".'[187] Where the family is unable to cope Tuke substituted an environment which sought to maintain the insane as a minor within a familial network in which reason retained the characteristics of the father.

With Pinel, however, there was no religious segregation. Yet the principle of moral regulation of life within the asylum and the values of the family and labour operated just as solidly: 'The asylum becomes, in Pinel's hands, an instrument of moral uniformity and social denunciation.'[188] But Pinel's means of dividing between reason and madness was, Foucault argues, more complex than that which operated at the *Retreat*. At the *Retreat* it was a question of a 'religious segregation for purposes of moral purification'.[189] With Pinel, however, the operation was relatively complex:

> To effect moral syntheses, assuring an ethical continuity between the world of madness and the world of reason, but by practising a social segregation that would guarantee bourgeois morality a universality of fact and permit it to be imposed as a law upon all forms of insanity.[190]

The *Retreat* was, Foucault argues, 'a space of nature and immediate truth'.[191] Pinel's asylum however, was 'a site of moral syntheses where insanities born on the outer limits of society were eliminated.'[192] This operated, Foucault argues, through three principal mechanisms, that of silence, a form of mirror recognition, and a perpetual judgment.[193] From the moment of entry into the asylum an indefinite process of surveillance, judgment and punishment operated:

> Formerly, unreason was set outside of judgment, to be delivered, arbitrarily, to the powers of reason. Now it is judged, and not only upon entering the asylum, in order to be recognized, classified, and made innocent forever; it is caught, on the contrary, in a perpetual judgment, which never ceases to pursue it and to apply sanctions, to proclaim its transgressions, to require honorable amends, to exclude, finally, those whose transgressions risk compromising the social order. Madness escaped from the arbitrary only in order to enter a kind of endless trial for which the asylum furnished simultaneously police, magistrates, and torturers; a trial whereby any transgression in life, by a virtue proper to life in the asylum, becomes a social crime, observed, condemned, and punished; a trial which has no outcome other than a perpetual recommencement in the internalized form of remorse. . . . The asylum of the age of positivism, which it is Pinel's glory to have founded, is not a free realm of observation, diagnosis, and therapeutics; it is a juridical space where one is accused, judged, and condemned, and from which one is never released except by the version of this trial in psychological depth – that is, by remorse.[194]

What united Pinel and Tuke despite their differences was that they both opened the asylum to medical knowledge. But rather than the introduction of a science, Foucault suggests that what

Pinel and Tuke introduced was a *personage* whose powers were of a moral and social order: 'If the medical personage could isolate madness, it was not because he knew it, but because he mastered it.'[195] Father and judge, family and law, the practice of the doctor in the asylum was, Foucault argues, to operate in terms of order, authority and punishment:

> Life in the asylum as Tuke and Pinel constituted it permitted the birth of that delicate structure which would become the essential nucleus of madness – a structure that formed a kind of microcosm in which were symbolized the massive structures of bourgeois society and its values: Family-Child relations, centred on the theme of paternal authority; Transgression-Punishment relations, centred on the theme of immediate justice; Madness-Disorder relations, centred on the theme of social and moral order. It is from these that the physician derives his power to cure; and it is to the degree that the patient finds himself, by so many old links, already alienated in the doctor, within the doctor-patient couple, that the doctor has the almost miraculous power to cure him.[196]

Along with the introduction of the figure of the doctor to the asylum Tuke and Pinel introduced, Foucault argues, the principle of 'liberty'. The 'liberty' which reigned in the asylum is enshrined in the legend of Pinel's founding gesture of removing the chains from the most violent of inmates.[197] The principle of truth, and of the loss of truth suffered by the mad person is less frequently remarked on. Foucault argues, however, that they are interdependent. The freeing of the insane from their chains at the same time freed the insane from their animality. And with this 'constitutive liberty' man was, Foucault argues, inextricably bound to that truth which he had lost in his madness: 'It is not a matter of the *liberation* of the insane towards the end of the eighteenth century; but of an *objectivation* of the concept of their liberty.'[198]

At the beginning of the nineteenth century, Foucault argues, madness came to be located in an anthropological discourse which was also a form of constraint, a constraint which functioned by means of the connection it established between the individual subject, the notion of the truth of the subject, and the introduction into the asylum of the person of the doctor who was to be the one to have access to this truth.[199] The French term '*aliéné*' expresses this situation better than the English notion of 'insane person'. The mad person in the nineteenth century, Foucault argues, was 'a stranger in relation to his self'.[200] Henceforth madness 'no longer indicates a certain relation of man to *the* truth – a relation which, at least silently, still implies liberty; it indicates only a relation of man to *his* truth.'[201]

It is this broad shift which Foucault identifies as having occurred toward the end of the eighteenth century which is central to the concerns of this and the following two chapters to examine the emergence of the modern notion of subject. It was, Foucault argues, through madness that there was to emerge the possibility of a knowledge of the subjectivity of the individual. Decisive in this shift is that madness could henceforth only be object, moreover object of medical knowledge. In place of the binary structure of unreason in the classical age, truth and error, was to emerge an anthropological structure composed of three terms – man, his madness and his truth.

Foucault suggests that a number of illnesses – general paralysis, monomania and moral insanity – mark the arrival of this decisive transformation. Of these moral insanity[202] is considered to have an exemplary value. On the one hand it was characterised by lucidity and entailed no impairment of the subject's reason; on the other hand it manifested itself as violent and furious outbreaks. Its persistence throughout the nineteenth century demonstrates, Foucault argues, that 'it was close to the essential structures of madness. More than any other mental illness, it manifested that curious ambiguity which made madness an element of interiority in the form of exteriority.'[203] Moral insanity, Foucault suggests, is almost a model for every possible psychology: 'it exhibits at the perceptible level of bodies, conducts, mechanisms and of the object, the inaccessible moment of subjectivity.'[204] Just as this subjective moment can only have a concrete existence as *object* of knowledge, in turn it is acceptable only by virtue of what it expresses of the *subject*. In this form madness, Foucault argues, is the first and principal means by which the truth of man becomes an object accessible to scientific perception:

> Madness is the purest form, the principal and primary form of the movement by which the truth of man passes over to the side of object and becomes accessible to a scientific perception. Man becomes *nature* for himself only in so far as he is capable of *madness*. As the spontaneous passage into objectivity, this is the constitutive moment in the becoming-object of man.[205]

Pinel may have freed the insane from the inhumanity of their chains. But through that very gesture, Foucault argues, the insane person was to be chained to the image of man and his truth: 'From that day, man has access to himself as a true being; but this true being is only ever given in the form of alienation.'[206]

Histoire de la Folie, as I have remarked already, is a history not of psychiatry but of psychiatry's conditions of possibility. It is also a history of the conditions of possibility of psychology understood as the science of the 'interior' of the individual, as that knowledge of man which operates on the hidden realm of his subjectivity. Not a study of successive discoveries, nor a history of ideas, but an investigation into the 'fundamental structures of experience' which made possible the appearance of psychology. In the nineteenth century the Western world saw emerge that 'massive postulate' – the human individual as a being defined by a truth which was both visible and yet hidden.[207]

Madness, Foucault proposes, in a phrase which translates poorly, can be regarded as '*absence d'oeuvre*'.[208] But the madness we know today, or more accurately the madness of the nineteenth century, is the product of a fantastic labour. Not necessarily a 'social construction',[209] but none the less the product of a massive 'work' of readjustment between the subject of madness and the subject as object of a positive knowledge.

What Foucault demonstrates in *Histoire de la Folie* is the process through which madness finally became object of a positive psychiatry. This process took place at a number of levels. I have tried in this chapter to follow Foucault's account of these different levels of events. These include the reorganisation of the world of internment; the changing nature of the judicial process; the image of the animality of the insane and its displacement in the second half of the eighteenth century; the difficulties encountered in attempting to produce a theoretical knowledge of madness; the reorganisation of the sphere of assistance; and finally the birth of the asylum.

There is much that I have had to omit in Foucault's account of how transformations in certain practices[210] made possible broader shifts in the mode of governing the population, maximising its resources, and dealing with disorder. Foucault's account of these processes effectively demolishes any notion that madness finally came to be treated as a result of the humanisation of attitudes towards the insane. Equally, Foucault demonstrates that the point of arrival of madness in nineteenth-century psychiatry was not the result of a progressive elaboration of a scientific knowledge attempting to break free from superstition and moral judgments. Foucault shows rather that madness was to be individualised not simply through a theoretical reflection, but also through a concern with government[211] and with the population conceived as source of wealth.

It may be tempting to some[212] to use Foucault's account of the conditions of emergence of psychiatry as 'evidence' against contemporary psychiatry. Indeed to have shown that madness was discovered in large part through a reorganisation of the moral world of unreason and disorder hardly provides support for the image of psychiatry as a disinterested scientific treatment of personal distress. Yet it would be wrong to use *Histoire de la Folie* in this sense. The importance of Foucault's account resides rather in that it demonstrates the surfaces of emergence[213] of madness, no more and no less. This demonstration may discomfort some. And this discomfort may be an appropriate response. But for my purposes here *Histoire de la Folie* is not of interest as a critique of the psychiatric profession.

The relevance of *Histoire de la Folie* for this study is in terms of the account it provides of the conditions of possibility of a positive knowledge of the subjectivity of the individual. In this respect Foucault's utilisation of terms such as 'experience', 'perception' and the 'subject-object' couple may seem misleading. The roughly phenomenological framework from which they may be considered to derive would seem to be at odds with my arguments concerning Foucault's genealogy of the subject. It would be wrong to view these terms in this way, however. The notions of experience and perception do not apply to the individual viewed as a subject. They are not subjective categories, but objective structures through which unreason was detected. The subject-object couple which recurs throughout *Histoire de la Folie* is absolutely central, but is not a given. Rather, it is through the different ways of construing unreason that different conceptions of man as a subject are proposed. And it is within a relation of knowledge that the modern subject is constituted.

Foucault's argument in *Histoire de la Folie* is, I argue, one component of what I have referred to above as his project of a genealogy of the modern subject. That it indicates the connection between the birth of the subject, the birth of a particular body of knowledge, and the problem of government is a useful corrective to attempts to have recourse to a universal category of subjectivity. It is also a useful corrective to the attempt to make the subject the *a priori* of liberation. Rather than making the subject both the unique locus of repression and the point of resistance to domination, Foucault shows most convincingly the correlative formation of the subject and object of knowledge. The relation of knowledge through which the modern subject emerges can, at the very least, be seen as a useful reminder of the materiality of knowledge, and of the relations between certain knowledges and other practices.

CHAPTER 5

THE BIRTH OF MEDICINE AND THE INDIVIDUALISATION OF THE BODY

•

A relatively short period in the history of medicine is perhaps a curious focus for my concerns in this study. Foucault's *Birth of the Clinic* concentrates in fact on that period from approximately 1760 to 1816 during which it is commonly acknowledged that contemporary medical practice established itself.[1] Yet rather than an esoteric history of medicine, what Foucault provides is a study of a crucial aspect of that process through which modern relations of power constituted man as object of specialised knowledge. The *Birth of the Clinic* is an important component of that project for a 'genealogy of the modern subject as a historical and cultural reality'[2] identified above[3] as Foucault's response to a philosophy of the subject. Medical thought, Foucault argues, is 'fully engaged in the philosophical status of man'.[4] It makes possible access to the 'truth' of man. Within the overall architecture of the human sciences it is, Foucault argues, 'closer than any of them to the anthropological structure that sustains them all'.[5]

There is nothing peripheral or marginal about Foucault's interest in medicine. At many points the analysis connects up with that of *Histoire de la Folie* and *The Order of Things*. And just as the history of madness was concerned with the conditions of possibility of psychiatry, so too *The Birth of the Clinic* charts the conditions of possibility of contemporary medicine rather than the history of medicine itself. There is, too, the same utilisation of paradox. Whereas the formation of psychology as knowledge of the subjectivity of the individual was achieved on the basis of unreason, knowledge of the individual body is, Foucault suggests, achieved through the conceptualisation of death. A central concern of Foucault's in *The Order of Things* is the formation of the notion of man's finitude. In *The Birth of the Clinic* the form of finitude, 'of which death is no doubt the most menacing',[6] is central also. With the reign of finitude 'the destiny of individuality will be to appear always in the objectivity that manifests and conceals it, that denies it and yet forms its basis'.[7]

At issue in *The Birth of the Clinic* is the question of the emergence of man as object of positive knowledge. With medicine as with psychiatry the point of arrival is that moment at which the individual becomes object of knowlege. But if it can be suggested that *The Birth of the Clinic* is one of Foucault's most strongly epistemological books, that it presents an account largely in terms of 'obstacles' to the emergence of a certain body of knowledge,[8] then it is equally accurate to argue that this epistemological concern is constantly related to a range of other levels of events. For the 'modern' field of medicine to be possible a spatial reorganisation of the hospital, a new definition of the status of the patient in society, a transformation in the sphere of assistance, and a new relation of language to observation were all necessary. The 'birth' of clinical medicine is an event within knowledge. It was, however, only possible by virtue of a number of transformations in spheres other than the strictly medical.

A POLITICS OF HEALTH

As Virchow remarked 'medicine is a social science and politics nothing but medicine on a grand scale.'[9] Foucault suggested more recently[10] that the formation of medicine in the nineteenth century cannot be divorced from the emergence of a 'politics of health' which entails 'the consideration of disease as a political and economic problem for social collectivities which they must seek to resolve as a matter of overall policy.'[11] Foucault does not suggest that the formation of a politics of health, a 'nosopolitics', was an absolute invention of the eighteenth century, that there had never previously existed a general concern with health and disease. What interests him rather are the *new* rules and objects which emerged at the end of the eighteenth century.

It is not to 'the State' that Foucault looks to account for the emergence of a politics of health. The Quakers in England,[12] charitable and benevolent associations, the eighteenth century Academies and the early nineteenth-century statistical societies were all to problematise the health and sickness of the population. But they did so from different sites in relation to which the role of the state was to vary considerably:

> Thus the eighteenth-century problematisation of nosopolitics does

> not correlate with a uniform trend of State intervention in the practice of medicine, but rather with the emergence at a multitude of sites in the social body of health and disease as problems requiring some form or other of collective control measures.[13]

The separation of questions of health from those of assistance is central here. Taking account of exceptions such as plague measures and regulations enforced during epidemics, Foucault suggests that until the end of the seventeenth century collective action towards disease was subsumed under assistance to the poor. 'Medicine' operated primarily through the various charitable foundations and was only one aspect of the distribution of food and clothing, provision for abandoned children, and projects of elementary education. Until the mid-eighteenth century sickness, Foucault argues, 'is only one among a range of factors, including infirmity, old age, inability to find work and destitution, which compose the figure of the "necessitous pauper" who deserves hospitalisation.'[14] The effacement of the pauper in the various procedures of assistance is one index of this shift during the eighteenth century, from which were to emerge distinctions between the good and the bad poor, the indolent and the unfortunate. In Foucault's words 'An analysis of idleness – and its conditions and effects – tends to replace the somewhat global charitable sacralisation of "the poor".'[15]

Without reducing this process to a response to the underlying needs of the labour process Foucault connects it to 'a general re-examination of modes of investment and capitalisation'.[16] The question of the sickness of the poor begins, he suggests, to be posed in relation to the requirements of increased productivity of the labour force. But alongside this process the question of the health of the population as a whole as one of the objectives of political power is also formed. This is not a matter of repairing the deficiencies, of supporting a marginal portion of the population. It is rather a question of 'how to raise the level of health of the social body as a whole.'[17] An 'imperative of health' which figures as an important component of the 'policing' of the social body. Delamare's *Treatise* on police[18] as well as Rau's *Medizinische Polizei Ordnung* (1764) and Frank's *System einer medizinische Polizei*[19] exemplify this shift toward a more generally medical notion of police and away from questions of charity.

If the eighteenth century witnesses a valorisation or synthesis of life into labour,[20] then this valorisation takes place in relation to a number of other instances which are to provide the possibility of psychology and medicine. But it would be wrong to regard this as simply a question of 'specialisation' or 'differentiation'. One could suggest instead that what connects the different categories of population which emerged during the latter half of the eighteenth century and the early years of the nineteenth is the question of *administration*. To say that Foucault's concern in *The Birth of the Clinic* is in part epistemological does not imply that it charts a changing relation between the subject and object of knowledge. It entails rather that one include the 'third term' in relation to which medical knowledge is transformed, the question of administration, or as Foucault puts it, the project of a 'technology of population'.

Within such a broad project Durkheim's *Suicide* of 1891 is perhaps only the culmination of that 'avalanche of statistics' which can be located as commencing in the 1770s, but as flourishing from the 1820s.[21] As Ian Hacking notes,[22] the concerns of these various statistical enquiries were wide-ranging: 'One name for statistics, especially in France, had been moral science: the science of deviancy, of criminals, court convictions, suicides, prostitution, divorce.'[23] And Wundt in 1862 was able to say that statisticians demonstrated that there are laws of love just as there are laws for all other human phenomena.[24] Foucault's analysis in *The Birth of the Clinic* of the individualisation of the body takes place in relation to this emergence of the population as 'more or less utilisable, more or less amenable to profitable investment . . .'[25] It is not only a question of subjection, but also one of a constant attempt to increase the utility of the population.

CLASSIFICATION, EPIDEMICS AND THE INDIVIDUAL

Foucault presents *The Birth of the Clinic* as concerned with 'the act of seeing, the gaze'.[26] This refers to a reorganisation of the overall field of the visible and the invisible. It is not a question of doctors at last seeing what they had previously failed to see. It concerns instead a transformation of knowledge such that certain phenomena were rendered a part of the field of the visible.[27]

The interest of this general shift at the level of knowledge for my concerns here is twofold. Firstly, the manner in which Foucault examines how this shift was made possible, what other events or levels of events enabled the formation of modern medicine, is central. Secondly, the 'result' of this reorganisation is the formation of the individual as object of a determinate knowledge, located within a precisely defined space, supervised according to norms of health.

At the level of its knowledge of diseases Foucault characterises the eighteenth century in terms of its classificatory schema, which he terms a 'primary spatialisation'. This was based on identifying diseases in terms of their resemblance and difference as located within a table of diseases. From Sauvages's *Nosologie*[28] of 1761 to Pinel's *Nosographie*[29] of 1798 Foucault argues 'the classificatory rule dominates medical theory and practice: it appears as the immanent logic of morbid forms, the principle of their decipherment, and the semantic rule of their definition. . .'.[30] Rather than locating disease in an organ within an individual body, disease is situated within families, genera, and species. A 'botanical model'[31] of which Sydenham was to comment:

> He who observes attentively the order, the time, the hour at which the attack of quart fever begins, the phenomena of shivering, of heat, in a word all the symptoms proper to it, will have as many reasons to believe that this disease is a species as he has to believe that a plant constitutes a species because it grows, flowers, and dies always in the same way.[32]

Within this model the individual patient is, Foucault argues, placed within parentheses. The doctor, he suggests 'must subtract the patient. . .'.[33] The patient's life-style, age, and predispositions only disturb the course of the disease. They do not serve to define its nature which is provided by the 'pure nosological essence'. Disease exists only within classificatory space. Its movement throughout the body, which may be accompanied by symptomatic changes, relies on the organs only as supports of the disease, 'They never constitute its indispensable conditions.'[34]

For eighteenth-century medical knowledge the individual is a negative element, an accident of the disease, something one must subtract. But one must also *reintroduce* the individual as that 'geometrically impossible spatial synthesis'.[35] Particular histories caused by qualitative variations of the essential qualities of diseases demand 'a renewed attention to the individual – an ever-more impatient attention, ever less able to tolerate the general forms of perception and the hasty inspection of essences.'[36] The patient is the 'rediscovered portrait of the disease'.[37] Foucault refers to this as the secondary spatialisation in which 'doctor and patient are caught up in an ever-greater proximity'.[38] But even here this 'acute perception of the individual' which is entailed 'need hardly dwell on this body for long, at least in its densities and functioning'.[39]

Foucault uses the term 'tertiary spatialisation' to refer to that range of processes which I have already indicated in the notion of a politics of health. Included here are 'heterogeneous figures, time lags, political struggles, demands and utopias, economic constraints, social confrontations'.[40] It was, Foucault argues, on the basis of this tertiary spatialisation that 'the whole of medical experience was overturned'.[41] Medicine as a corpus of institutions and practices confronts here the medicine of classes, and it is the latter which Foucault suggests is displaced.[42]

The eighteenth-century conception of epidemics illustrates this 'confrontation' between the dominant theoretical medicine of species and classes, and the 'policing' role of medicine. Opposed to a nosology at the level of its theoretical configuration, the eighteenth-century notion of epidemics was connected at another level, that of the tertiary spatialisation of diseases. An epidemic in the eighteenth century was not considered to differ fundamentally from an individual disease. Epidemics were regarded as quantitative or mathematical phenomena which occur when a particular illness is reproduced a number of times in the same place and at the same time. An epidemic was no more than a 'nucleus of circumstances', Marseilles in 1721, or Bicêtre in 1780.[43] Central to this notion is the examination of the particular process the epidemic follows, which varies according to circumstances from one epidemic to another. Contagion is not primary in such an account, and whilst it may figure this would only be as one aspect among others.

But whether regarded as contagious or not an epidemic possesses an 'historical individuality' which dictates the necessity for a complex method of observation capable of describing the event in great detail. The possibility of such a detailed form of observation on a national scale was provided for the first time with the decree of 1776 which created the *Société Royale de Médecine*.[44] With this decree was initiated the most important of the administrative enquiries of the eighteenth century, and although in many regards a failure,[45] it provided an 'avalanche of statistics' in reply to a range of meteorological questions. The immediate objective of the Society was to break the isolation of the provincial doctors and put them in touch with lists of clinical signs and forms of treatment for countering epidemics. More broadly, however, it sought to specify sanitary standards for hospitals, prisons, and military camps, and the gradual enlargement of its role as a control body for epidemics led to its becoming a focus for the centralisation of knowledge and an authority for the arbitration of all medical activity. In many respects the *enquêtes* of the *Société Royale de Médecine* can be taken as an indication that health and disease had come to be recognised as problems requiring a form of collective control. And although in conception and organisation an institution of the *Ancien Régime*, the *Société Royale de Médecine* can be regarded not so much as a representative of a monarchical political order, but more accurately as a 'portent of things to come'.[46]

MEDICALISATION, NORMALISATION AND A CONTRACTUAL SOCIETY

It may be that this perception of epidemics as unique and unrepeatable events, and the attempts by the *Société Royale de Médecine* to chart their course, is opposed at all points to the medicine of classes which was still dominant. But when it is a question of their common task of supervising the health of the population they are, Foucault argues, subject to the same requirements:

> The definition of a political status for medicine and the constitution, at state level, of a medical consciousness whose constant task would be to provide information, supervision, and constraint, all of which 'relate as much to the police as to the field of medicine proper'.[47]

At issue in this 'medicalisation' of French society at the end of the eighteenth century was not simply a question of distributing medical knowledge uniformly, but an attempt to combine a *collective* medical perception with a knowledge and supervision of *individual* lives. Within this framework medicine was to base itself on a notion of healthy functioning in which the cure entails returning the sick individual to a norm. Foucault argues that medicine thus:

> assumes a normative posture, which authorizes it not only to distribute advice as to healthy life, but also to dictate the standards for physical and moral relations of the individual and of the society in which he lives.[48]

With this shift, as J.-P. Peter has argued, doctors were to become 'men of power; their knowledge entitles them to practise. Men of order also: to cure is to restore a natural order, to return the living being to its norm.'[49] Treatment in such a schema consists in an evaluation of 'men and their habits according to norms of life and health defined sovereignly by the medical world'.[50] Doctors may well have as their aim diagnosis and cure, but as Georges Canguilhem has argued, this principle of cure cannot be separated from that of normalisation: 'To cure is in principle to return a function or an organism to the norm from which it has deviated.'[51]

Normalisation here refers to a perceived necessity for a regulation of those individual lives which reside outside certain boundaries, and which remain a potential threat to the model of *healthy* man. Medicine as 'policing' was to establish itself within a field divided according to the bipolarity of the normal and the pathological. Hence, Foucault argues, the 'unique character' of medicine – as science of man it is inseparable from the positive role that it occupies as norm.

Foucault does not locate this normalising role of medicine solely at the level of an abstract specification of conceptions of healthy functioning. The operation of such a normalising or policing role for medicine demanded at the end of the eighteenth century an entirely reorganised medical apparatus which would legitimate medical competence as well as provide a system of training for doctors. A congruence, that is, between a *political ideology* and a *medical technology* which would provide a medicalisation of French society, yet in accordance with the requirements of individual liberty.

There were, it is true, attempts under the *Ancien Régime* at providing medical establishments which combined teaching and treatment. But examples such as the Paris College of Surgery which existed from 1774–93,[52] although indicative of an emergent body of medical practitioners, and although they were to play a prominent part in the 'reform' of the hospital, were the exception rather than the rule. In any case the Paris College of Surgery operated principally as a research rather than a teaching institution.[53] And like the *Société Royale de Médecine* and the other medical institutions of the *Ancien Régime* it was to be abolished in 1793. From this date it was some years before the hospital was to emerge as a specifically medical establishment equipped with teaching, treatment and research facilities.

But the transformation of the hospital in the decade following 1793 from a generalised site of assistance into a place of medical treatment is crucial in the individuation of the patient as object of medical knowledge. With this shift the hospital was no longer a space in which death was awaited, it became instead a politically preferable site of *treatment* of illnesses.[54] Through these displacements the hospital was finally to become established as a 'curing machine' (*machine à guérir*).

The Revolution was faced with the task of abolishing the privileges of medicine which had existed under the *Ancien Régime* and which still continued, whilst at the same time securing an effective supervision of the nation's health. That is, a demand both for liberty as well as for stricter control in order to protect against charlatans and to prevent the continuation of the corruption and closed practices associated with the Faculties. A demand which we can now regard as that of a request for medicine as a liberal-contractual profession, a liberty which can only be assured through the provision of a medicine which is itself strictly supervised.

By this time Foucault suggests that medicine had already established a corpus of knowledge in which the unity of clinical teaching, its combination of treatment and training, would be defined. But the absence of an institutional correlate meant that the reorganisation of medicine could not be achieved. Throughout the early years of the Revolution Foucault argues that:

> an indispensable structure was lacking: a structure that might have given unity to a form of experience already defined by individual observation, the examination of cases, the everyday practice of diseases, and a form of teaching that everyone knew ought really to be given in the hospital rather than in the Faculty.[55]

Foucault's account here in terms of a fundamental 'absence' or 'obstacle' is in one sense disquieting. It gives the impression of supplying a retrospective coherence to an otherwise disparate and non-unified number of events. But what Foucault demonstrates is not a lacuna specified at the level of a model. Rather he shows how it was impossible for a particular form of medical knowledge to install itself without the support of a number of other practices.

The overturning of the eighteenth-century nosologies did not, Foucault argues, operate entirely at the level of knowledge as theoretical grid. The reorganisation of medical knowledge for Foucault is intimately connected with that process through which clinical institutions and methods were established.[56] The reform of medical teaching after 1793[57] is hence a crucial aspect of that process through which medicine was to establish itself as scientific knowledge, as a 'domain in which truth teaches itself'.[58] After this date what occurred was 'the restructuring, in a precise historical context, of the theme of "medicine in liberty": in a liberated domain, the necessity of the truth that communicated itself to the gaze was to define its own institutional and scientific structures.'[59] It is worth fixing some of the main stages of this process which Foucault recounts, and through which 'A way of teaching and *saying* became a way of learning and *seeing*.'[60]

The Fourcroy Report of Year III proposed the establishment of a single school for the whole of France in which officers of health would be trained to staff the hospitals, and especially the military hospitals.[61] The defence here against any possible suggestions that this might represent a return to the old corporations and privileges was that medicine was a practical science of benefit to the whole nation, that 'by setting up a school, one is not favouring a small handful of individuals, but, through qualified intermediaries, one is helping the people to feel the benefits of truth.'[62] It is its immediate relationship with 'nature' that makes medicine a body of knowledge of use to all citizens, as opposed to the Faculties and their brand of esoteric knowledge. Ackerknecht comments on the 'practical' character of these proposals:

> The Fourcroy report designated as the core of the new law the practical character of instruction – the preponderance and immediacy of clinical teaching. The new Paris student did not begin with theoretical instruction. From the first day on, he was trained on the wards.[63]

As a result of objections to these proposals the law itself[64] provided for the setting up of three schools of medicine at Paris, Montpellier and Strasbourg. These were to provide courses of teaching lasting over three years. What characterised this reform was that it not only emphasised the clinic as the site of medical practice but counterbalanced this with a 'much broader theoretical teaching'.[65] Experimentation on sick individuals was to be combined with a conception of medicine as encyclopaedic knowledge.[66] However Foucault argues that this measure failed entirely to achieve the results intended. The insufficient number of schools, the absence of examinations, and the teaching provided by the schools all conspired to prevent the formation of a body of qualified doctors. This led to demands for restoring a medical profession which would be defined both by qualifications and laws. A series of Reports by Cales, Vitet and Cabanis enables this development to be traced.

Cales's project,[67] in an attempt to gain acceptance for re-establishing a body of professional doctors, opposed the notion that physicians were to be confined to the towns, surgeons to the countryside, and apothecaries to the treatment of children. All three categories were henceforth to attend the same courses, and their studies would be checked by examinations. Foucault argues that under this guise of an attempt to rationalise the system of teaching, Cales's project sought principally to re-establish a body of doctors whose competence would be substantiated by a 'system of standardized studies and examinations'.[68] It was, however, to be violently attacked both for the relatively minor place it accorded the clinic and its suggested return to the old Faculties.

With one important modification it was revived in large part in Vitet's project of 17 Ventose Year IV. Five schools of medicine were to be set up with a council of health in each department concerned with epidemics and preserving the health of the inhabitants. The crucial innovation of these proposals was the 'requirement of a clinical test'.[69] This was the first time that 'the criteria of theoretical knowledge and those of a practice that can be linked only to experience and custom were found together in a single institutional framework.'[70] Within the framework of normal studies the value of practice acquired in the hospital was recognised.

However, Vitet's project was to generate as much opposition as that caused by Cales's proposals. What was at issue here, Foucault argues, was the question of the very practice of medicine, a problem whose resolution fixed the possibilities for resolving the reform of medical teaching. The impasse which was reached by this time was conceptual and political, and demonstrated that the principal question was not that of the number of *Écoles de Santé* or their programme; it was rather 'the very meaning of the medical profession and the privileged character of the experience that it defines'.[71]

Foucault suggests that the basis for a resolution of this stalemate can be detected in a report by Cabanis made only a few months later. This relatively minor chronological distance belies, he argues, that 'this text already belonged to another age; it marked the stage at which ideology was to take an active, and often determining part in political and social restructuring.'[72] Presented as an attempt to specify the conditions for a practical solution 'it sought, above all, to provide the outline of a theory of the medical profession.'[73] In addition to proposals concerning examinations, the essential part of the text relates to the very nature of the medical profession, to the problem of assigning it to a 'closed domain' without either returning to the corporative structures of the *Ancien Régime* or a form of centralised state control. It sought to achieve this by suggesting that the public must delegate control over medical practice to the state precisely in order to secure individual liberty. Since the object of medicine concerned the human individual 'about whom any error may prove fatal',[74] and since its merits were not immediately visible, it was open to both error and fraud; there was hence a need to provide a measure of the competence of the doctor. The control which the public delegates to the state is not over the objects produced, something contrary to the principles of economic freedom, but over the producer. Doctors were to be supervised as those who treat the producers of wealth, a form of control which was seen as neither restricting the operation of industry nor the freedom of the individual.

Whilst these proposals made by Cabanis were not immediately accepted they indicate what was ultimately to provide the 'solution'. With the law of 19 Ventose Year XI medicine was to be accorded the status of a liberal profession, a status it has preserved until this day. A two-tier level of medical provision was to be supplied: doctors in medicine and surgery qualified in one of the six schools on the one hand; on the other hand officers of health who would provide 'the most ordinary care' which could in principle be based entirely on experience in a hospital or as a doctor's assistant.[75] Legal backing in the form of fines and imprisonment were provided for those who practised medicine yet did not fit either of these two categories.

This definition of the 'closed' nature of the medical profession avoided both the old corporative model and a form of control over medical acts which would have offended the principles of economic liberalism. The notion of competence defined in terms of the capacities of the person of the doctor retained both the principle of choice and its control. At the same time the distinction between doctors and officers of health which it installed provided a difference of level which is 'no longer a question of a difference in the object, or the way in which the object is manifested, but of a difference of level in the experience of the knowing subject.'[76] This distinction had as its 'objective correlate' that the officers of health were to treat 'the industrious and active people'. This was a continuation of the eighteenth-century notion that the labouring classes, and especially those in the country 'led a more simple, moral, and healthy life than others, and were subject primarily to the external illnesses that came within the competence of the surgeon'.[77] With the legislation of Year XI this distinction became a social one and the officer of health was assigned the task of treating the people who generally suffered only 'primitive accidents' and 'simple indispositions'.

The important distinction on which this difference of level was based, and which Foucault argues constituted the most innovatory factor of the law of Year XI, was that between the years of *practice* required of an officer of health, and the *clinical* experience which complemented the theoretical training of a doctor. The practice required of the officer of health was that of a 'controlled empiricism' in which 'experience was integrated at the level of perception, memory, and repetition, that is, at the level of the example'.[78] In the clinic, however, 'it was a question of a much more subtle and complex structure in which the integration of experience occurred in a gaze that was at the same time knowledge, a gaze that exists, that was master of its truth, and free of all example.'[79] A difference, that is, of epistemological status correlate with the institutional conditions under which each was to operate. Whilst medical practice was *opened* up to the officers of health the doctors were to *reserve* the clinic for themselves.

CONTRACTUALITY AND CLINICAL OBSERVATION

Together with this new definition of the clinic there took place a reorganisation of the hospital which served to fix the terms within which the clinical gaze was to operate and on whom it was to be exercised. During Year VI there occurred a revitalisation of the economic and moral criticisms raised against the principle of hospitalisation at the outset of the Revolution and before. However, this revitalisation took place in a climate in which any hope of erasing hospitals entirely from the social landscape was absent. Widespread poverty, the fear of popular movements, and suspicions regarding the possible political use of individual assistance demanded that a framework be found 'for the preservation of both the hospitals and the privileges of medicine, that was compatible with the principles of liberalism and the need for social protection'.[80]

The 'solution' to this question was found by discharging the government of all obligation to provide hospital space and returning them to their civil status. Municipal authorities were now to be responsible for their organisation and the state was freed from any necessity of providing assistance. The regulation of poverty took place more in accordance with the economic-contractual principles of liberalism:

> The system of obligation and compensation between rich and poor no longer passed through the law of the state, but, by means of a sort of contract, subject to variation in space and suspension in time, it belonged more to the order of free consent.[81]

Alongside this modification a further contractual relation was being established. This took place on the one hand between the hospital as site of treatment for the poor and the clinic as a place of medical training, and on the other hand between the individual patient and medical knowledge. What was at stake here was the moral problem posed by the transformation of a patient compelled to seek assistance at the hospital into an object of clinical observation. Foucault suggests that this issue was resolved through the contractual relation itself which implied that 'to look in order to know, to show in order to teach' was not only acceptable but was demanded 'by virtue of a subtle right that resides in the fact that no-one is alone, the poor man less so than others, since he can obtain assistance only through the mediation of the rich'.[82]

This principle of contractual obligation had already been contained in the proposals concerning the conversion of hospitals into medical schools made by Nicholas Chambon de Montaux (1748–1826), physician at the Salpêtrière, in 1789.[83] Chambon considered that the shelter, care, and medical remedies provided by the teaching hospital were the inverse of the patients' donation of their bodies to society. Lacking means of payment the poor provided in return for treatment 'the history of their infirmities . . . and the means by which they have been cured'.[84] In a hospital as opposed to private practice, the 'secrets of the body' were rendered public and made 'the subject of lessons'.[85] The contractual relation between the individual and society therefore does not cease ever in the case of illness.[86] As Chambon argued:

> The suffering man does not cease to be a citizen; if there is a way in which he can contribute to the public welfare, his infirmities do not exempt him from a duty which gratitude and humanitarianism likewise imposed on him.[87]

This debt in which the individual patient stood was, moreover, not simply to 'society', but more specifically to the medical profession. The 'clinical contract' was 'a special application of the ideology of the social contract between the monarchical state and its constituent individuals'.[88] The monarchical state required hospitals since without such charitable institutions:

> discontent or 'demoralization' of the poor was inevitable. This could easily lead to 'general disorder' which ultimately threatened property owners much more than the working class. *Chambon recognized the hospital as an instrument for social order and control, and the clinical contract as a refinement of that function.*[89]

If, as Gelfand argues, Chambon 'vigorously defended the sanctity of the individual',[90] this should not be a cause for surprise since at issue here was not a monarchical form of power but the emergence of a liberal-contractual medicine. This 'contractual' medicine dictated that disease can only be cured through the intervention of others and their knowledge and resources. The reciprocal structure entailed here was such that 'what is benevolence towards the poor is transformed into knowledge that is applicable to the rich.'[91] The 'contract' established a basis for clinical medicine through combining a certain epistemological modification in medical *savoir* with a political investment which was at the same time a *demand to know*:

> In a regime of economic freedom, the hospital had found a way of interesting the rich; the clinic constitutes the progressive reversal of the other contractual part; it is the *interest* paid by the poor on the capital that the rich have consented to invest in the hospital; an interest that must be understood in its heavy surcharge, since it is a compensation that is of the order of *objective interest* for science and of *vital interest* for the rich. The hospital became viable for private initiative from the moment that sickness, which had come to seek a cure, was turned into a spectacle. Helping ended up by paying, thanks to the virtues of the clinical gaze.[92]

The formation of the clinic, Foucault argues, is the emergence of a site in which 'the sovereignty of the gaze gradually establishes itself'.[93] This is not simply a process which takes place in reference to a particular theoretical knowledge of disease. It is equally a 'political' process. The clinic is not simply a space of observation, of a gaze conceived as sight. It is 'no longer the gaze of any observer, but that of a doctor supported and justified by an institution, that of a doctor endowed with the power of decision and intervention'.[94] A gaze that was both calculating and 'always receptive to the deviant'.[95] The formation of the medical gaze in the clinic entailed both that new objects were presented, and that, at the same time 'the knowing subject reorganizes himself, changes himself, and begins to function in a new way.'[96] Within this reorganisation the changed relationship of the symptom to the disease, and the introduction of probabilistic thought[97] were each to play their role. The clinic, Foucault argues, is a field made 'philosophically "visible" by the introduction into the pathological domain of grammatical and probabilistic structures'.[98]

The clinical gaze, Foucault argues, is a 'perceptual act sustained by a logic of operations. . .'.[99] There is, moreover, no difference between the clinic as 'science' and the clinic as teaching. The pathological and the pedagogical are connected in the operation through which the clinic transforms the visible into language. One 'sees the visible only because one knows the language'.[100] This is not a question of speaking in a language which is not widely understood,[101] rather an 'operational mastery over things is sought by accurate syntactic usage and a difficult semantic familiarity with language'.[102] A 'balance' between speech and observation, 'the great myth of a pure Gaze that would be pure Language: a speaking eye.'[103] The visible is to be expressible, and it is visible only *because* it is expressible. But this dream of complete reversibility of the visible in the expressible remained, Foucault argues, 'a requirement and a limit rather than an original principle'.[104]

BICHAT, LOCALISATION AND DEATH

The final level at which Foucault's account of the formation of modern medicine operates is that of the transformations effected first with Bichat and then with Broussais, Bichat's innovation[105] was, Foucault argues, not to 'discover the corpse'. Dissection had already been taking place before the end of the eighteenth century. Foucault comments that 'there was no shortage of corpses in the eighteenth century, no need to rob graves or to perform anatomical black masses; one was already in the full light of dissection.'[106] Rather, what Bichat achieved was the spatialisation of disease according to the 'thinness of the tissue'. Tissues are seen here as elements of the organs, as traversing them, relating them together, and forming 'systems' through which 'the human body finds the concrete forms of its unity'.[107] Against Morgagni whose thought was organised entirely on the basis of the organs, Bichat sought to reduce organic volume to tissular space. Bichat's gaze, Foucault suggests, was not a surface gaze in the same way that early clinical experience was a surface gaze. Rather, it related the phenomena of the disease to the surface of membranes and supplied pathological anatomy with an 'objective, real, and at last unquestionable foundation for the description of diseases'.[108] As Francois Jacob has commented, referring to Bichat, 'it is no longer the shape alone that gives an organ its properties: it is first and foremost the specific nature of its component tissue.'[109]

The medical gaze now had to relate the symptomatic surface to the tissual surface, the manifest to the hidden. Through this step anatomo-clinical experience separated itself from the original clinical experience which had implied an external, deciphering subject able to identify a range of characters spread out over the surface of the body. Now it was necessary for the medical gaze to see the disease as it penetrated the body itself. It is 'no longer a pathological species inserting itself into the body wherever possible, it is the body itself that has become ill.'[110]

Entailed here, Foucault argues, was a transformation of the entire epistemic field which made it possible for particular objects to appear, and for the observing subject to occupy that site, both conceptual and institutional, from which they could be known.

> What is modified in giving place to anatomo-clinical medicine is not, therefore, the mere surface of contact between the knowing subject and the known object; it is the more general arrangement of knowledge that determines the reciprocal positions and the connexion between the one who must know and that which is to be known.[111]

This development was, Foucault argues, not that of a modification of an existent practice, but the formation of a quite different one organised according to different rules. Amongst these rules is the substitution of the principle of localisation for that of the recording of frequencies, and the ordering of the chronological series of symptoms according to the 'ramification of lesional space'.[112] Through the three reference points of localisation, site and origin the analysis of anatomo-clinical perception modifies what was previously the essentially temporal reading of the clinic. The notion of the seat[113] of the disease as original site replaces that of class, and removes from this notion of seat the causal implications it had with Morgagni.

The changed conceptualisation of death which was possible

with Bichat is complementary to this transmutation in medical *savoir*. In eighteenth century medical thought death was seen both as the end of life and also as the end of the disease. Early clinical medicine did not question this conception of death, yet with pathological anatomy death was provided with an account which served to differentiate it from the phenomenon of the disease.

Bichat tried to distinguish two questions which had not been separated with Morgagni's anatomy: 'manifestations contemporary with the disease and those prior to death'. The coming of death was provided with an existence, partly autonomous, which referred to a different process from that of the disease itself.[114] Divided up into time and space, death was accorded both a chronological ordering as well as a spatial picture of the interactions between the deaths of various parts of the organism, identified in three main relays – heart, lungs, and brain. Death was to become 'multiple, and dispersed in time. . .'.[115] No longer that 'absolute, privileged point at which time stops and moves back; like disease itself, it has a teeming presence that analysis may divide into time and space.'[116]

Death was distinguished through this development both from the process of life and from that of disease. Endowed with its own mechanisms and organic network death now acts as a 'point of view' on the pathological.[117] It provides access to the *truth* of the disease and its different chronological phases. A tripartite division is established between life, disease, and death, with death at the summit, a configuration which resembles that established in *Histoire de la Folie* between 'the insane person, man, and the truth of man'.[118]

Against the more frequently noted 'vitalism' of Bichat Foucault counterposes what he terms his 'mortalism', in relation to which the irreducibility of the living to the mechanical he regards as secondary. The analysis of disease is no longer based on the essence of the living. Rather it is carried out from the point of view of death, a death which by definition life resists. Life is both opposed to and exposed to death, measured by the strength of internal resistance to external pressures leading towards death.[119]

Together with the changed nature of the relation between the sign and the symptom of a disease this conceptualisation of death was, Foucault argues, to allow the possibility of a scientific discourse on the individual. From the point of view of the corpse, disease now has 'a land, a mappable territory' [which paradoxically] . . . enables us to perceive it living'.[120] Spatialised in the organism and entwined with the process of life itself, disease assumes the appearance of a living process, a deviation within life. Disease no longer attacks life but is understood rather through the notion of 'pathological life'; disease is the pathological form of life, a phenomenon to be *treated*.

This was not the first time that the passage from health to disease, and from disease to death, had been observed. But from Bichat onward this relationship was 'scientifically conceived or structured in medical perception'.[121] Death is both the absolute point of view over life and opens onto its truth, as well as being that to which life is opposed. Deviation in life is located in relation to a life that is perpetually moving toward death.

Hence the importance of the concept of 'degeneration' for pathological anatomy.[122] A concept which already had a history, from Bichat onward it was to be gradually accorded a positive content. In so far as degeneration was conceived as a return to the inorganic, this was so only to the extent that it was 'infallibly orientated towards death'.[123] Degeneration lies at the very principle of life, of a life caught up in a process of self-destruction, demonstrating both the necessity of death and the most general possibility of disease. From the moment that death was situated as the third term in the conceptual trinity of life, disease, and death, disease was both spatialised and individualised.

BROUSSAIS AND THE REORGANISATION OF THE MEDICAL EPISTEME

The shift in medicine which Foucault locates with Bichat does not entail simply a closer inspection of that which had already been observed with Morgagni. It is not a question of the subject of knowledge penetrating further toward the truth of the object and its secrets. It is rather an adjustment of both terms in relation to each other. Foucault argues that it is a reorganisation which:

> bears jointly on the type of objects to be known, on the grid that makes it appear, isolates it, and carves up the elements relevant to a possible epistemic knowledge (*savoir*), on the position that the subject must occupy in order to map them, on the instrumental mediations that enables it to grasp them, on the modalities of registration and memory that it must put into operation, and on the forms of conceptualization that it must practice and that qualify it as a subject of legitimate knowledge.[124]

What is modified with Bichat is that very relation of knowledge which determines the positions and connections between that which is to be known, and the one who is to know. A 'recasting' at the level of what Foucault terms 'epistemic knowledge' itself (*savoir*) and not at the level of increasingly accumulated and refined knowledge (*connaissances*). The new relation between the sign and the symptom which was possible with Bichat opens up a new role for medical knowledge in constituting the objects of its investigation.[125] In the early forms of clinical medicine the sign, Foucault argues, was not by nature different from the symptom. 'Every symptom was a potential sign, and the sign was simply a read symptom.'[126] But with anatomo-clinical medicine 'the symptom may quite easily remain silent'.[127] The sign is not a symptomatic expression of the disease, the anatomo-clinical sign 'can refer only to a lesional occurrence, never to a pathological essence'.[128] The sign, Foucault argues, 'no longer speaks the natural language of disease; it assumes shape and value only within the questions posed by medical investigation. There is nothing, therefore, to prevent it being solicited and almost fabricated by medical investigation.'[129]

With this transformation of medical analysis Foucault suggests that 'A discourse on the individual is once more possible, or rather, necessary.'[130] The principle of visibility which remains dominant, despite the introduction of different sensorial fields,[131] has as its correlate the differential reading of cases. It is 'the constant possibility of an individual modulation',[132] which defines anatomo-clinical medicine. And this is a modulation which cannot be explained in terms of the environment or the temperament of the subject. From now on 'Only individual illnesses exist: not because the individual reacts upon his own illness, but because the action of the illness unfolds in the form of individuality.'[133]

What is finally offered to scientific knowledge is that 'forbidden, imminent secret: the knowledge of the individual'.[134] The old Aristotelian law which proscribed a scientific discourse on the individual is, Foucault argues, finally lifted. But there is a further level in relation to which one can locate these shifts and transformations within the sphere of knowledge. This Foucault identifies with the name of Broussais and his critique of the theory of essential fevers. It is, Foucault argues, only with Broussais that anatomo-clinical medicine finds its 'equilibrium', a point on which he has been mildly rebuked by Dagognet[135] for its implied homogeneity and continuity after such an event. But what is important here is the break which Foucault suggests was finally established with Broussais from the nosology of the eighteenth century.

Eighteenth-century fevers[136] were characterised according to a number of features: they were understood as reactions of the organism against a pathogenic attack, and were directly related to its visible symptoms such as shivering, increased pulse rate, and sweating. The circulatory system was held to be an essential element in the process by which fever is generalised, the phenomenon of heat being regarded as only the superficial culmination of fever as opposed to the movement of the blood through which the essential nature of the fever was determined. Eighteenth-century fever had 'its own qualities, a sort of substantial, differentiated solidity that makes it possible to divide it up according to specific forms'.[137]

It was, Foucault argues, only with Broussais's 1816 *Examen de la Doctrine généralement admise* that the separation of pathological anatomy from nosology was finally achieved. Ackerknecht has remarked also on the significance of this text:

> The great change came in 1816. The old concentration on symptoms and essentialism was replaced with astonishing speed by a new orientation towards lesions and localism. It was introduced by a man now almost forgotten: Francois Joseph Victor Broussais, the inventor of 'physiological medicine'.[138]

Whilst Foucault does not adopt this language of invention he nevertheless attributes to Broussais a pivotal space. What Broussais challenged, Foucault argues, through a utilisation of Bichat's tissual principle was Pinel's continuing adherence to a notion of the essential nature of diseases.

Rather than situate Pinel as the first to 'localise' fever, Foucault suggests that what Pinel localised was not the disease but the signs, which still depended on the principle of the essential nature of a disease manifested through its symptoms. With Broussais, however, the localisation of disease was achieved through an identification of the surface of the organic attack, through the principle of tissual alteration, each tissue possessing its 'own mode of alteration'. From this moment the organic space of the localisation is, Foucault argues, finally rendered independent of the space of the nosological configuration.

With this change was inverted the relation between the absolute principle of visibility retained even with Bichat, and that of localisation as secondary. With Broussais it is the *local* nature of disease which renders it in a secondary way visible. Localisation takes precedence over the principle of visibility and disease 'exists in space before it exists *for sight*'.[139] From this moment on sickness in an organism is located 'only in relation to the solicitations of the external world, or of alterations in its functioning or anatomy'.[140] Broussais was able to situate the principle of localisation in the context of an enveloping causal schema. The local space of the disease is then immediately a causal space. The 'great discovery' of 1816 resides, Foucault argues, in the disappearance of the 'being' of the disease. It is now 'caught up in an organic web in which the structures are spatial, the determinations causal, the phenomena anatomical and physiological'.[141] Henceforth there are no essential diseases or essences of diseases, disease is nothing other than a complex reaction of tissues to an irritating cause. Foucault acknowledges that Broussais's 'revolution' was carried out on the basis of a number of out-dated notions such as those of sympathy and irritation. But these reversions were, he argues, 'structurally necessary if a medicine of organs was to appear in all its purity and if medical perception was to be liberated from all nosological prejudice'.[142]

CONCLUSION

The Birth of the Clinic tends to be regarded as the most opaque of Foucault's texts discussed in this study. I am inclined to suggest against this that it is Foucault's best book. As with *Histoire de la Folie* it is not a history of a discipline but of the conditions of possibility of a discipline. In this case it is the surfaces of emergence of a liberal-contractual medicine which Foucault charts. It is again the individual which is the point of arrival of Foucault's history, although in *The Birth of the Clinic* it is the individual body rather than the subjectivity of the individual of which knowledge is finally produced.

Foucault demonstrates brilliantly how the formation of modern medicine depended on a complex of shifts at a number of different levels: through a politics of the population; through an overturning of the 'botanical model' of classification of diseases; through the establishment of medicine as both a teaching and a curing profession; and finally through the theoretical principle of the localisation of diseases. Rather than reduce the shifts at the level of knowledge to the effects of the political *context* of an emergent medicine, Foucault shows how the relations between these different levels and the uncertain unity between them allowed the installation of a new medical order.

What is central for the purposes of this study is the way Foucault demonstrates the connection between a particular *savoir*, the question of the government of the population and the maximisation of its resources, and the formation of the individual as object of knowledge. It is, I suggest, the conjunction which Foucault establishes between the question of government and the fabrication of the individual within a range of practices which allows him to overcome the difficulties I identified with the concepts of domination and ideology discussed in previous chapters. Firstly, it avoids the problems I suggested resided in the words of Horkheimer, Marcuse and Habermas in their attempts to posit subjectivity as unique locus of domination and point of resistance. Secondly, it avoids the shortcomings of Althusser's attempt to locate the production of subjectivity at the level of a formal and ahistorical mechanism of subjectification. Foucault demonstrates how the individual was produced as object of certain knowledges, how particular technologies assisted this knowledge,[143] and how these knowledges interlaced with a transformation in the mode of government of populations. The individual in Foucault's account is not simply target of strategies of government, but is also the mechanism through which such a mode of government is rendered possible, a mechanism which has its own effectivity and its own conditions of emergence.

To describe the birth of clinical medicine Foucault employs the image of the lifting of the Aristotelian prohibition of a scientific knowledge of the individual. What is crucial for the purposes of this study is that it is the interior of the individual which emerges as object of medical practice as well as object of psychiatric practice. In *Histoire de la Folie* Foucault demonstrates the appropriateness of the French term *aliéné*[144] to describe the operations through which the insane individual became object of psychiatric knowledge. From that point on madness and the mad person could, Foucault argues, only be *object* of knowledge. As I have argued this is not to return to an account presented in terms of the process by which a subject is reduced to an object. It is simply to register that the emergence of the individual as object of positive knowledge depended on that knowledge being obtained through operations performed by the psychiatrist and the doctor. The individual only emerges as object of medical knowledge to the extent that the symptoms can be identified by *another*, by the doctor. From Broussais onwards medicine was able to confront a sick organism. But more important, perhaps, is that from 1816 a knowledge of the *individual* could be produced which operated according to a division between the normal and the pathological,[145] a knowledge whose conditions were specified from within medical thought. It is this reorganisation of knowledge, this correlative formation of the subject and object of knowledge, which Foucault argues made possible both psychiatry and modern medicine. And one can suggest that this event was, at the very least, of importance to the new strategies of government of the liberal-contractual society in the process of establishing itself in France in the early nineteenth century.

The emergence of medical knowledge in Foucault's account is absolutely central to the emergence of a liberal politics of health. A concern with maximising the health of the population as a whole is linked with efforts to optimise the functioning of the human individual. Such a programme in a liberal society, however, could not be *imposed*. Medical knowledge of the individual was to be conducted in large part through the 'curative machine' of the hospital, a contractual model for the operation of a politics of health. The role which the new medical knowledge was to play in this was crucial, but was always fully inscribed within an institutional and governmental practice. Norms of health could henceforth provide a basis for assessing the condition of the individual and the population as a whole. It is, I argue, at this level that we should understand Foucault's account of power throughout his works, despite the fact that at this stage he did not use this term to describe his concerns. The installation of a new normalising knowledge of the individual, and of a set of institutions and practices through which this could operate, is fundamental to the formation of modern relations of power. What Foucault was to call later the disciplinary mode of power, and which is discussed in chapter 7 below, is concerned centrally with the 'calculated management of life'. Medical knowledge in its modern form is absolutely central to this project.

CHAPTER 6

THE HUMAN SCIENCES AND THE BIRTH OF MAN

•

Foucault's 'response' to a philosophy of the subject has assumed a number of forms. *Histoire de la Folie* charted the emergence of the modern subject as a being defined by a truth which it was psychiatry and psychology's privilege to track down. The givenness of the human body was challenged in *The Birth of the Clinic* through an investigation into the diverse conditions which rendered the body visible within modern medical knowledge. Central to both these studies was the examination of the interplay between institutional, administrative, theoretical and political practices. *The Order of Things* is very different in its approach from these studies, although it is an integral component to the project of a genealogy of the modern subject. The transformations it charts reside entirely at the level of knowledge. Rather than a demonstration of the non-discursive conditions of possibility of a particular discourse, Foucault remains at the level of discourses. It is, in particular, with the discourses of life, labour and language that Foucault is concerned. As its sub-title indicates, *The Order of Things* is an archaeology of the human sciences and not an archaeology of knowledges in general.[1] In it Foucault provides us with what is perhaps his most iconoclastic statement – that man is an 'invention' produced through the transformation in certain knowledges which occurred around 1800. The iconoclasm should, however, not mislead. Foucault is simply describing what he depicts as an 'event'[2] which took place within knowledge. *The Order of Things* is an attempt to follow the details of this transformation at the archaeological level of knowledge, at the level of what Foucault calls the *episteme*.[3]

Foucault's project of an archaeology and the notion of *episteme* have been the target of considerable criticism.[4] It is worth briefly considering what Foucault means by these terms before proceeding to an examination of the substance of his argument. The project of an archaeology depended, Foucault tells us in a foreword to the English edition of *The Order of Things*, on the suggestion that empirical knowledge, at a given time and in a given culture, might possess a 'well-defined regularity'.[5] What, he asks, 'if the very possibility of recording facts, of allowing oneself to be convinced by them, of distorting them in traditions or of making purely speculative use of them, if even this was not at the mercy of chance?'[6] In short, what if 'the history of non-formal knowledge had itself a system?'[7]

Foucault addressed these questions, however, not through a search for a *Weltanschauung*. Instead he tells us that he sought to identify 'an epistemological space specific to a particular period'.[8] That is, he attempted to reveal 'a *positive unconscious* of knowledge: a level that eludes the consciousness of the scientist and yet is part of scientific discourse'.[9] Foucault undertook this by attempting to elicit the 'rules of formation' which allowed naturalists, economists and grammarians to define the objects of their study. The concept of *episteme* gains its meaning in the suggestion that these different fields of study exhibit common rules of formation:

> It is these rules of formation, which were never formulated in their own right, but are to be found only in widely differing theories, concepts, and objects of study, that I have tried to reveal, by isolating, as their specific locus, a level that I have called, somewhat arbitrarily perhaps, archaeological.[10]

In undertaking his project of an archaeology of the human sciences in *The Order of Things* Foucault sets aside both the problem of causality and the problem of the subject. Rather than asking 'What made such a discovery possible?', 'Why did this new concept appear?', Foucault prudently confines himself to charting the transformations in conceptual structure of the sciences of life, labour and language. To a certain extent questions of causality had been broached in his earlier studies.[11] Foucault admits, however, to both a dissatisfaction with traditional explanations – spirit of the epoch, interests, social or technological factors – and to an inability to offer an alternative causal account.[12]

In refusing to base his project for an archaeology on the category of the subject Foucault expresses a preference for exploring knowledges in terms of the rules that come into play in their very existence. What was it, he asks, that enabled certain discourses to qualify as naturalist, economic or grammatical? An analysis, that is, which rejects the postulate of a transcendental consciousness in favour of a theory of discursive practice:

> Discourse in general, and scientific discourse in particular, is so complex a reality that we not only can, but should, approach it at different levels and with different methods. If there is one approach that I do reject, however, it is that (one might call it, broadly speaking, the phenomenological approach) which gives absolute priority to the observing subject, which attributes a constituent role to an act, which places its own point of view at the origin of all historicity – which, in short, leads to a transcendental consciousness. It seems to me that the historical analysis of scientific discourse should, in the last resort, be subject, not to a theory of the knowing subject, but rather to a theory of discursive practice.[13]

I have attempted in this chapter to offer a reading of *The Order of Things*, one which alters the balance of the book in two ways. Firstly, I have not done justice to Foucault's detailed examination of general grammar, natural history and the analysis of wealth in the classical age. In the confines of this study it is not realistic to hope to supply examples which adequately illustrate Foucault's arguments. As far as possible I have tried to overcome this difficulty by indicating where relevant secondary material. Secondly, I have more or less neglected Foucault's account of the Renaissance at the beginning of the book. This is on the grounds that it is neither pertinent to the concerns of this study nor central to Foucault's enterprise in *The Order of Things*. Foucault does not accord the Renaissance the attention that the classical age receives, and it is reasonable to suggest that it functions to a large extent as a negative in relation to the classical age, neither so rigorously demarcated nor so carefully examined. This is not to devalue its seriousness as historical analysis. Indeed the works of both Ian Hacking[14] and Francois Jacob[15] examine the systems of thought of the Renaissance in ways which are similar in a number of important respects to Foucault's approach. It is simply to note that, as with Foucault's two previous studies, in *The Order of Things* his concern was to chart the nature of the classical age and its disruption toward the end of the eighteenth century.

I begin the discussion of *The Order of Things* by offering an outline of Foucault's account of the nature of the *episteme* of the classical age, its dependence on the notion of representation and the figure of the *table*. The importance of the classical age for the purposes of this study is principally in terms of that which Foucault argues it could not sustain as a figure of knowledge. The classical age is interesting just as much in its dissolution during the last quarter of the eighteenth century as in the period of its stable functioning. I continue by examining Foucault's account of the formation of the human sciences in the *episteme* which he argues was established at the beginning of the nineteenth century. Finally, I examine Foucault's account of the emergence of psychoanalysis, ethnology and linguistics from within the *episteme* of the nineteenth century, as knowledges opposed to a general theory of man. In conclusion I offer some reflections on the relevance of Foucault's history of the human sciences for the concerns of this study.

THE CLASSICAL AGE AND THE SCIENCE OF ORDER

Foucault's starting point in *The Order of Things* is the *episteme* of the Renaissance which is marked, he argues, by *similitude* as the form of knowledge. Renaissance knowledge is defined by the absence of a distinction between objects and signs, between the existence of the world and its signification. The historian of science Francois Jacob has remarked in similar terms on the Renaissance form of knowledge:

> In order to know things then, it was necessary to detect the visible signs which nature had placed on their surfaces precisely to permit man to comprehend their relationships. It was necessary to discern the system of resemblances, the network of analogies and similitudes providing access to certain of nature's secrets.[16]

At the beginning of the seventeenth century this 'age of resemblance' begins, Foucault suggests, to be displaced. And with this shift classical thought establishes itself as a mode of knowledge based on the principles of identity, difference, measurement, and order. Henceforth resemblance, Foucault argues, is examined in terms of identity and difference discovered through measurement with a common unit, or position within an order. Knowledge no longer seeks to reveal kinships and intrinsic similarities, but discriminates and establishes identities only to locate them on successive points in a series. History and science are separated from one another, the former consisting of erudition and the interplay and disagreement between authors' opinions, the latter consisting of 'the confident judgements we are able to make by means of intuitions and their serial connections'.[17] The written word is no longer the form of truth and the signature of things;

whilst words may continue to translate the truth of things they can no longer be considered a mark of it.

Classical knowledge for Foucault is distinguished through the relation which it maintains with the *mathesis*. This is not an attempt to mathematise empirical knowledge, but refers to a universal science of measurement and order. This link with the *mathesis* was, Foucault argues, to remain a constant until the end of the eighteenth century. On the one hand, whilst based on the principles of order and measurement, it was always possible within this configuration to reduce problems of measurement to problems of order. The relation of knowledge to the *mathesis* hence becomes that of the possibility of establishing an order, even if this is a non-measurable one. On the other hand a number of empirical fields – general grammar, natural history and the analysis of wealth – were to be defined for the first time, most of which did not depend on any mathematicisation, yet all of which relied on a possible science of order. The particular instrument of these new forms of knowledge was, Foucault argues, the *system of signs*, manifested in general grammar, natural history, and the analysis of wealth. None of these empirical studies which mark the boundaries of the classical period (approximately from 1660 to 1800) could, he maintains, have been established without their relation to the project of a universal science of order.

The first half of the seventeenth century is held to witness an alteration in the entire organisation of signs. No longer bound by its mark as resemblance or affinity, the sign finds its place *within knowledge*. Signs could no longer reside undiscovered, but could only exist within a '*known* possibility of substitution between two *known* elements'.[18] Signs are only constituted through the act of knowing since 'it is within knowledge itself that the sign is to perform its signifying function; it is from knowledge that it will borrow its certainty or its probability.'[19]

The relation of the sign to that which it signifies is, Foucault argues, also altered with the advent of classical thought. Whereas similitude in the sixteenth century drew things together and united them, in the seventeenth century the sign is characterised by its dispersion, by its ability to be both part of that which it designates and yet separate from it. The sign is inseparable from analysis and a result of it. It is at the same time its instrument and 'enables things to become distinct, to preserve themselves within their own identities, to dissociate themselves or bind themselves together'.[20]

Foucault argues that the sign can also, from the seventeenth century onwards, assume the value of either nature or convention.

Not that the sixteenth century had been unable to formulate this distinction, but rather that it was unable to separate artificial signs from their fidelity to natural signs which were the foundation of all others. The seventeenth century, Foucault argues, made the man-made sign 'the sign at the peak of its activity'.[21] As Jacob remarks: 'Henceforth, science was less concerned with the divine will secretly ruling beings and things than with the grid that had to be placed on nature to decipher its order.'[22] Conventional signs were henceforth able to permit the analysis of things into their simplest elements, to enable the decomposition of things into their origins, and to demonstrate the possibility of the combination of those elements. Jacob comments that:

> First limited to mathematical objects, the search for order progressively extended to empiric domains which at first sight appeared beyond the reach of this type of analysis. Gradually the reduction of complexity to its underlying simplicity and the rules of the combinative method applied even to what could not be directly measured. The most varied objects, substances, beings and even qualities finally lent themselves to classification.[23]

The sign system is crucial to the reorganisation of knowledge which Foucault suggests was installed with the classical *episteme*. It was 'the sign system that linked all knowledge to a language, and sought to replace all languages with a system of artificial symbols and operations of a logical nature.'[24] In terms of an archaeology of classical thought it was this dissociation of sign and resemblance in the early part of the seventeenth century which permitted the emergence of the themes of probability,[25] analysis, combination, and universal language system, as 'a single network of necessities'.[26]

However, Foucault argues that the most fundamental property of signs for the classical *episteme* consists in the relation of the sign to its content. No longer guaranteed by the order of things in themselves, it resides now in the connection established within knowledge between 'the *idea of one thing* and the *idea of another*'.[27] The triple system based on resemblance characteristic of the Renaissance is replaced by a strictly binary organisation which was clearly stated in the *Logic of Port Royal*: 'The sign encloses two ideas, one of the thing representing, the other of the thing represented; and its nature consists in exciting the first by means of the second.'[28] But one condition is required if the sign is to play this role. It can, Foucault argues, do so only if it manifests, in addition, its relation with that which it signifies. Its representation must also be represented, and a sign can fulfill its task of representation 'not only because a bond of representation can be established between them, but also because this representation can always be represented within the idea that is representing'.[29]

In classical thought signs are, Foucault argues, co-extensive with representation, and with thought as a whole. There is, moreover, no possibility of a theory of signification since 'if phenomena are posited only in a representation that, in itself and because of its own representability, is wholly a sign, then signification cannot constitute a problem.'[30] Indeed it is not even visible. And yet Foucault argues that this binary nature of the sign is linked with a general theory of representation, an 'ideology' which provides a philosophical account of 'all forms of representation, from elementary sensation to the abstract and complex idea'.[31]

Foucault suggests that the Classical *episteme* and its relation to a knowledge of order is made possible through two principal mechanisms. The ordering of simple natures is achieved through recourse to a *mathesis*, of which the universal method is algebra; the ordering of complex natures, of empirical representations in general, is achieved through constituting a *taxinomia*, which necessitates establishing a system of signs. However, this separation is not absolute, and the *taxinomia* relates to the *mathesis* in so far as empirical representations are analysable into simple natures; likewise, since the *mathesis* is only one particular case of *taxinomia*, it cannot be held to subsist independently. Figure 6.1[32] demonstrates this relation.

Figure 6.1 General science of order

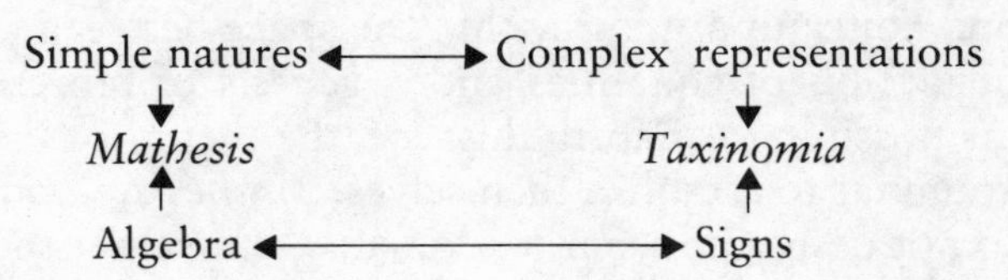

However, to the extent that the *taxinomia* also implies a certain continuum of things, the possibility of a science of empirical orders requires an analysis of knowledge that permits the reconstitution of this hidden continuity of being. It is this, Foucault argues, which leads to the necessity, manifest throughout the classical age, of questioning the origin of knowledge.

Foucault's argument concerning this general project of identifying an origin for thought and ideas is supported in a brief discussion of language analysis before Saussure by Jonathan Culler:

> Condillac set out to demonstrate that reflection can be derived from sensation and that the mechanism of derivation is a 'linking of ideas' brought about through the use of signs. The precise nature of his argument is not important; what is important is the direction in which it leads him. Trying to show that thought has a natural origin, that the existence of reflection and abstract notions is something which can be explained, he went beyond the claim that language is a picture of thought (the seventeenth-century position) to argue that abstract ideas are a result of the process by which signs are created. He had therefore to demonstrate that there was a natural process by which a language of conventional signs could arise from a primitive and non-reflective experience. He had to concern himself with *the origin of language*.[33]

Empirical analyses are already included within the demands of a knowledge posited as the establishment of order. The limits of the classical episteme are set on the one hand by a *mathesis* as the science of calculable order, and on the other by a *genesis* as 'the analysis of the constitution of orders on the basis of empirical series'.[34] Within these limits resides that figure which Foucault argues is fundamental to the classical age, the *table*. As knowledge it involves providing a sign for all representations and articulating these into distinct subregions.

It is here, Foucault argues, within the space between a *mathesis* as the calculation of equalities and a *genesis* of representations, that it was possible for natural history, the theory of money, and general grammar to establish themselves. *Mathesis*, *taxinomia* and *genesis* do not designate separate domains, but rather the network which is held to define the possible forms of knowledge in the classical age, within which the central place is occupied by the *table*. It is this network and its positivity to which Foucault's archaeology addresses itself, a network which does not impose a principle of homogeneity on all that takes place within it, but which defines the conditions which make division and controversies possible.

LANGUAGE AND REPRESENTATION

That representation provides the 'key' to the classical episteme is aptly demonstrated through the case of language.[35] In the seventeenth and eighteenth century Foucault argues that words have the task and the capacity of 'representing thought'. But representation here is not understood in the sense of a reproduction exterior to thought. There is, Foucault argues, 'no essential and primitive act of signification, but only, at the heart of representation, the power that it possesses to represent itself'.[36] In the classical age, nothing is given that is not given to representation. Representations do not depend on a world which gives them meaning but 'open of themselves on to a space that is their own, whose internal network gives rise to meaning'.[37] Language in the classical age does not express thought as its exterior effect, but is 'caught in the grid of thought, woven into the very fabric it is unrolling'.[38] Language does not 'exist', Foucault argues, rather it 'functions', its entire existence is exhausted in its representative role; it has 'no other locus, no other value, than in representation'.[39] Once the 'existence' of language has been eliminated it is only its representative role that remains, its status as discourse which is 'merely representation itself represented by verbal signs'.[40]

Language, however, has a peculiar status by virtue of the particularity of its system of signs. Foucault argues that what enables language to be distinguished from all other signs and to play a decisive role in representation is 'that it analyses representation according to a necessarily successive order'.[41] Language has to arrange thought in a linear order which paradoxically both distinguishes it from representation and from signs. Located neither in a position of exteriority in relation to thought, nor opposed to other signs as the arbitrary to the natural, it replaces the contemporaneous with the successive. In installs an order which is regulated according to the principle of linear succession.[42]

Foucault locates general grammar as '*the study of verbal order in its relation to the simultaneity that is its task to represent.*'[43] Its object is not an individual language but *discourse* conceived as a sequence of verbal signs. General grammar is distinct from comparative grammar[44] in that its generality does not reside in the discovery of grammatical laws common to all linguistic domains. Instead its generality consists in its attempt 'to make visible, below the level of grammatical rules, but at the same level as their foundation, the representative function of discourse'.[45] There can still be different general grammars (French, English, Latin, German) since general grammar does not seek to define the laws of all languages;[46] rather it takes 'each particular language, in turn, as a mode of the articulation of thought upon itself'.[47] Foucault argues that general grammar seeks to establish the *taxonomy* of each language, the system of identities and differences which in each language establishes the possibility of discourse.[48] It achieves this through what Foucault terms the *quadrilateral* of language, the four theories – of the proposition, of articulation, of designation, and of derivation – which are presupposed within general grammar's study of the representative function of words.

Proposition: The proposition is the most general and elementary form of language since without it discourse no longer exists. It is the proposition which 'constitutes a word as a word and raises it above the level of cries and noises'.[49] Of the three elements in the proposition – the subject, the predicate, and the link between them – it is the verb which has an irreducible function. It is 'the indispensable condition for all discourse; and whenever it does not exist, at least by implication, it is not possible to say that there is language.'[50] The verb has an 'invisible presence' whose first appearance constitutes the threshold of language. Its essential function resides in its capacity to 'affirm the existence of an attributive link between two things'.[51] The function of the verb can, Foucault argues, be 'reduced to the single verb that signifies *to be*'.[52] The verb *to be* is 'the representation of being in language; but it is equally the representative being of language – that which, by enabling language to affirm what it says, renders it susceptible of truth or error.'[53] The verb designates the representative character of language, its mode of existence, a function which was to be dissociated as soon as the domain of general grammar was itself to disappear.[54]

Articulation: The possibility of discourse acting as representation resides also in that 'it is made up of words that *name*, part by part, what is given to representation.'[55] In its very nature the word is a noun or a name, and as such is always directed towards a particular representation. But unless there are to be as many nouns as there are things to name, nouns require a generality which can be acquired in two ways. Either by a 'horizontal' articulation which establishes generalities by progressing from the individual to the species, or by a 'vertical' articulation which is linked to the first, but which distinguishes 'substance' from surface characteristics. These two modes of articulation of language intersect at the point of the common noun, midway between the proper noun and the adjective. Language preserves its representative function in its function of nomination which enables language to be 'entirely comprised within the general form of the proposition'.[56]

Designation: This theory of 'generalised nomination' indicates, in addition to the propositional form of language, a particular relation to things which is of the order of indication or designation. The origin of language is, Foucault argues, revealed in 'the primitive moment in which it was pure designation'.[57] Language is detached from nature in so far as it rests upon 'the reversible and analysable relations of signs and representations'.[58] It is constituted through the difference between words and things, the separation between language and that which it is the task of language to designate. This enables one to explain both the substitution of the sign for the thing designated, as well as the relation it achieves with what it names, the permanence of the designation of the sign.[59]

Derivation: Words can, however, shift from their original signification and alter their meaning, their form, and their field of application. Whilst the modifications of form obey no rule, Foucault argues the alterations of meaning obey fixed principles, which are all of a spatial order. Alphabetic writing, as opposed to figurative writing, is based on reconstituting in space not ideas but sounds, from which can be formed a relatively small number of signs whose combination enables the formation of all possible words. Whereas symbolic writing is inherently limited, as is a culture based on it, with alphabetic writing 'the history of men is entirely changed.'[60] Language can enter the general domain of analysis, thereby 'allowing the progress of writing and that of thought to provide each other with mutual support'.[61] And yet, although writing is the support of the possibility of progressive refinements of analysis, 'it is neither their principle nor even their initial movement. This latter is a slipping movement common to attention, to signs, and to words.'[62] The movement of language away from its primary designations is hence attributed to the capacity of a representation to become attached to a single element of the thing, or to be used as analogy. The progressive analysis and articulation of language 'are not the effect of a refinement of style; on the contrary, they reveal the mobility peculiar to all language whenever it is spontaneous.'[63] And this capacity of words to change their meaning is dependent on their location within a *tropological space*.

The four elements of this 'quadrilateral' interrelate, Foucault argues, both around the periphery as well as diagonally across it. At the point where the two diagonals intersect there resides the nexus of the entire classical experience of language, the *name*. To name is both to provide a verbal representation of a representation, as well as to place it within a general table. It might even be said, Foucault suggests, that 'it is the Name that organizes all Classical discourse.'[64] Speaking and writing do not return us to intentional subjects. Instead they indicate 'the sovereign act of nomination'.[65] The four theoretical segments – proposition, articulation, designation, and derivation – indicate the limits within which it was possible for the classical analysis of language to exist. And whilst it is the proposition which enables language to exist, the three other segments impose their own requirement, the necessity for 'resemblances that posit themselves from the very start'.[66] Below the level of identities and differences resemblance 'still constitutes the outer edge of language: the ring surrounding the domain of that which can be analysed, reduced to order, and known'.[67] But this is not a return to the sixteenth century and the principle of similitude, because resemblance is now located within a propositional relation based on the verb *to be* and the network of *names*.

NATURAL HISTORY AND THE ANALYSIS OF WEALTH

The domain of natural history in the classical age is, Foucault argues, dependent on the same figures as those which established the possibility of general grammar. It was made possible at that same moment when words and things were separated and when the space opened up in representation enabled visible characteristics to be transcribed into words. Natural history, Foucault argues, is 'nothing more than the nomination of the visible'.[68] Between the sixteenth and seventeenth century what changed was 'not the desire for knowledge, but a new way of connecting things both to the eye and to discourse'.[69]

However, natural history and language are not connected through the transference of a method. Their linkage resides instead at the level of that which establishes the conditions of possibility of a knowledge of beings such as to enable them to be represented in a system of names. This Foucault terms the historical *a priori* and suggests that it authorises the dispersion of projects and divergences of opinion within the parameters of veridical discourse established in the classical age.

> This *a priori* is what, in a given period, delimits in the totality of experience a field of knowledge, defines the mode of being of the objects that appear in that field, provides man's everyday perception with theoretical powers, and defines the conditions in which he can sustain a discourse about things that is recognised to be true.[70]

Natural history exists side by side with general grammar in the seventeenth and eighteenth century as a 'well-constructed' language, designating each being and clearly indicating the place it occupies within the order of the whole. This it achieves on the one hand through the theory of *structure* which regroups into a unity the two functions of the proposition and articulation; on the other hand the theory of *character* superimposes itself on the place occupied by the figures of designation and derivation. This, Foucault argues, makes it possible 'both to indicate the individual and to situate it in a space of generalities that fit inside one another'.[71] Francois Jacob has remarked that:

> In order to classify plants, they must be represented by symbols – that is, named. To give a name is already to classify. The two operations are inextricably interwoven. They are two aspects of a single combinative system which must be articulated with that of visible structures, namely, the system of surfaces and volumes to whose rearrangement plants owe their diversity. The meeting point, the pivot of what can be seen, named and classified, is the *character*. According to Linnaeus: 'A plant should be mutually known from its specific name, and the name from the plant, and both from their proper character, written in the former and delineated in the latter.' Linked to the details of structure, the character constitutes the 'proper mark' of the plant. It represents the trace which must persist in thought after examination and description of a plant.[72]

Until the end of the eighteenth century Foucault argues that the category of life does not exist, that there exists only a multiplicity of living beings ordered in relation to each other. Francois Jacob also has suggested that it was only at the end of the eighteenth century that living beings were 'definitely separated from things'.[73] The threshold between the living and the non-living during the eighteenth century did not constitute a serious problem, and the naturalist was concerned instead 'with the structure of the visible world and its denomination according to characters. Not with life.'[74] Natural history, Foucault argues, is interwoven with language in so far as 'it is essentially a concerted use of names and since its ultimate aim is to give things their true denomination.'[75] The relation between language and natural history is crucial in that the knowledge of nature which it offers attempts 'to build upon the basis of language a *true* language, one that will reveal the conditions in which all language is possible and the limits within which it can have a domain of validity.'[76] This interrelation was only to be dissociated when in the nineteenth century life was to attain its autonomy in relation to the concepts of classification, and to become one object of knowledge among others, a transformation which Foucault argues took place at the level of the *episteme* itself.

The analysis of wealth in the classical age Foucault presents as constituted in relation to the same dominant figures of the *episteme* which made possible general grammar and natural history. However, he suggests that its formation and eventual dispersion retained a singularity through its investment in a range of practices and institutions. The sixteenth century had located the ability of money to measure commodities and its exchangeability in terms of its intrinsic value. The seventeenth century was to invert this and make the exchanging function the foundation for its properties of measure and substitution. Money is held to receive its value from its pure function as sign, and the value which things assume in relation to each other is represented through this monetary sign. Without this property as sign 'wealth would remain immobile, useless, and as it were silent.'[77] Yet as the same time in order to function as representation money must have characteristics which render it adequate to its task, and hence precious. Money 'cannot signify wealth without itself being wealth. But it becomes wealth because it is a sign.'[78] Money only becomes real wealth in so far as it operates as representation, and the relations between wealth and money are no longer of the order of the 'preciousness' of metal, but are based on circulation and exchange. Circulation hence becomes one of the fundamental categories of analysis since the different forms of wealth are related to each other only within an overall system of exchange.[79]

Foucault suggests that the analysis of wealth can be regarded in terms of the same configuration which he uses to characterise natural history and general grammar. The theory of value corresponds with the attributive function of the verb which in general grammar is the condition of possibility of language. Value is that which makes it possible to explain how one thing can function within the system of exchanges as the equivalent of another. At the same time, since value is defined and limited within the overall system of exchanges, it also assumes the role of articulation recognised in general grammar. Foucault suggests that value occupies 'exactly the same position in the analysis of wealth as *structure* does in natural history'.[80] On the other hand, he argues, the theory of money and trade corresponds to the function of *designation* and derivation within general grammar. It explains 'how any given form of matter can take on a signifying function by being related to an object and serving as a permanent sign for it'.[81] It explains also modifications in this relation. The theory of money and prices 'functions in relation to wealth in the same way as *character* does in relation to natural beings'.[82]

The 'quadrilateral' identified by Foucault in relation to the theory of language is held to operate then not only in the domain of natural history, but also in the analysis of wealth:

> The order of wealth and the order of natural beings are established and revealed in so far as there are established between objects of need, and between visible individuals, systems of signs which make possible the *designation* of representations one by another, the *derivation* of signifying representations in relation to those signified, the *articulation* of what is represented, and the *attribution* of certain representations to certain others.[83]

Within classical thought, at the level of its *episteme*, Foucault suggests that natural history and the analysis of wealth have the same conditions of possibility as language. This indicates, he argues, that 'order in nature and order in the domain of wealth have the same mode of being, for the Classical experience, as the order of representations as manifested by words.'[84] Moreover, as a system of signs words are privileged when it is a question of the order of things such that a well-organised natural history and a well-regulated theory of money are able to function in the same way as language.

There are of course distinctions to be made between the domain of language and that of wealth or natural history, and also between natural history and the theory of value and prices. However, they are, Foucault argues, united at the archaeological level, at that level which 'defines a certain mode of being for language, natural individuals, and the objects of need and desire'.[85] And this mode of being is that of representation. It is within the space opened up inside representation that the classical *taxinomia* and its ability to arrange things in an order of identities and differences is made possible. It was, Foucault suggests, only with the decline of representation that the classical *episteme* was itself to disintegrate.

THE DISRUPTION OF THE CLASSICAL EPISTEME

Foucault argues that a discontinuity manifests itself across the entire surface of knowledge in the last years of the eighteenth century, such that wealth, living beings, and discourse no longer appear through the transparency of words. A transformation, that is, at the level of the *episteme*, and through which a series of new figures appears. Knowledge is no longer organised through a general *taxinomia* but constitutes instead an area composed of organic structures, their internal relations, and their overall function. The organising figures of this space are, Foucault argues, those of *analogy* and *succession*. It is no longer the identity of the elements which establishes the link between things, but rather 'the identity of the relation between the elements . . . and of the functions they perform'.[86] If organic structures are still located adjacent to each other this derives not from the principle of classification but rather 'because they have both been formed at the same time, and the one immediately after the other in the emergence of the successions.'[87] This reorganisation of the Western *episteme* took place, Foucault argues, in two phases whose outer limits are marked by the years 1775 and 1825, and which overlap around the years 1795–1800.

The first phase of this 'event' in Western culture Foucault presents as a dislocation of the stability of representation and its constitutive role within the classical *episteme*. What is modified at this stage is the way in which, within general grammar, natural history, and the analysis of wealth, the representative elements function in relation to each other, how they perform their double role of designation and articulation through which an order is established. A first stage perhaps, but one which was crucial in that it provided the conditions of possibility for that event, the announcement of which is perhaps the most notorious aspect of *The Order of Things* – the invention of man as object of knowledge.[88]

Whilst Adam Smith is not accorded the role of founder of political economy,[89] Foucault's account nevertheless accords him a decisive place in the transformation of the classical analysis of wealth. Smith did not, Foucault argues, invent the concept of labour, instead he displaced it from its function of expressing exchange in terms of need and revealed its irreducibility. Whilst still a representative element, what it represents from Smith onwards is no longer desire but labour. In distinguishing between the reasons behind exchange and the measurement of that which is exchanged, Smith introduces labour as an irreducible principle of the order of exchanges. Equivalence is henceforth established through that which is heterogeneous to the objects exchanged. The possibility of exchange and the regulation of its order is dependent on labour and the conditions under which it takes place, conditions which are exterior to their representation. From this moment the analysis of capital and production is constituted as a domain governed by its own internal laws.

Within natural history a similar displacement was taking place during the same period based on the introduction of the principle of *organic structure*.[90] As a basis for taxonomies this principle displaced the domain of the visible since it was no longer reducible to a representative role. The notion of character, by means of which individuals and species are grouped into more general units, is no longer based on visible structure, but rather on the existence of functions essential to living beings.[91] Character is 'nothing in itself but the visible point of a complex and hierarchized organic structure in which function plays an essential governing and determining role.' Francois Jacob has remarked on this change that:

> Thus at the end of the eighteenth century there was a change in the relations between the exterior and the interior, between the surface and the depth, and between organs and functions of a living being. What became accessible to comparative investigation was a system of relationships in the depth of a living organism, designed to make it function. Behind the visible forms could be glimpsed the profile of a secret architecture imposed by the necessity of living.[92]

The notion of life becomes crucial to the ordering of living beings, and the visible attains importance only to the extent that it can be related to the invisible.[93] Just as the notion of labour was not invented by Smith, so too the concept of organic structure had already existed in eighteenth-century natural history. However the crucial displacement occurs at that moment when the concept of organic structure becomes a foundation for the ordering of nature, when classification and nomenclature are dissociated.

From this moment on the division between organic and inorganic becomes fundamental and enables the possibility of a biology within which vitalism can be regarded as a 'surface effect' of a mutation at the archaeological level.[94]

Finally, it is in general grammar that Foucault argues the first stage of this mutation in the Western *episteme* can be detected. The privileged place of language analysis within the field of representation meant, he suggests, that the changes occurred here at a slower pace than in the other two domains.[95] For the seventeenth and eighteenth century the representative mode of being of words and their foundation in an initial designation served as the basis for the 'horizontal' comparison of languages. However in the last years of the eighteenth century comparisons between different languages assume a different function through the modification in status of the phenomenon of inflection. The shift to comparative grammar at the beginning of the nineteenth century has been referred to by Jonathan Culler in the following terms:

> The shift of attention from roots to inflectional patterns (which had always been the most difficult items for philosophic etymologists to deal with) reflects a change in the notion of what language is: no longer is it simply representation, a series of forms ordered by the rationality they represent and through which one moves to grasp thought and the processes of mind itself. It is a system of forms which are governed by their own law, which possess an autonomous formal pattern.[96]

Whereas previously inflectional phenomena had been analysed in terms of their representative value, from the end of the eighteenth century one can already detect 'a more complex relation between the modifications of the radical and the functions of grammar'.[97] The dimension of the purely grammatical begins from this moment to appear to the extent that in addition to its representative role, language 'consists also of formal elements, grouped into a system, which imposes upon the sounds, syllables, and roots an organization that is not that of representation'.[98] Languages are no longer to be compared through their representative function, but rather through the manner in which words are arranged in relation to each other. From this point on there is, Foucault argues, 'an interior "mechanism" in languages which determines not only each one's individuality but also its resemblances to the others'.[99] The word, Foucault argues,

> is no longer attached to a representation except in so far as it is previously a part of the grammatical organization by means of which the language defines and guarantees its own coherence. For the word to be able to say what it says, it must belong to a grammatical totality which, in relation to the word, is primary, fundamental, and determining.[100]

The 'event' which Foucault locates as having occurred toward the end of the eighteenth century is, he suggests, analogous in its structure in all three spheres. Henceforth it is *labour* which gives objects their value; it is the *organic structure* of living beings which enables their characterisation; and it is the *inflectional system*, the 'internal architecture' of language, the modification of words through their grammatical position in relation to each other, which makes it possible to define a language. The unity which underlies these diverse events resides, Foucault argues, at the level of 'the relation of representation to that which is posited in it'.[101] Representation can no longer establish the connection of representations to each other through an immediate visibility in the space of the table. Things now have their own internal space, their own organic structures, even though at this stage representation has not entirely lost the constitutive role it possessed within the classical *episteme*.

In the sphere of philosophy a correlate of this mutation in general grammar, natural history, and the analysis of wealth is located by Foucault in the works of Kant where it is a question not simply of representations but of what renders representation possible in general.[102] Kant's answer is in terms of proposing the conditions which define their universally valid form, the basis on which all representations may be posited. Whilst only empirical observations can be based on the contents of representation 'Any other connection, if it is to be universal, must have its foundation beyond all experience, in the *a priori* that renders it possible.'[103] In this respect, the Kantian critique marks, Foucault argues, the 'threshold of our modernity' in that it 'sanctions for the first time that event in European culture which coincides with the end of the eighteenth century: the withdrawal of knowledge and thought outside the space of representation.'[104] But at the same time as demonstrating the metaphysics of representation it provides the conditions of possibility of another metaphysics 'whose purpose will be to question, apart from representation, all that is the source and origin of representation'.[105] It is this space that the question 'what is man' comes to occupy, a question whose possibility is established with the dissolution of the classical *episteme*.

Foucault suggests that the dissolution of the *mathesis* as a general science of ordered representations gave rise on the one hand to the theme of a transcendental subject as the condition of possibility of knowledge of objects, and on the other hand to new empirical fields defined by the value of things, the organic structure of living beings, and the grammatical structure of languages. Labour, life and language as three new and distinct positivities are, Foucault suggests, in correspondence with the founding of a transcendental philosophy. Indeed they are themselves 'so many "transcendentals" which make possible the objective knowledge of living beings, of the laws of production, and of the forms of language'.[106] They are both outside knowledge, yet at the same time are the conditions of knowledge. But just as the new positivities correspond with the transcendental field, they also differ from it in residing on the side of the object, on the side of *a posteriori* knowledge instead of the *a priori* possibility of experience as such. And with this shift, Foucault argues, the empirical domains of the knowledge of living beings, of the laws of production, and of the forms of language 'become linked with *reflections on subjectivity, the human being, and finitude*, assuming the value and function of philosophy, as well as of the reduction of philosophy or counter-philosophy'.[107]

It is of course true that Foucault presents all this as only a first stage in that reorganisation of the Western *episteme* which made possible the formation of the human sciences. However, it was, Foucault argues, 'the beginning of a certain *modern* manner of knowing empiricities'.[108] Only on the basis of this primary decomposition was it possible to establish a transcendental field of subjectivity and the 'quasi-transcendentals' of life, labour and language, a transformation of 'knowledge itself as an *interior and indivisible mode of being between the knowing subject and the object of knowledge*'.[109] And it was, Foucault argues, only on this basis that Ricardo was able to secure that space opened up by Adam Smith, Cuvier that marked out by Lamarck and others, and Bopp that which was established with the first philologists. With this second stage language finally lost its transparency and the representative function of the word ceased to be its constitutive element. The fundamental position which language occupied in relation to all knowledge as 'the initial, inevitable way of representing representations',[110] was at last to be dissipated. Henceforth language was to be characterised by laws of its own and was to become one object of knowledge among others. With this 'dispersion' of language man was at last constituted as an object of knowledge, accorded a specific domain and investigated within it.

THE FINITUDE OF MAN

Despite the constitutive role played by representation within the classical *episteme*, a crucial absence in the 'table' which it constructs is the very being for whom representation exists. Indeed until the last years of the eighteenth century Foucault argues that *man did not exist*, that 'there was no epistemological consciousness of man as such. The Classical *episteme* is articulated along lines that do not isolate, in any way, a specific domain proper to man.'[111] The concept of human nature as it existed in the seventeenth century and eighteenth century excluded, he argues, the possibility of a science of man. Nomenclature established human nature within a linear succession of identities and differences and denied the possibility of establishing a well-constructed domain regulated by a number of 'laws' and organised in accordance with them. As Jacob remarks:

> Until the end of the eighteenth century there was no clear boundary between beings and things. The living extended without a break into the inanimate. Everything was continuous in the world and, said Buffon, 'One can descend by imperceptible degree from the most perfect creature to the most shapeless matter, from the best organized animal to the roughest mineral'. There was as yet no fundamental division between the living and the non-living.[112]

Within the classical *episteme* nature and human nature are interrelated functional elements and man 'as a primary reality with his own density, as the difficult object and sovereign subject of all possible knowledge, has no place in it'.[113] Whilst the 'transparency' of language persisted, an individualised domain of knowledge concerned with man and his particular mode of being could not be formed, Foucault argues, precisely because classical language 'contained the nexus of representation and being'.[114] As the common discourse of representation and things, and the point of intersection of nature and human nature, the 'invisibility' of classical language prevented the constitution of that entity for whom representation existed from being questioned in its own right and according to its own laws. The possibility of the Cartesian transition from the 'I think' to the 'I am' is exemplary in this regard since it links together representation and being in an immediate form. It was, Foucault suggests, only with the dissolution of the classical *episteme* that the questioning of the second half of this couple was rendered possible. A discourse could then be held on the individual without seeking its confirmation in the originary being of the 'I think'.

Foucault's account of the constitution of man as object of knowledge at the beginning of the nineteenth century stands in relation to a number of figures in the same way as the four elements of the general theory of language identified in the classical *episteme* functioned as a common point of articulation for natural history and the analysis of wealth. The first of these segments marks the emergence of man 'in his ambiguous position as an object of knowledge and as a subject that knows'.[115] It is the *finitude* of man which is indicated with the emergence of biology, economics, and philology since it is man as a being governed by labour, life, and language which is designated through the space which they constitute. The finitude of man, Foucault argues, 'is heralded – and imperiously so – in the positivity of knowledge; we know that man is finite, as we know the anatomy of the brain, the mechanics of production costs, or the system of Indo-European conjugation.'[116] The knowledge of man as an individual who lives, speaks and works in accordance with the laws of an economics, a philology, and a biology is possible only against the background of his own finitude. This finitude underpins all the empirical positivities through which man is known.

The second element is that within this 'analytic of finitude' man, Foucault argues, is an 'empirico-transcendental doublet', it is through man that knowledge is attained of what renders all knowledge possible. But this is not the same as the attempt in the classical age to make representation the condition of possibility of knowledge in general. It is now a question, not of representation, but of man in his finitude; it is a question of 'revealing the conditions of knowledge on the basis of the empirical contents given in it'.[117] The 'threshold of modernity' is located, Foucault argues, at precisely that point at which man is constituted as an 'empirical-transcendental doublet'. At this moment two types of analysis emerge, one of which led to the discovery that knowledge has anatomo-physiological conditions, that 'there is a *nature* of human knowledge that determines its forms and that can at the same time be made manifest to it in its own empirical contents.'[118] On the other hand emerged analyses which demonstrated that knowledge had social and economic conditions, that 'there was a *history* of human knowledge which could both be given to empirical knowledge and prescribe its forms.'[119] With this search for a nature or a history of knowledge are presupposed a number of divisions, the most fundamental of which is that of *truth* conceived in terms of the order of the object or that of discourse. A truth that is both gradually outlined and expressed as well as a truth which makes it possible to employ a language that will be true, that is scientific.[120]

The third element resides in that as an empirical-transcendental doublet man can no longer posit himself in the immediacy of a *cogito*. At the same time, however, the *cogito* is not abandoned but revived in a movement which seeks 'the articulation of thought on everything within it, around it, and beneath it which is not thought, yet which is nevertheless not foreign to thought'.[121] The modern *cogito* cannot affirm itself with the force of the 'I am' but leads instead to an interrogation of that being which entails 'for the first time, man's being in that dimension where thought addresses the unthought and articulates itself upon it'.[122] This results not simply in the disappearance of an immediate reflexive knowledge.[123] More positively what is made possible is for 'an objective form of thought to investigate man in his entirety'.[124] The unconscious, or to be more precise, the 'unthought in general', is, Foucault argues, an archaeological contemporary of the formation of man as object of knowledge at the beginning of the nineteenth century. It is both 'Other' in relation to man as well as inseparable from his appearance within knowledge. It reveals, moreover, what man is *in his truth*, and leads to the attempts to return man's essence to his empirical being. Man thus appears as a dual being, as both subject and object of knowledge. It is essential then that thought 'should be both knowledge and a modification of what it knows, reflection and a transformation of the mode of being of that on which it reflects'.[125] 'Modern thought', Foucault argues, is ceaselessly attempting to bring the unthought nearer to itself, to advance 'towards that region where man's Other must become the Same as himself'.[126]

The final element which defines the manner in which man was constituted within knowledge at the beginning of the nineteenth century concerns what Foucault terms 'the relation to the origin'.[127] Origin in the eighteenth century was, Foucault argues, conceived in terms of the duplication of representations and 'the origin of knowledge was sought within this pure sequence of representation'.[128] In modern thought, however, this origin can no longer be maintained since labour, life, and language now possess their own historicity, their own laws. These historicities are indeed contemporaries of the formation of man who 'can be revealed only when bound to a previously existing historicity'.[129] In so far as these historicities are still directed towards an origin it is one which is possible only on the basis of the previously constituted histories of labour, life, and language. But at the same time these three domains 'conceal their truth (and their own origin) from those very beings who speak, who exist, and who are at work'.[130] The dual nature of man as both subject and object of knowledge permits the articulation of a conception of origin which locates him 'within a power that disperses him, draws him far away from his own origin, but promises it to him in an imminence that will perhaps be forever snatched from him'.[131] Since man is not contemporaneous with his being, things assume a time which is their own, thereby returning us to the point of departure in the notion of finitude, a finitude which now appears at the level of the 'insurmountable relation of man's being with time'.[132]

Foucault argues that at the archaeological level knowledge is organised, from the beginnings of the nineteenth century, in accordance with this quadrilateral whose segments have a *prima facie* symmetry and resemblance to those which constituted general grammar in the classical age. Yet this initial correspondence conceals, he suggests, the fundamental transformation which took place once representation no longer characterised knowledge. In contrast to the notion of a linear sequence of representation the constitution within knowledge of man as a finite being takes place through a dispersion which is no longer that of observable identities and differences. Whilst one still finds four theoretical segments, their function is entirely displaced once a theory of representation no longer occupies a fundamental place within knowledge. And with this transformation 'man appears as a finite, determined being, trapped in the density of what he does not think, and subject, in his very being, to the dispersion of time.'[133]

THE HUMAN SCIENCES AND THEIR POSITIVITY

The human sciences, Foucault argues, were only able to emerge once man was formed as object of knowledge at the beginning of the nineteenth century. Their appearance is made possible, he suggests, by the dissociation of the classical *episteme*. This event which shattered the possibility of a *mathesis* as the organising space of knowledge introduced the modern *episteme*, a 'volume of space open in three dimensions'.[134] In one of these Foucault argues the mathematical and physical sciences are located; in another reside the sciences of life, labour and language; in the third is situated the field of 'philosophical reflection' and 'those regional ontologies which attempt to define what life, labour, and language are in their own being'.[135]

Foucault does not locate the human sciences within this tripartite division, but suggests that they exist instead 'in the interstices of these branches of knowledge, or more exactly, in the volume defined by their three dimensions'.[136] It is precisely this location which on the one hand renders them a threat to these three domains of knowledge, and on the other hand explains 'their precariousness, their uncertainty as sciences, their dangerous familiarity with philosophy, their ill-defined reliance upon other domains of knowledge, their perpetually secondary and derived character, and also their claim to universality'.[137] The opaqueness of the human sciences is attributed not to that 'difficult' object man, but to the 'epistemological configuration' through which they emerge, their relation to all three of its dimensions.

It is in relation to the sciences of life, labour, and language that Foucault argues the human sciences must be situated. But at the same time, he suggests, neither biology, philology, nor economics can themselves be regarded as human sciences. The domain of the latter is constituted, not simply by the designation of man as a particular entity, but through the emergence of a living being who 'constitutes representations by means of which he lives, and on the basis of which he possesses that strange capacity of being able to represent to himself precisely that life'.[138] It is only through the representation of economics that man as a labouring being enters the arena of the human sciences. Likewise, language is not an object for the human sciences, although man's relation to language is, in so far as the object of the human sciences is 'that being which, from the interior of the language by which he is surrounded, represents to himself, by speaking, the sense of the words or propositions he utters, and finally provides himself with a representation of language itself'.[139] Moreover the human sciences are not an extension of the sciences of economics, language, and biological mechanisms. In relation to these domains which take man as object they are instead in a position of 'duplication'. The domain of the human sciences is covered, Foucault proposes, by three interconnected sub-regions: the 'psychological region' which borders on the domains of biology, the 'sociological region' which is situated adjacent to the analysis of production, and the study of literature and myths which arises in relation to the laws and forms of language.

The 'positivity' of the human sciences is largely regulated by what Foucault terms 'constituent models' which 'make it possible to create groups of phenomena as so many "objects" for a possible branch of knowledge'.[140] Operating as 'categories' they ensure an empirical interconnection of phenomena which have already been established in their proximity. These models are, Foucault argues, borrowed from the fields of biology, economics, and philology. Biology supplies the categories of functions and norms, economics those of conflict and rules, and linguistics those of signification and system. Foucault argues that together these three pairs 'completely cover the entire domain of what can be known about man'.[141]

Whilst providing a formal demarcation of the various domains these concepts are not restricted to functioning separately and exclusively in a relation of adjacency to the respective sciences of life, labour and language. Indeed all three pairs 'occur throughout the entire volume common to the human sciences and are valid in each of the regions included within it'.[142] The boundaries between the human sciences thus become blurred, and although it is in principle possible to identify the positivity of psychology in terms of functions and norms, and that of sociology in terms of conflicts and rules, Foucault admits that 'in the end their proper object may even disappear altogether.'[143]

Foucault suggests also that historically these three models have covered the history of the human sciences. A first stage he identifies as dominated by the biological model and the identification of man in terms of organic functions. This is followed by the economic model and the ascendancy of conflict as the locus of man's activity. Finally, the linguistic era and its analysis in terms of meanings and signifying systems induces 'a vast shift [which] has led the human sciences from a form more dense in living models to another more saturated with models borrowed from language.'[144]

A further shift has, Foucault argues, led the first term in each of the models to cede constituent place to the second. Goldstein,[145] Mauss[146] and Dumezil[147] mark that moment at which norm, rule, and system emerged with a greater strength than the tripartite division of function, conflict, and signification. The inversion of function and norm meant that the normal and the non-normal could no longer be identified primarily by virtue of their function, but required the constitution of a pathological psychology which would operate alongside normal psychology. Similarly, with Durkheim a pathology of societies was made possible once conflict no longer took precedence over rule.[148] And finally, when signification no longer carried more weight than system it was not possible to confine meaning to one domain of human activity. The ascendancy of norm, rule, and system thus provided each area with its own principles of coherence and demarcation. 'By pluralizing itself – since systems are isolated, since rules form closed wholes, since norms are posited in their autonomy – the field of the human sciences found itself unified.'[149]

The ability of these broad categories to 'structure the entire field of the human sciences'[150] resides, Foucault suggests, not in their empirical generality but rather in their capacity to establish 'the basis on which man is able to present himself to a possible knowledge'.[151] They permit also the dissociation of consciousness and representation in so far as they are based on the ability to provide representations of man as an empirical being without requiring that this be present to consciousness. Foucault argues that the human sciences 'speak only within the element of the representable, but in accordance with a conscious/unconscious dimension, a dimension that becomes more and more marked as one attempts to bring the order of systems, rules, and norms to light.'[152] The dichotomy of the normal and the pathological is perhaps, Foucault suggests, being replaced by that of consciousness and the unconscious.

Foucault's account of the formation of the human sciences places them in the curious position of having as their object what is in fact also their condition of possibility. They operate, he suggests, through a process of 'unveiling' which always has as its horizon 'the project of bringing man's consciousness back to its real conditions, of restoring it to the contents and forms that brought it into being, and eludes us within it'.[153] For this reason the problem of the unconscious, the question of its status and the possibility of knowing it, is for the human sciences 'a problem that is ultimately coextensive with their very existence'.[154] The attempt to uncover and gain a knowledge of the unthought is, Foucault argues, 'constitutive of all the sciences of man'.[155]

Foucault's celebrated announcement of both the birth and death of man is the most radical possible. It entails a demonstration of the conditions of possibility of man as object of knowledge. The identification and individuation of the human sciences themselves is not made on the basis of that object known as man. It is not man that constitutes them and provides them with a specific domain. Rather it is the arrangement of the *episteme* which makes them possible and provides them with a space in which they are then able to individuate man as an object to be known according to a number of different domains. It is to the conditions of emergence of the human sciences within the Western *episteme* that one looks in response to the archaeological question of the appearance, and possible disappearance, of man. The human sciences exist 'not whenever man is in question, but whenever there is analysis – within the dimension proper to the unconscious – of norms, rules, and signifying totalities which unveil to consciousness the conditions of its forms and contents'.[156]

Located within the modern *episteme* the human sciences are, Foucault argues, not sciences, although this does not thereby situate them within the terrain of 'ideology'. Neither are they impure admixtures of rational and irrational elements, the latter forming a negative element in relation to the possibility of one day achieving maturity.[157] To grasp their emergence they must, Foucault argues, be located instead within the 'epistemological configuration' particular to those knowledges which are incapable of becoming sciences yet which do not thereby exist in a relation of deficiency to the domain of scientific knowledges. They constitute 'in their own form, side by side with the sciences and on the same archaeological ground, *other* configurations of knowledge'.[158] They cannot be sciences, Foucault argues, precisely by virtue of their adjacency to the sciences of life, labour and language, a relationship which 'presupposes, in fact, the transposition of external models within the dimension of the unconscious and consciousness, and the flowing back of critical reflection towards the very place from which those models come'.[159] The inability of the human sciences to become sciences does not derive from the characteristics of man, his complexity or irreducibility. It derives instead from the position they occupy within the modern *episteme* and the possibility which this provides of constituting 'a being who, by one and the same interplay of reasons, must be a positive domain of *knowledge* and cannot be an object of *science*.'[160]

THE DISPERSAL OF MAN

There is, Foucault suggests, a final stage of transformation that one can identify at the level of the *episteme*. This is one which undermines, he argues, the figure of man. It concerns the disciplines of psychoanalysis, ethnology and linguistics. Foucault depicts these as 'counter-sciences' which provide 'a perpetual principle of dissatisfaction, of calling into question, of criticism and contestation of what may seem, in other respects, to be established'.[161] That is, they both emerged from within the nineteenth century *episteme*, whilst at the same time challenging the figure of man as their articulating principle.

Nothing, Foucault argues, is 'more alien to psychoanalysis than anything resembling a general theory of man or an anthropology'.[162] Directed as it is at the unconscious, psychoanalysis does not remain within the configuration of the representable but moves beyond it and indicates that which makes it possible. Outside the sphere of the representable it outlines 'the three figures by means of which life, with its functions and norms, attains its foundation in the mute repetition of Death, conflicts and rules their foundation in the naked opening of Desire, significations and systems their foundation in a language which is at the same time Law.'[163] And whilst death, desire, and the law 'can never meet within the knowledge that traverses in its positivity the empirical domain of man',[164] they nevertheless 'designate the conditions of possibility of all knowledge about man'.[165]

Ethnology on the other hand, whose own condition of possibility resides in the history of Western culture in its relation with other societies, is oriented toward the articulation of the human sciences with the domains of biology, economics, and philology. Focussing as it does on 'the normalization of the broad biological functions, the rules that render possible or obligatory all the forms of exchange, production, and consumption, and the systems that are organized around or on the model of linguistic structures',[166] ethnology places its own limits in relation to the three positivities of life, labour and language. Along with psychoanalysis it addresses not man himself but the terrain which makes knowledge of man possible. To the extent that it emerged through the dominant relation of the Western *ratio* to other cultures it 'avoids the representations that men in any civilisation may give themselves of themselves'.[167] Instead it concentrates, just as psychoanalysis does, on 'that which, outside man, makes it possible to know, with a positive knowledge, that which is given to or eludes his consciousness'.[168]

Foucault argues that both psychoanalysis and ethnology 'dissolve man' in so far as they 'go back towards that which foments his positivity'.[169] They are articulated upon each other through an intersection at one point only, where 'the signifying chain by which the unique experience of the individual is constituted is perpendicular to the formal system on the basis of which the significations of a culture are constituted.'[170] At this point of exclusion of possibilities and specification of possible choices both for the individual and the social structure 'is formed the theme of a pure theory of language which would provide the ethnology and the psychoanalysis thus conceived with their formal model'.[171] Linguistics resides at this point as a 'perfectly founded' science which deals solely with language as a positivity exterior to man. No more concerned with man than psychoanalysis or ethnology it provides the most general challenge to the field constituted through the human sciences. Together, Foucault argues, 'these three counter-sciences threaten the very thing that made it possible for man to be known.'[172]

In relation to this question of the dissolution of the modern *episteme* language continues to occupy the fundamental position Foucault attributes to it both in the functioning of the classical *episteme* and its dissociation in the last years of the eighteenth century. Linguistics[173] does not operate on concepts formed elsewhere, for instance in the sphere of the human sciences, but is constitutive of its very object. Hence the question of the 'being' of language, a problem 'so intimately linked with the fundamental problems of our culture, reappears in all its enigmatic insistence'.[174] And in this reappearance of the question of language, Foucault argues, a decisive shift is taking place in which man can no longer occupy the central place:

> From within language experienced and traversed as language, in the play of its possibilities extended to their furthest point, what emerges is that man has 'come to an end', and that, by reaching the summit of all possible speech, he arrives not at the very heart of himself but at the brink of that which limits him; in that region where death prowls, where thought is extinguished, where the promise of the origin interminably recedes.[175]

It is in literature, in the works of Artaud, Roussel, Kafka, Bataille, and Blanchot, as well as in the domain of the formalisation of thought that Foucault argues this 'return' of language emerges, not as a novel discovery but rather as 'the strict unfolding of Western culture in accordance with the necessity it imposed upon itself at the beginning of the nineteenth century'.[176] It is through the organisation of the modern *episteme*, which still provides the terms within which we think, that Foucault argues the question of language was formed with such urgency. The works of Ricardo, Bopp, and Cuvier both constituted man as that object which is to be known, whilst at the same time providing the conditions for his dispersion.

Foucault conjectures whether 'man is in the process of perishing as the being of language continues to shine ever brighter upon our horizon?'.[177] There is a sense in which Foucault posits a teleology of dispersion of the figure of man as inherent in contemporary culture. By their very position within the Western *episteme* the sciences of life, labour, and language were faced with the prospect of never acceding to that figure of man. Indeed as Foucault has suggested, the further they pushed the less they discovered the figure of man.[178] It was ultimately the structures of language and the unconscious which were to be revealed, not the being of man. As Foucault prophetically suggests, it is reasonable to assume that if the arrangement of knowledge which was established at the beginning of the nineteenth century were itself to disintegrate, then 'man would be erased, like a face drawn in sand at the edge of the sea'.[179]

CONCLUSION

Foucault's two previous studies discussed in earlier chapters[180] have both been appropriated for a certain mode of critique of domination. *Histoire de la Folie* has been used as ammunition for a denunciatory attack on psychiatry,[181] and *The Birth of the Clinic* has provided a similar basis for a critique of the medical profession.[182] The hegemony of these two allied professions has been identified as a means of accounting for a mode of domination of individuals specific to the industrialised West. However *The Order of Things* has not been seen to provide fuel for any such onslaught against the human sciences. This is not surprising since Foucault does not connect the knowledges he examines in *The Order of Things* with particular strategies of government. He does not attempt, for example, to demonstrate that the emergence of the human sciences made possible a new form of administration of populations. He has commented himself on some of the distinctions between the archaeology of discourse undertaken in *The Order of Things*, and the more explicit concern with power in his later writings. In *The Order of Things*:

> What is in question is that which governs statements and the manner in which they govern one another in order to constitute a set of scientifically acceptable propositions which may, in consequence, be verified or falsified by scientific procedures. In short, a problem of the regime or politics of the scientific statement. At this level, it is a question not of knowing what power weighs on the science from outside, but what effects of power circulate among the scientific statements; what is, as it were, their internal regime of power; how and why at certain moments it is modified in a global manner.
>
> It is these different regimes which I tried to locate and describe in *The Order of Things*, all the while saying clearly that I was not, for the moment, attempting to explain them, and that it would be necessary to try to do that in a subsequent work. But what my work lacked was this problem of the 'discursive regime', or the effects of power peculiar to the statemental game. I confused it too much with systematicity, theoretical form, or something like the paradigm. At the point of junction of *Histoire de la folie* and *The Order of Things*, there was, under two very different aspects, this central problem of power which I had still only very poorly isolated.[183]

The description of *The Order of Things* is to my mind more accurate than the self-criticism for failing to isolate the issue of power in his early studies. As I have argued, Foucault's inclusion in *Histoire de la Folie* of the issue of 'police', of the supervision and government of populations, places it under the same general set of concerns as his self-declared investigations into power.

The Order of Things can usefully be viewed as an account of the conditions of possibility for the emergence of modern humanism. This humanism can, Foucault suggests, be regarded as dependent on the process through which man was produced as object of knowledge at the end of the eighteenth and beginning of the nineteenth century.

In another interview Foucault has remarked that:

> In *The Order of Things* I wanted to show the various elements which composed man at the end of the eighteenth and the beginning of the nineteenth century. I attempted to characterise the modernity of this figure and what seemed to me important to demonstrate was this: it

> was not so much as a result of a moral concern for the human being that one had the idea of knowing him scientifically, but on the contrary because one constructed the human being as object of a possible *savoir* that the moral themes of contemporary humanism developed, themes which one finds in woolly marxisms, in Saint-Exupery and Camus, in Teilhard de Chardin, in short in all those pallid figures of our culture.[184]

Sartre is perhaps the perfect example of this humanism, especially in his attempt to unite Marxism and humanism in the promise of a dialectical reconciliation of man with himself.[185] In this sense Marxism and humanism are, Foucault remarks, equivalent in their adherence to a philosophy of history in which man regains his authenticity. The concept of dialectic provides, as it were, an accessory for the realisation of this process.

The dream of returning man to his essence is, Foucault argues, dependent on the invention of man as object of a positive knowledge. Man could only be seen to be capable of becoming a subject of his own liberty once he had become an entity that could be known in his determination and his alienations. Georges Canguilhem, in what is the most penetrating article written on *The Order of Things*,[186] has commented on what was at stake in this formation of man as object of knowledge. It was, he remarks, only with Kant that was formulated the notion of a *cogito* which could not arrive at a knowledge of itself. Kant was, he argues, necessary before the 'I think' of Descartes could assume the form of a philosophical event:

> In a sense it is not the invention of the *Cogito* by Descartes that constituted, for more than a century, the essential merit of its inventor. It was necessary for Kant to bring the *Cogito* before the critical tribunal of the *I think* and to refuse it all substantialist bearing in order for modern philosophy to acquire the habit of referring itself to the *Cogito* as the philosophical event that inaugurated it. The kantian *I think*, a vehicle for the concepts of the understanding, is a light which opens experience to its intelligibility. But this light is in our back and we are unable to turn round to face it.

Foucault uses the term 'anthropological sleep' to designate what Canguilhem refers to as 'the calm assurance with which the contemporary promotors of the human sciences take as a given object, given in advance of their progressive studies, that which at the outset was only the project they were constituting.'[187]

Now it is true that Foucault's closing remarks in *The Order of Things* suggest that this figure of man is in the progress of being eroded. A non-dialectical culture is, Foucault proposes, emerging as a result of the disciplines of linguistics, psychoanalysis and ethnology. Nietzsche is a crucial figure in this disruption of the modern *episteme*, the death of God being also, Foucault remarks, the death of man.[189] I do not propose to attempt here an evaluation of the extent to which the disruption of the nineteenth-century *episteme* has developed. It would, however, be possible to identify the beginning of such a shift both at the level of the particular knowledges Foucault cites as well as at the level of the operationalisation of such practices as psychological techniques.[190] But one can suggest at the very least that the figure of man may well prove resistant to a displacement of such magnitude that would entitle one to talk of a change of *episteme*.[191]

Foucault has remarked of Sartre's *Critique of Dialectical Reason* that it is the attempt of a man of the nineteenth century to understand the twentieth century.[192] In this sense one can suggest that there are many more such 'men of the nineteenth century' who are living in and seeking to understand the twentieth century. One can indeed regard critical theory as discussed above as an influential example of such 'anachronisms'. However, anachronisms or not, Foucault's archaeology of the human sciences helps one to understand the critique of domination undertaken by Horkheimer, Marcuse and Habermas. In discussing these theorists I criticised their respective attempts to construe domination as bearing on the subject as unique locus of effects. I criticised also their attempt to have recourse to the subject as point of liberation. Bearing in mind Foucault's methodological stricture to treat discourses as practices,[193] we can perhaps better appreciate now the basis on which critical theory established itself.

Foucault's researches direct our attention toward the functioning of those knowledges which operate through the imperative to discover the truth of man. The formation of man as subject and object of knowledge, and as 'empirical-transcendental doublet', is what provides the basis of Foucault's account of the inability of man to liberate himself through the positing of an unfettered subjectivity. What differentiates Foucault from critical theory is that he shows the futility of appealing to the subject as that entity which is to break with domination. For one can suggest that it is precisely through the attempt to produce a *knowledge of the subject* that man remains trapped within the finitude of a knowledge which can only ever be a knowledge *of* the subject. Rather than a critique of the objectification[194] entailed in such knowledges, *The Order of Things* explores what it is that renders such empirical knowledges possible. *The Order of Things* is, I argue, central to the project of a genealogy of the modern subject. It locates the basis of critical theory's denunciation of domination in Western industrialised societies. And in so doing helps to alert us to the limitations of an analysis which effects a polarisation according to a view of the human individual as object of domination and subject of liberation.

CHAPTER 7

FROM DISCIPLINARY POWER TO GOVERNMENTALITY

•

It was around about 1970, the story goes, that Foucault began to talk about power.[1] Rudely introduced to the reality of power by the events in Paris in 1968 he was from then on to incorporate the question of power into his studies. The dust-laden task of genealogy[2] was to be instilled with a political urgency. The studies of the prison and of sexuality which were to follow can, so this interpretation continues, be read according to this acknowledgment of the significance of power.

The evidence for such an interpretation can be found. We have, to begin with, the word power itself. With the appearance of this word Foucault can be seen to name the real object of his researches. He says as much himself.[3] And with the appearance of *Discipline and Punish* in 1975 we have a monument to this concern with power. For is not the prison the symbol of power, a power which dominates the individual, to which the individual must submit? The prison, some might say, was a symbol which had a striking obviousness for this concern with power.

My argument is that Foucault's researches from 1970 onwards do not mark a wholly new concern with power. Nor do they serve to register a concern with power which had been implicit in all his previous works. Of course it would be foolish to deny that *Discipline and Punish* and *The History of Sexuality* each mark new stages in Foucault's work.[4] But this is not in itself surprising. The same can be said of all of Foucault's studies, although this is not to suggest that they can therefore be viewed as a series of case studies.[5] However there is a novelty to the issues addressed in Foucault's writings after 1970. This is that they come explicitly to address the individualisation and incorporation of the subject into networks of surveillance which are also mechanisms for producing knowledges of the subject. I have argued that this is a theme which is present in Foucault's earlier studies. In *Discipline and Punish*, the three volumes of his *History of Sexuality*,[6] and in his discussions of what he termed 'governmentality', this investigation of discourses, categories and practices of the self, of individualisation, is a constant. That this common concern should be related to a wide range of practices and institutions is not surprising. Nor is it surprising that Foucault should utilise different terms to describe those practices which address the subject – disciplinary power, bio-power, techniques of the self, and governmentality. After 1970, however, the *regulatory* dimension of these practices is explicitly identified and named. As Foucault's researches developed they identified different contexts and different historical periods within which occurred the processes of constitution and regulation of subjects. The variety of institutions in relation to which these regulatory practices of the self function may explain in part the range of terms Foucault uses. This does not weaken, however, the overall concern with the notion of the subject, the conditions for producing a truth of the subject, and for regulating the subject according to this truth.

The inaugural lecture Foucault was to deliver at the Collège de France[7] contributes to this concern to investigate those practices which take as their ambition the production of the truth of subjects and their regulation. It provides both a reflection on previous studies, in particular *The Archaeology of Knowledge*, and a mapping out of new areas of research. Its focus is the phenomenon of discourse and some of the principle mechanisms which serve to regulate its production and functioning. Foucault argues that in every society the production of discourse is controlled, selected, organised and distributed by a variety of procedures which seek to master it. One such procedure is negative, that of *prohibition*. We cannot, Foucault points out, speak of anything in any circumstances, and not everyone has the right to speak of anything. There are taboos on the object of speech, the ritual of the circumstances of speech, and the privileged or exclusive right of the speaking subject. A second mechanism concerns not prohibition but a *division and a rejection*. The most prominent example of this in his writings is the opposition between reason and madness. Since the Middle Ages the discourse of the mad has been nullified, rendered void, deprived of truth and worth. The third mechanism concerns the *opposition between the false and the true*. Foucault refers to this as a 'will to truth', a mechanism which across the centuries and in varying forms has governed the will to knowledge. This will to truth rests, as do the other mechanisms, on a whole strata of practices and institutions. But it is also the focus of the other two mechanisms, the point towards which they are drifting. There are of course other groups of procedures which permit the control of discourse. But it is the tripartite group of procedures of prohibition, division, and the will to truth which are of central importance to his later studies, and to the question of the uncovering of the truth of the subject. In criminality and modes of punishment, sexuality, and in the conduct of the self Foucault was to pursue this study of those practices which seek to promote subjectivity as a mode of regulation of the lives of individuals, and at the same time to produce a true knowledge of this subjectivity.

DISCIPLINARY POWER AND NORMALISATION

There are three images which stand out in the discussions in Britain of *Discipline and Punish*.[8] The first is that of carceral forms of discipline which exercise over the individual a perpetual series of observations and modes of control of conduct. The prison epitomises such discipline but it occurs elsewhere, in asylums, factories and schools. The second is of the Panopticon, that ideal mechanism of power formulated as an architectural proposal. This circular building with a central observation tower was to provide the model for numerous correctional institutions. It was, as Gilles Deleuze was to emphasise,[9] a diagram of power, an abstract machine. It was power reduced to its ideal form. To inspect the individual without being seen was to provide a principle of functioning for a whole range of practices of supervision in modern societies. The third was the notion of a disciplinary society. The prison was not the only site for the exercise of disciplinary power. The whole of society down to its smallest details offered a site for its deployment. There was always the danger that such a notion be interpreted in too zealous a fashion. A disciplin*ary* society would be mistaken for a disciplin*ed* society. The distinction was between a society in which all individuals obediently conformed to the demands placed upon them, and a society in which individuals constantly escape, evade and subvert the functioning of discipline. The latter was clearly the conception Foucault had intended.

These three images of *Discipline and Punish* are not incorrect. They provide much of the focus of the book. They need, however, to be located in relation to another set of issues, those which concern the redefinition of modes of punishment by a knowledge of the individual. Located on this register Foucault's study can be clearly distanced from any interpretation of it as a crude sociology of control mechanisms.[10] Foucault is not concerned in *Discipline and Punish* with simply repeating the sociological accusation and critique that societies control the conduct of their members. His project is as much epistemological as it is sociological. His concern in *Discipline and Punish* in this respect carries forward, albeit in modified form, the concerns of his previous studies with forms of knowledge of the individual organised around norms of truth. It continues also the concern with how such processes undertake a project of subjectification, a dual process which seeks to endow individuals with a certain type of subjectivity whilst at the same time operating over them a subjection.

There is no excuse for the epistemological dimensions of *Discipline and Punish* to have been so neglected. Perhaps readers were distracted by the gruesome spectacle of the death of Damiens the regicide recounted in the opening pages. But immediately following this Foucault comes to the point. Such corporal forms of punishment which operated a carefully calculated infliction of pain on the body of the condemned were to be replaced by a new mode of punishment. This was one in which physical pain was no longer the constitutive element of the penalty. The new way of punishment was one which operated on the soul of the individual. This was to replace the executioner by a whole army of technicians of the soul – warders, doctors, chaplains, psychiatrists, psychologists and educationalists. As Mably was to put it 'Punishment, if I may so put it, should strike the soul rather than the body.'[11] With this shift 'crime' itself was to be transformed, its quality, its nature, the very substance of the punishable element. The passions, instincts, anomalies, infirmities, maladjustments, effects of environment, drives and desires were to enter the process of judgment. These might appear only to be shadows, lurking behind the case, but it is these shadows that are judged and punished.[12] It is no longer the offence which is to be punished but the individual, his dangerous state of mind, his criminal tendencies.

It was in this process of judgment that psychiatric expertise, criminal anthropology and criminology were to find their precise functions.[13] The offence was to be inscribed in the field of objects susceptible to scientific knowledge. They were to provide the means by which the soul of the criminal could enter with full honours the process of punishment. The nature of the criminal act and of the person who carried it out were to become central questions in this new modality of punishment. Questions were to arise as to what field of reality the act might belong. Was it a fantasy, a psychotic reaction, or a delusional episode? How could one assign the causal process that produced it. A new truth was to enter the process of punishment, a truth which was to bear on the individual and turn the demonstration of guilt into a scientific-juridical complex.

Central to this transformation was the intrusion of the phenomenon of madness into the legal process. According to the 1810 French penal code, madness was dealt with only in terms of article 64. This stated that in cases where the offender was of unsound mind at the time of the act there was neither crime nor offence. A person could not be both guilty and mad. Once declared mad, the legal process was interrupted and the hold of the law was loosened over the author of the act. But this opposition was soon to be weakened. Degrees of guilt and of madness were to enter the legal process. Soon it came to be accepted that one could be both guilty and mad. Perhaps one was less guilty the madder one was, but none the less someone to be put away and treated. Not just guilty, but dangerous also because sick.

The sentence was gradually to take account of this dimension. The terms of the legal punishment were to entail judgment of normality, attributions of causality, and anticipations as to the offender's future. Henceforth the judge was not to be alone in judging. Around the judge were to swarm a series of subsidiary authorities: psychiatric or psychological experts, educationalists and members of the prison service, all of whom were to fragment the legal power to punish. The sentence, one might say, was to come to be adjusted to the nature of the individual upon whom it was brought to bear. Psychiatric expertise was to become a particularly significant part of this process, and continues to be so to this day.[14] From its beginning psychiatric expertise was called upon to formulate 'true' propositions on the individual and the part played by liberty in the acts committed. In its intersection with the new modality of punishment which was emerging in the nineteenth century psychiatric expertise was to participate in what might be termed the medico-judicial treatment of the offender. Criminal justice was to be redefined by those knowledges which could lay claim to the truth of the individual.

Foucault was to describe the enterprise he was engaged upon in *Discipline and Punish* in the following manner:

> This book is intended as a correlative history of the modern soul and of a new power to judge; a genealogy of the present scientifico-legal complex from which the power to punish derives its bases,

> justifications and rules, from which it extends its effects and by which it masks its exorbitant singularity.[15]

This investigation was, Foucault suggested, to assist the understanding of how man, the soul, the normal or abnormal individual have come to 'duplicate' crime as objects of penal intervention. How was it that 'a specific mode of subjection was able to give birth to man as an object of knowledge for a discourse with a "scientific" status.'[16] The new technology of the soul and the knowledges on which it was to be based were born out of methods of punishment, supervision and constraint. The supervision and training of madmen, children at home and in the school, and those who are stuck at a machine and supervised for the rest of their lives. This, Foucault argues, is the historical reality of the modern soul, the element on which power and knowledge are articulated, each giving rise to, extending and reinforcing the effects of the other. Various concepts and fields of analysis were to be carved out from this point of reference. The psyche, subjectivity, personality, consciousness and the moral claims of modern humanism which were built on these foundations. Foucault argues that modern man, whom so many invite us to free, is inhabited, brought into existence, and subjected to his very depths by this soul.

Detention was to become, in a short space of time, the most general form of legal punishment, and labour was to be an important element of its reforming ambitions. The lazy individual was to be transformed into one with a liking for work, forcing the individual back into a system of interests in which labour was more advantageous than idleness. Isolation was to be added to labour with the same ambition of correction. And the partitioning of daily life according to a strict timetable was to bring with it its own obligations and prohibitions. Together these different processes were aimed to effect a transformation of the individual as a whole, of his body, his habits, his mind and his will.

The most important feature of detention in Foucault's account, however, was that the control and transformation of behaviour were brought about through the development of a knowledge of individuals. Perpetual notes and observations of the behaviour of individuals made it possible to divide prisoners up not so much according to their crimes as according to the dispositions they revealed. An entire corpus of individualising knowledge was to be organised around the person and the potentiality of danger which lay hidden in them, but which might be detected in their everyday observable conduct. The prison was to function in this enterprise as an 'apparatus of knowledge'.[17]

The prison was to participate in this way as a central element in the formation of an 'art of the human body'.[18] The ambition of such a project was the development of mechanisms which would make the individual more obedient and more useful. Discipline was to seek to produce in this way 'docile' bodies. But these were not simple automatons, conditioned to respond to commands. Discipline understood in this way was a positive force. It was to produce an 'aptitude', a 'capacity'. Discipline, Foucault was to argue, 'makes' individuals. Individuals were to be the object and instrument of its exercise. And discipline was to normalise. Individual actions were to be referred to a whole that was to be a field of comparison and a space of differentiation. Individuals were to be differentiated from one another. The 'nature' of individuals was to be measured in quantitative terms, their abilities placed on a hierarchical grid. A limit was to be defined which traced the frontier of the abnormal. Normalisation was to become one of the great instruments of disciplinary power.

We should not be misled by the subtitle of *Discipline and Punish*. It is not the birth of the prison or even strictly speaking a new form of punishment which it addresses. Its concern is rather with the emergence of a whole new panoply of techniques for the normalised regulation of individual lives. The prison was, one might say, an enormous laboratory in which a number of techniques were to be invented. So too was the workshop, the school and the army. Foucault used the term discipline to designate this transformation of the ways in which Western societies since the early nineteenth century have sought to produce a knowledge of the individual which was also to provide the basis for an ethics of personal conduct. The knowledges of the human individual, particularly those which have the preface psycho-, are inseparable from this formation of a vast new project of supervision of the lives of individuals. There were to develop a plethora of new technicians of behaviour, engineers of personal conduct, 'orthopaedists of individuality' as Foucault was to term them. The departure from the norm, the anomaly, was to haunt the prison and the courtroom, but also the asylum and the school. The social enemy was to become the deviant, identified by the omnipresent judges of normality. We are, Foucault argued, 'in the society of the teacher-judge, the doctor-judge, the educator-judge, the "social worker" judge; it is on them that the universal reign of the normative is based.'[19] The carceral network is only one dimension, part product part constitutive element of this normalising judgment exercised over individual lives. The person as a knowable entity, their soul, individuality, consciousness or conduct was the object and effect of this new modality of power. As medicine, education, psychology, psychiatry and social work come to assume an ever increasing importance in the regulation and normalisation of individual lives, the prison begins to lose its specificity and some of its purpose. One might suggest that today what requires investigation is no longer detention as a process of normalisation, but the proliferation of regulatory practices of the self across the whole of society.[20] Carceral power opened up the entire fabric of society to a normalising regulation, but it no longer provides the exclusive model.

Punishment and the human sciences are not two separate figures which intersect – one coming to be utilised in the operations of the other. They are part of a single matrix, an 'epistemologico-juridical' formation. Delinquency was to be the most productive object which was to emerge out of this formation. Delinquency, with the generalised police surveillance that was deployed in its detection, engendered an apparatus which made it possible to supervise, through the delinquents themselves, the whole social field. The delinquent is to be distinguished from the offender not so much by his act as by his life. Disciplinary punishment bears in this way on a life, seeking to reconstitute it in all its petty detail in the form of knowledge. A biographical knowledge and a technique for correcting individual lives. Upon this basis develops an entire psychological causality. The delinquent is linked to his acts not only as a freely acting subject, but as a being characterised by a whole bundle of instincts, drives and tendencies. Delinquency comes in this way to be understood not so much in terms of the law as of the norm. The task which emerges is to define the illegal acts of the delinquent in terms of a scientific knowledge of the individual *qua* delinquent. The delinquent made it possible to constitute under the authority of medicine, psychology or criminology, an individual who was both the offender of the law and the object of a scientific technique. With this development criminal justice, authenticated by the 'sciences', was able to function according to criteria of 'truth'.[21]

The term power may well be an appropriate one for the processes Foucault charts in *Discipline and Punish*. If it is to be utilised it should be understood in this context as constituting the very tissue of social reality.[22] And we need also to remind ourselves that the disciplinary programmes Foucault addresses in that text are precisely that – programmes. His concern was not with 'real life' in the prison.[23] It was with those features of social life which operate in such a manner as to make the distinction between true and false implicit in the evaluation of the ways men 'direct', 'govern' and 'conduct' themselves. Yet even with these points fully registered the notion of power in *Discipline and Punish* suffers from an overloading. The critics who chided Foucault for ignoring class relations were drastically wide of the mark, as Paul Patton demonstrates so well.[24] Capitalist production and disciplinary power function well together, and it would be unwise to hope to separate them historically. But there seems something a little foolish in suggesting what amounts to an inversion of the historical materialist principle by identifying power as, more or less, the motor of history, with capitalism one of the phases disciplinary production goes through.[25] This is one example of the 'overloading' of the notion of power which *Discipline and Punish* tends toward. It occurs also in the way in which discipline comes to be defined as a project which embraces the whole of society, and which is extended over each and every individual through innumerable mechanisms. If one interprets power as Foucault does in *Discipline and Punish* as the very tissue of society there is of course a sense in which this description is accurate. And it does not imply that our society is a disciplin*ed* society, a society of entirely obedient citizens. But to refer to discipline as a generalised project which ultimately comes to be exerted over the whole of society, on each and every individual, detracts from its actual mode of exercise. This is one in which disciplinary normalisation conducted according to criteria of truth deploys itself around certain privileged objects. This may, as Foucault argues in *Discipline and Punish* be the delinquent. Or it may be the child and its health as during the inter-war years in Britain.[26] Or it may be the dissatisfied or redundant worker.[27] All of these are objects of intense interest to those specialised knowledges of the person which operate most importantly by locating a knowledge of the individual in relation to a particular norm and set of regulatory techniques. But such enterprises should not be viewed as part of a generalised project directed at the individual on behalf of society. There may well be a number of tactical alliances formed between these distinct strategies. But to impute to society a generalised disciplining ambition *vis-à-vis* the individuals who compose it is to risk returning us to the sociologies of control against whom Foucault's enterprise so impressively stands out.

SEXUALITY AND POWER OVER LIVES

It is not surprising that Foucault's genealogy of the modern subject, and of those techniques and knowledges which supply access to its truth, should have come to focus on sexuality. As one commentator has remarked, today to know how one loves is to know who one is.[28] In 1976, in the first volume of his *History of Sexuality*[29] Foucault provided an introduction to the themes and methodological protocols which might guide such research. Central to this was his critique of what he called the 'repressive hypothesis'. This referred to the story of an imperial prudery which descended on sexuality. On the question of sex, silence, reticence and repression were to become the rule. Foucault fundamentally challenged such a notion on the grounds of an observation and of a methodological principle for the analysis of power. The observation was that rather than silence and repression, what has occurred since the seventeenth century has been an explosion of discourses on sexuality. With the emergence during the eighteenth century of the concept of population as an economic and social problem the question of sex was to be identified as central. It became urgent to analyse the age of marriage, legitimate and illegitimate births, and the frequency of sexual relations. For the first time a society affirmed publicly and consistently that its fortune and future were connected, not simply to marriage rules and family organisation, but to the manner in which each made use of his own sexuality. Sex became, between the state and the individual, a public stake in which a whole web of discourses, knowledges and analyses invested. Through various sites sexuality became something around which arose a web of procedures and observations, a multitude of 'incitations to speak', a multiplication rather than a reduction of sexualities.

It was not that the West finally discovered in sex its truth, its essence. Foucault's concern with sex is not because after all it holds the key to our being. It is rather that it was within a multiplication of discourses around the population that sexuality was identified as central. Sexuality provides a clue to our existence not because of what we *really* are, but because of its centrality to a range of strategies which provide a knowledge of the subject and a set of norms around which the behaviour of the subject can be regulated. The general issue here, as Foucault has put it elsewhere, was the entry into discourse of 'the life of infamous men'.[30] Between the mid-seventeenth and mid-eighteenth century there commences an 'exhaustive murmuring' from which no aspect of the individual's life should escape. Archives of confinement, of police, petitions to the king and *lettres de cachet* were to be some of the mechanisms through which the minutiae, the banality and the intimacy of the lives of individuals were to enter discourse. Christianity had exerted a hold over the commonplace of life around the confession. This subjected the minuscule world of the everyday and its banal faults to a dissection effected by language, and offered an effacement by the very act of utterance. An astonishing constraint imposed on everyone to say everything in order to efface everything, to admit all the wrongs of one's life in the first person.

Around the end of the seventeenth century this mechanism was to be surrounded by another which was no longer religious but administrative. The objective however was the same: to bring everyday life into discourse, to survey the unimportant irregularities and disturbances. But the avowal is displaced from the central role which Christianity had accorded it. In its place were to be substituted procedures of denunciation, indictment, inquiry, the report, the use of informers and interrogation. The minutiae of misconduct and misery were no longer to be conveyed by the avowal but were to accumulate in the form of written traces. Disputes between neighbours, quarrels between parents and children, domestic misunderstandings, excesses of wine and sex and public bickerings were to be summoned into discourse.

With the nineteenth century this theatrical recounting of everyday life was to be transformed again. A finely differentiated and continuous network of institutions, central to which are medicine and psychiatry, were to develop a language claiming to be that of observation and of neutrality. The 'efficacious but grey grid of administration, of journalism and of science'[31] was to emerge to subject the life of the individual to a perpetual reporting. The confession, however, was to remain central to the production of true discourses on sex. Yet during the nineteenth century it too was to be considerably transformed. A confession-science was to be created which combined the confession with the examination and the use of various procedures by which to inscribe the confession within a field of acceptable scientific observations. A postulate of a general and diffuse causality was to be introduced by which sex could be the 'cause of everything and anything'. A principle of a latency intrinsic to sexuality was asserted which by means of sexuality could be viewed as something which might be hidden from the subject, something which required that the *extraction* of a confession be articulated with scientific practice.

And the confession was to be medicalised, the domain of sex was no longer to be governed by principles of sin and transgression, but to be defined under the regime of the normal and the pathological.

Sexuality, Foucault argues, can be understood according to these coordinates of the confession and the mechanisms for government of the intimate lives of individuals. In this sense sexuality is central to the relations of power characteristic of Western societies. Foucault was to provide a set of methodological principles by which this power might be understood and investigated. These were that power should not be understood according to the model of a generalised domination exerted by one group over another. Power must be understood as a multiplicity of force relations which are immanent to the domain in which they operate and are constitutive of their own organisation. Power does not derive from a single point of origin but is to be found where it operates, at the mobile and unstable interrelation of force relations at local levels. Power is neither an institution nor a structure; it is not a force that can be located. It is 'everywhere', it is 'the name that one attributes to a complex strategical situation in a particular society'.[32] Power relations are not external to and causally related to other types of relations such as economic processes or knowledges, but are immanent to them. Power comes from below, from the multiple force relations operating in the apparatuses of production, families and institutions which cut across the social body. Power relations are intentional, yet they are non-subjective, that is to say they are marked by a calculation of aims and objectives, but do not result from the choice or decision of an individual subject. And finally, where there is power there is resistance. Power is a relational phenomenon which exists through a multiplicity of points of resistance which are present throughout the networks of power.

These methodological postulates have been rehearsed often enough already. They have given cause for concern as well as for celebration,[33] and are a useful corrective to the ways political theorists and sociologists have viewed power.[34] But in themselves they are a little stark. They do not really fulfill the promise of a method if this is understood as a universal formula which is valid at all times and in all places. As a method it is really an extrapolation of a number of points from previous studies, a philosophical reflection on historical researches. It is not in the section headed 'Method' that one finds the heart of Foucault's argument. This is to be found instead in the last chapter entitled 'Right of death and power over life'. Here Foucault fuses historical observation with conceptual elaboration in a much more instructive and subtle manner than when he openly declares a methodological interlude.

The image which depicts Foucault's notion of power here is that of a contrast between the limited power of the sovereign to require the death of a subject, and the immense power involved in the right of the social body to ensure, maintain and develop its life. Power, Foucault argues, consists of a positive influence over life, an attempt to administer and optimise it, to subject it to precise controls and comprehensive regulations. That the new discipline of sociology should take suicide as one of its first objects of study is not surprising. Suicide testified to the limits and borders of power, an individual and private sphere which posed a challenge to a society in which power sought to administer life. The term Foucault coined to describe this power over life was bio-power. This referred to a project of the calculated management of individual lives and of the population as a whole. This was to occur in various sites – schools, barracks, workshops, in the concern with the birthrate, longevity, public health, housing and migration. An indispensable element in the development of capitalism, yet also a phenomenon worthy of study in its own right, and conditioned by factors other than the contradictions of capital. Sexuality is just one of the objects which has emerged in the operation of such a form of power. It is through sex that the individual has to pass in order to have access to his or her intelligibility. Sex is merely one of the dimensions, albeit an important one, to be addressed in a genealogy of the modern subject. The value of Foucault's study of sexuality lies in what it tells us of the conditions of emergence of a whole series of techniques and knowledges of the self.

GOVERNMENTALITY AND TECHNOLOGIES OF THE SELF

After 1976 one can detect in Foucault's writings a further inflection to the project of investigating the bases on which modern practices of subjectivity have been constructed. This entailed rendering explicit the two dimensions identified previously – a micro-concern with the individual and a macro-concern with the population taken as a whole. To use Foucault's own terms, these two dimensions can be called respectively 'technologies of the self' and 'governmentality'. By the first is meant those techniques which allow individuals to effect, by their own means, various operations on their own bodies, souls, thought and conduct, and in such a manner as to transform themselves, modify themselves, and attain a state of perfection and happiness. The latter refers to the practices which characterise the form of supervision a state exercises over its citizens, their wealth, their misfortunes, their customs and their habits. It addresses the population as a whole, and seeks, amongst other things, the improvement of its condition, the increase of its wealth, its longevity and health.

These two dimensions to Foucault's concerns after 1976 are not at odds with each other. Rather they each provide the conditions for the exercise of the other. To govern a population is to exert over it a supervision which penetrates to its depths. And to exert over oneself a perpetual watchfulness is to provide the conditions under which a state can be managed. One might view this development in Foucault's work as providing an oblique reply to those who had complained that he had ignored the imposing reality of the state. Aside from the misplaced nature of this criticism, and the implication that one knew exactly what the phrase 'the state' refers to today, there was also a methodological problem. The analysis of 'the state' is, as Foucault has remarked, an indigestible enterprise. Would it not be better to approach the question from a different angle? To look at the specific rationalities which have sought to constitute both the elements over which the state exercises its rule – the individual subject – and the principles and rationalities which inform the management of citizens taken as a group.

This concern with the political management of society and its interdependence with practices for the regulation of the self had been identified in Foucault's earlier studies as well as by his co-workers. His studies of madness, medicine, crime and sexuality had all addressed individualisation as the specific modality for the exercise of power. In a recent lecture[35] Foucault was to argue for the need to examine how the regulation of the self comes to be combined with the centralised power of the state. Two particular sets of doctrine were important to the latter: *reason of state* and the *theory of police*.[36] The former was, Foucault argued, to come to be defined as an 'art', as a technique conforming to certain rules, not as arbitrary and violent. *Reason of state* was to derive its rationale from a specification of that to which it was devoted – the state. This was not a statement of the obvious but a departure from the model of the art of government as that of God imposing his laws upon his creatures. *Reason of state* sought to produce principles capable of guiding an actual government, principles concerned with what the state is, what its exigencies are. The aim of such an art of governing is to reinforce the state itself. And it is to achieve this through knowledge: concrete, precise and measured knowledge as to the state's strength, its capacity, the means to enlarge it, the strength and capacity of other states. *Political statistics or arithmetic* was to become indispensable for correct government.[37]

Police, in the seventeenth and eighteenth century, was a very different phenomenon from that which goes under this name today.[38] It referred to a governmental technology peculiar to the state – domains, techniques and objects on which the regulatory power of the state should bear. 'Police' in the seventeenth and eighteenth centuries referred to an administration heading the state, yet one which branched out into all of the people's conditions. Police included everything, but from an extremely particular point of view. The relationships between men and things, their coexistence on a territory, what they produce, how they live, the diseases and accidents which befall them. A living, active, productive individual was the object of perception of police. As one of the first authors to propose such a schema was to suggest in the early seventeenth century: 'The police's true object is man.'[39] One might say that the role of 'police' is to supply the people with a little extra life, and in so doing to supply the state with a little extra strength. Delamare, a prominent theorist in the 'police' tradition was to identify eleven things to which 'police' must attend within the state: religion; morals; health; supplies; roads, highways, town buildings; public safety; the liberal arts; trade; factories; manservants and labourers; the poor. 'Police' is the term which covers an entire new field in which centralised political and administrative power could intervene.

But 'police' was not just a grouping together of a range of disparate activities under the duties of the state. It had a focus, which was variously defined as 'happiness', social relations carried on between men, and 'living'. The last provides the clearest definition of the object and logic of 'police' as a governmental strategy. Religion is dealt with from the point of view of the moral quality of life; health and supplies concerned the preservation of life; trade, factories, workers, the poor and public order concerned the production and maintenance of the conveniences of life; and theatre, literature and entertainment concerned life's pleasures. One might say that the object of police was *life* – to ensure that people live, survive, and do even better than that was the purpose of police. And to develop those elements constitutive of the lives of individuals in such a way that their development also fosters that of the strength of the state. To foster the lives of citizens and the state's strength.

'Governmentality' was the term Foucault was to coin to describe the various techniques and rationalities by which states addressed themselves to the maintenance and improvement of the condition of their citizens. '*Reason of state*', 'police', and in the second half of the eighteenth century 'population'[40] were the different perceptions through which the art of government was to be elaborated. These programmes were formulated at the level of the state, but they also touched the depths of the individual. But there was another set of practices which took the individual subject as their starting point. These Foucault has described as 'technologies of the self', 'arts of existence'. They concern first and foremost the question of how to govern oneself, how to regulate one's conduct. From this follow recommendations as to how to govern others. It was these concerns Foucault was to address in the second and third volumes of his *History of Sexuality*.

The interrelation between practices and notions of sexuality and those of subjectivity has already been noted. The project of a 'history of sexuality' was conceived not as a documenting of conducts and sexual practices, but as an investigation into those processes through which individuals have come to recognise themselves as subjects of 'sexuality'. This project was finally to emerge as rather different from that initially outlined. It was to appear in the form of a genealogy of those practices by which individuals have come to devote attention to themselves, to understand themselves as subjects of desire. Sexual behaviour was the route through which this was to be achieved, though it was not its exclusive domain. A more general preoccupation animated Foucault's research: to analyse the formation of the modern subject through the mechanisms by which the individual's relation to their own self was to enable the individual to constitute and recognise him- or herself as a subject. And a subject of which the truth could be known. To the truth of the mad person analysed in *Histoire de la Folie*, the truth of the living, speaking and working being analysed in *The Order of Things*, and the truth of the criminal studied in *Discipline and Punish* was to be added an investigation into the truth of the human individual as a subject of desire.

A very general question guided this research: how, why and in what ways did sexual behaviour become the object of a moral preoccupation, one which at certain times and amongst certain groups was to appear to be of greater importance than eating habits or the performance of civic duties? What were the conditions through which the human individual came to be problematised in this way and accorded such an identity? This very general question however did not have just a scholarly significance. It was to provide some clues to the understanding of those practices to which Foucault gave the name 'arts of existence': those means through which individuals not only fix for themselves rules of conduct, but seek to effect a transformation of their selves, to make of their life an enterprise subject to aesthetic values and questions of style. The study of the problematisation of sexual behaviour in Antiquity should be viewed as one component in a broader project of investigation of 'techniques of the self'.

The details of Foucault's investigation into the codes of sexual conduct in Antiquity and amongst the early Christians are less important for my purposes here than the general principles of analysis they suggest. In relation to my concern with the issue of power and subjectivity one of these is of capital importance. This is the relationship Foucault identifies between freedom and the regulation of the conduct of the individual. One might have supposed that freedom was the reverse of supervision. This could have appeared to be one of the lessons which emerged from *Discipline and Punish*. However, Foucault argues the opposite in *L'Usage des Plaisirs*. Power, he suggests, presupposes freedom.[41] The codes which prescribed modalities of sexual behaviour in Antiquity sought not to limit freedom but to promote it. Freedom was an objective to be installed and preserved. It was a certain form of relationship which the individual was to establish with their self, and it was also an indispensable element for the functioning of the state. The attitude of the individual toward himself,[42] and the manner in which he assumed the liberty of his desires was a constituent element in the happiness and good order of the city. To be free in regard to pleasure was not to be a slave to them. The objective rather was to exert over oneself a power, but not that of a universal legislation defining those acts which were allowed and those forbidden. The principle rather was to be that of a specific use of pleasure, a knowledge, an art which would prescribe the modalities of its use, its force, its intensity, its frequency, and its timing. The end state to which this was directed was that of an active freedom, an existence in which the individual's relation to his self enabled him to constitute himself as the subject of a moral conduct. A means of elaborating, albeit for free males only, an aesthetics of existence, an art of freedom which was also the play of power. What Foucault provided in *L'Usage des Plaisirs* and *Le Souci de Soi* was, if one accepts his definitions, a 'history of sexuality'. But it was also much more than that. It was an important element in that genealogy of the subject and of those discourses and practices which have produced subjectivity as a mode of functioning of power.

ON INDIVIDUALISATION, SUBJECTIVITY AND POWER

Foucault's researches since 1970 cover a vast field. However, there is a preoccupation common to them. This is with those various practices and discourses which have as their objective to install individualisation as a mode of living. In *Discipline and Punish* this had been conceived principally according to an *objectivation* of the subject through disciplinary power. The emphasis was to be changed in volumes two and three of the *History of Sexuality*. The subject in these was to be constituted in a field of freedom, governed by an ethics which had as its goal to produce a subjectivation of the self. In this respect these more recent works can be seen to indicate a refocussing on the theme of the subject, on those discourses which seek to promote subjectivity through various rules for the conduct of the self.

One complaint concerning these most recent volumes might be that the 'history of the present' Foucault declared himself to be undertaking seems to be one which recedes ever further into the past. There is, however, a striking relevance to the present in the concern of these studies with the elaboration of various prescriptive models for the exercise of the freedom of the individual through self-government as an end in itself and as a modality for the government of society. 'Techniques of the self', 'arts of existence', and a general ethics of life according to which the individual might regulate his or her life. These are precisely the issues around which a society calling itself liberal offers a political rationality and a model for the conduct of economic life. As Gerhard Oestreich remarked: 'beside freedom of information and debate, democracy presupposes discipline on the part of the citizen, a discipline which serves the common good.'[43] In such a society the entrepreneurial self is not just an economic figure but an individualising formula by which the person may conceive and articulate their life as an enterprise. Such a political rationality combines with a series of interventions addressed to the psyche and subjectivity of the person. Once again freedom and the play of power enjoy a reciprocal functioning. The merit of Foucault's researches is to alert us to the fact that such a mutual reinforcement is not unusual, but rather one of the characteristics of power.

CONCLUSION

Comparative assessments of the writings of critical theory and Foucault are beginning to emerge. Not surprisingly, in view of the current interest in the writings of Habermas, these tend to focus on comparing his achievements with those of Foucault. Such evaluations are long overdue. There has for some time appeared to be a reticence to address the issues at stake, almost an unacknowledged moratorium. The tragic death of Foucault may well turn out in this respect to have a positive role to play in encouraging such debate, once the initial and justly earned respectful tributes have been paid.[1]

We should perhaps be grateful that we have been spared endless polemic or mutual congratulation between what I have argued are two quite distinct traditions. We do, however, have some fragments from the participants themselves from which one might begin the task of attempting to elicit the underlying preoccupations of each tradition. In a recent interview Foucault has reminded us of some fascinating aspects to the non-intersection of his work with that of critical theory.[2] In France, he points out, very little was known about the tradition of enquiry which goes from Weber to Habermas. Despite the fact that representatives of the Frankfurt School went to Paris in 1935 in hope of refuge, Foucault remarks that as a student he never once heard of the Frankfurt School from his professors. This 'minor historical problem' is certainly intriguing, especially in view of the relevance for the whole of Europe of the preoccupations of the Frankfurt School at the time. What is more interesting for my concerns in this study than the simple fact of this non-intersection of two schools of thought is the way Foucault discusses it. He remarks that if he had been aware of the Frankfurt School, he would have avoided detours in his own work and would have been able to follow avenues already opened up. Referring to his own work in relation to that of critical theory he speaks of 'two very similar types of thinking'.[3] In confirmation of this 'similarity' we also find

Habermas praising Foucault for his 'masterly description of the bifurcation of reason', the bifurcation of a given moment. We also have Foucault's comments in his essay on Kant and the question of enlightenment which draws attention to the proximity of his concerns to those of critical theory.[4] He distinguishes between a critical philosophy framed as an analytical philosophy of truth in general, and a critical thought which takes shape as an ontology of ourselves, an ontology of the present. It is the latter, he suggests, which underlies the work of the Frankfurt School as well as his own concerns. And we also have Habermas's comments on the same issue in his tribute to Foucault.[5]

One can, however, take these self-declarations too literally. For when pressed Foucault clarifies the extent of the similarity between his own work and that of Habermas. He argues that the Frankfurt School were preoccupied by *one* bifurcation of reason. Foucault, in contrast, was concerned with an endless, multiple bifurcation. His concern was not with the point at which reason became instrumental. His concern has not been to seek out *the* reason with which one might oppose technical rationality. For Foucault there is no single bifurcation of reason but an abundance of branchings, breaks, ramifications. An investigation which centres on the forms of rationality applied by the human subject to itself. What were the forms of rationality and the historical conditions which led the human subject to take itself as the object of possible knowledge? And also at what price? What were the effects of locating the mad person as other, of problematising and analysing the speaking subject, the working subject, the living subject? And what is at stake in a system of punishment which seeks the truth of criminal subjects in what can be known of their selves? What connects these heterogeneous enquiries is not the bifurcation of reason, but 'the relation of self to self and of telling the truth'.[6]

The puzzle we need to address is twofold. Firstly, the non-intersection of two schools of thought. Secondly, the *different levels* at which one can identify similarity and difference between critical theory and the work of Foucault. The preoccupation with forms of rationality, with critique and enlightenment may provide one line of enquiry. That which I have pursued here is of a different kind. It has centred on an attempt to identify the type of reflection which critical theory has undertaken with a view to analysing the operation of mechanisms of domination and of liberation. On what basis is critique founded, on what foundations might reason be re-established? This project of critique seems to me to be at the heart of critical theory. It seems also to depend to a significant extent on notions of the essential subjectivity of human individuals, for identifying the existence and extent of domination and for identifying the possibility of liberation. The critique of domination has in this way been a predominantly philosophical critique. I have argued that this is not just an underlying concern of critical theory, but a source of limitation in the project of critique which it has sought to develop.

In Foucault's writings I have identified a quite distinct concern with the question of power. Despite reservations I have expressed with the word power, as well as those Foucault himself has voiced, it has seemed useful to retain it here as a way of indicating a difference of approach between the work of Foucault and that of critical theory. Foucault's investigations into the question of power have taken the form, I have argued, of a series of inquiries into the varied forms of knowledge of the subject, of the divisions, rejections and classifications of subjects which have accompanied them. The micro-level investigation has been linked with a concern to chart the operation of power at what can be termed a macro-level. This is not a question of detecting the societal origins of the micro-level, of identifying a constant concern emanating from the social totality to control and classify. It emerges rather in relation to a specific rationality. It is no accident, for example, that the bulk of Foucault's studies cover a similar period, the classical age, and seek to demonstrate what has been at stake in the emergence of our modernity. What has been at stake in particular is the construction of a diverse range of projects for the management of populations of human individuals according to a 'liberal' principle of investing in the human individual with a view to promoting in him or her a constant attention to their conduct, to their health, and to their contribution to society as a whole. The term 'liberal' has to be understood here in its broadest sense, and not as entailing any necessary seal of approval. It also has to be noted that it is a question of programmes of ideal government which has been at issue, not the actual functioning of concrete institutions. One might chide Foucault for not having undertaken this task also. It would be wrong, however, to view the project Foucault did undertake as illegitimate in its own right.

One tendency which can be detected in assessments of the work of critical theory and Foucault is a differentiation according to the principles of generality and particularity. Critical theory is depicted in this view as having a commitment to generality, to universality, and against relativism. In a culture which is increasingly moving towards particularity, towards emphasising the local and the fragmentary (Foucault), universality and comprehensiveness (Habermas) provide some reference point and a set of criteria by which we might appraise the present. It would to my mind be foolish to place too much hope of resolving current intellectual and political dilemmas by a doctrine of universality which bears little past evidence of success. More importantly, however, it would be inaccurate to push too far this counterposing of Foucault and Habermas as the particular to the general, the specific to the universal. I have argued that underlying the work of critical theory, at least in the three writers discussed here, is a general project. Despite the differences I have argued exist between this project and that of Foucault, I have identified a strong continuity in the latter's researches with the general question of unravelling the various strands of a preoccupation with producing a knowledge of the subject. At this level there is a strong element of generality in Foucault's concerns.

What differentiates Foucault's researches is not some *a priori* fascination with the particular as opposed to the general. Where a strong concern with particularity does emerge is in his examinations of the conditions of emergence and functioning of a knowledge of madness, and of the sick person. At the risk of proposing a crude formal model which is wide open to criticism I would identify a number of elements to Foucault's concern to investigate these conditions of emergence of the question of the subject. Firstly, a concern to chart the structure of those knowledges which seek to produce a knowledge of the subject. This is a question of those concepts central to a particular body of knowledge, and also of the mechanisms through which it operates (the doctor-patient relation for example). Secondly, a concern with the institutional framework through which such knowledges operate. This might be the hospital, the asylum, the prison or the business school. All such institutions exist, one can argue, in intimate association with a complex body of theoretical knowledge. In their present form such institutions are unthinkable without such knowledges which begin by being adjacent to them, but gradually find their operation to be more or less inseparable from them, the knowledge becoming an element internal to the institution. Thirdly, there is what one might refer to as administrative or governmental programmes for the regulation of society as a whole. These each embody their own rationality, set their own objectives, and indicate a range of mechanisms through which they can develop. The system of 'police' so well developed in

Germany and France in the classical age is an example of this, as is our very different contemporary concern to promote an entrepreneurial culture of the self, a model for social relations which can apply not only to the economic sphere but also to the spheres of health care and the culture of the psychological self.

I am aware of the dangers of even suggesting that one might be able to elicit from Foucault's writings anything resembling a 'method'. No doubt I shall be duly reprimanded for my foolishness in proposing this triptych, with its emphasis on the relations between the three elements, as at least a starting point. It does, however, seem to me to be of use. This is for our own investigations as well as for making sense of some of the complexity in Foucault's own analyses, in particular *Histoire de la Folie* and *The Birth of the Clinic*.[7]

At the risk of causing even further consternation, I would like to suggest that Foucault's writings offer insights into a question which has proved a serious sticking point in so many debates, that of the state. I have argued above that Foucault's concern has been with the question of human subjectivity. One way of expressing this is to say that Foucault's underlying concern has been with the phenomenon of life, with how it can be observed, detected, measured, improved, classified, regulated and improved. This concern with the regulation of social life has been a continuing theme throughout Foucault's researches. The interrelation of bodies of knowledge, institutional frameworks and programmes of government has given content and direction to this concern. The 'state' in contrast, is a rather empty notion, unless one gives it shape by reference to questions of force, of 'bodies of armed men', or to its functional role within society or *vis-à-vis* the reproduction of social relations. Foucault's work draws attention to another and perhaps more important dimension of the existence of the state, one which has a less obvious profile, a weaker visibility. The 'governmentalisation' of the state is a term Foucault coined to describe such a phenomenon. The state may well turn out to be a composite reality, composed not just of force but of a variety of factors. Central to these would be the very process of definition of the boundaries between the public and the private, what is within the competence of the state and what is not. The state in this view becomes a more 'personal' phenomenon, it knows the individual better. Knowledges of the individual as a subject, the linkages between these knowledges and programmes for the regulation of society, and the institutions through which such programmes obtain their conditions of exercise are central to this project of actually defining and elaborating what the limits of the state are. Such an investigation would be guided, however, not by the obviousness of the term the 'state', but by the project of government to be deciphered, a project which may well turn out to be pursued as actively by non-state as state agencies, particularly in the current political climate.

The researches Foucault has undertaken open out onto a rich field of investigation which may help to render intelligible our present. But not according to an ideal of reason which had no practical efficacy. The project of critical theory gives rise I have argued to a less fruitful series of investigations, and provides also some misdirections for the process of political critique. It is not by appeal to an *a priori* notion of reason and subjectivity (or intersubjectivity) that one will be better equipped to decipher the shape of a better society. Indeed the abyss between the present and the ideal is a feature which marks the work of all the critical theorists discussed in this study. Against this it would be foolish to propose a Foucauldian model of political critique which one can simply apply to the problems at hand. A politics of health, or a politics of psychiatry is a much more complex issue than that.[8] Foucault's work none the less alerts us to the different levels which such a politics must address. Not simply the institutions, but the complex interrelation between political programmes, institutions, and the specialised bodies of knowledge. It is in demonstrating the subtle interplay between these different practices and the constructivist principle according to which they work which is Foucault's greatest achievement, not the programming of an alternative politics.

Perhaps I should add in conclusion that I am aware that one might have approached the task of a comparative assessment of critical theory and Foucault in very different terms to those undertaken here. And that this would have produced a different account of the two traditions. To have examined them in terms of their approach to the role of critical intellectuals for instance might well have led to an interpretation which placed critical theory and Foucault closer together than I have here. This is, however, only to reiterate that it is a matter of the level at which one chooses to conduct one's analysis that determines what is left out. The approach adopted here has clearly neglected much that would be relevant to a different study of these two traditions. None the less the interrelation between the concept of subjectivity and analyses of domination and power seems to me to highlight some important differences between the works of critical theory and Foucault. It is these differences and their implications I have sought to elicit for they highlight issues of central importance to the respective traditions.

NOTES

NOTES—INTRODUCTION

1 Cf. L. Althusser, *For Marx* (Harmondsworth, Allen Lane, The Penguin Press, 1969); L. Althusser and E. Balibar, *Reading Capital* (London, New Left Books, 1970).

2 Cf. L. Althusser and E. Balibar, *op. cit.*, p. 180.

3 Cf. L. Althusser, 'Ideology and Ideological State Apparatuses', in *Lenin and Philosophy and Other Essays* (London, New Left Books, 1971).

4 *Ibid.*, p. 160.

5 L. Althusser, 'Reply to John Lewis', in *Essays in Self-Criticism* (London, New Left Books, 1976).

6 Cf. E. P. Thompson, 'The Poverty of Theory', in *The Poverty of Theory and Other Essays* (London, Merlin Press, 1978).

7 M. Pêcheux, *Les Vérités de la Palice* (Paris, Maspéro, 1975). Translated as *Language, Semantics and Ideology* (London, Macmillan, 1979).

8 Cf. J. Lacan, *Écrits* (London, Tavistock, 1977); A. Lemaire, *Jacques Lacan* (London, Routledge & Kegan Paul, 1977).

9 Cf. R. Coward and J. Ellis, *Language and Materialism* (London, Routledge & Kegan Paul, 1977).

10 M. Weber, *The Theory of Social and Economic Organization*, T. Parsons, ed. (New York, Oxford University Press, 1947), pp. 152–4.

11 P. Q. Hirst, *Social Evolution and Sociological Categories* (London, George Allen & Unwin, 1976).

12 H. H. Gerth and C. W. Mills, *From Max Weber* (London, Routledge & Kegan Paul, 1948). References are to Routledge Paperback edition, 1970, p. 253.

13 *Ibid.*, p. 257.

14 *Ibid.*, p. 261.

15 W. Hennis, 'Max Weber's "central question" ', *Economy and Society*, vol. 12, no. 2 (May 1983).

16 Critical theory is of course simply a name given to a group of social theorists. It is used in the context of this study to refer to the writings of Max Horkheimer, Herbert Marcuse and Jurgen Habermas.

17 *History and Class Consciousness* (London, Merlin Press, 1971), is the collection of essays for which

Lukács is best known in England.

18 *Ibid.*, pp. 95–9.

19 G. Therborn, 'A Critique of the Frankfurt School', in *New Left Review*, no. 63 (1970); and 'J. Habermas: The New Eclecticism', in *New Left Review*, no. 67 (1971).

20 *Considerations on Western Marxism* (London, New Left Books, 1976).

21 S. Lukes, *Power: A Radical View* (London and Basingstoke, Macmillan, 1974).

22 For recent examples of the continuing debate, cf. for instance, T. Benton, ' "Objective" interests and the sociology of power', *Sociology*, vol. 15 (1981), and B. Hindess, 'Power, interests and the outcomes of struggles', *Sociology*, vol. 16, no. 4. (1982).

23 Benton, *op. cit.*, p. 179.

24 Hindess, *op. cit.*

25 Cf. N. Poulantzas and R. Miliband, 'The problem of the capitalist state' in R. Blackburn (ed.), *Ideology in Social Science* (London, Fontana, 1972).

26 N. Poulantzas, *State, Power, Socialism* (London, New Left Books, 1978).

27 *Ibid.*, p. 67. A sensitive evaluation of the relevance of Foucault's studies to Marxism is carried out by Barry Smart in *Foucault, Marxism and Critique*, (London, Routledge & Kegan Paul, 1983).

28 Cf. M. Foucault, 'The subject and power', in H. L. Dreyfus and P. Rabinow, *Michel Foucault: Beyond Structuralism and Hermeneutics* (Brighton, Harvester Press, 1982).

29 Cf. on this point C. Gordon, 'Afterword', in C. Gordon (ed.), *Power/Knowledge* (Brighton, Harvester Press, 1980). Canguilhem's output is immense, but see in particular, *La Connaissance de la Vie*, 2nd edn (Paris, Vrin, 1980); *Études d'Histoire et de philosophie des sciences* (Paris, Vrin, 1968).

30 Cf. M. Foucault, 'On governmentality', *Ideology and Consciousness*, no. 6. (Autumn 1979).

31 Cf. M. Foucault, 'The politics of health in the eighteenth century', in C. Gordon (ed.), *op. cit.*

32 Cf. M. Foucault, *The History of Sexuality, Vol. 1. An Introduction* (Harmondsworth, Penguin, 1981). See especially Part Five, 'Right of death and power over life'.

33 R. Castel, *Le Psychanalysme* (Paris, Maspéro, 1973); *L'ordre psychiatrique* (Paris, Les Editions de Minuit, 1976); R. Castel, F. Castel and A. Lovell, *The Psychiatric Society* (New York, Columbia University Press, 1982).

34 J. Donzelot, *The Policing of Families* (London, Hutchinson, 1980); *L'Invention du Social* (Paris, Fayard, 1984).

35 Cf. G. Procacci, 'Social economy and the government of poverty', *Ideology and Consciousness*, no. 4 (Autumn 1978).

36 Cf. P. Pasquino, 'Theatrum politicum. The genealogy of capital – police and the state of prosperity', *Ideology and Consciousness*, no. 4 (Autumn 1978).

37 Cf. P. Miller, 'The territory of the psychiatrist', *Ideology and Consciousness*, no. 7 (Autumn 1980). 'Psychiatry – the renegotiation of a territory', *Ideology and Consciousness*, no. 8 (Spring 1981). See also P. Miller and N. Rose (eds), *The Power of Psychiatry* (Cambridge, Polity Press, 1986).

CHAPTER 1 MAX HORKHEIMER AND CULTURAL CRITIQUE

1 The English translation of this article referred to in the following discussion is to be found in Max Horkheimer, *Critical Theory*, New York, Seabury Press, 1972.

2 M. Horkheimer, 'Traditional and critical theory', *Zeitschrift für Sozialforschung*, 1937, in his *Critical Theory*, *op. cit.*, p. 204.

3 *Ibid.*, p. 211.

4 *Ibid.*, p. 197.

5 *Ibid.*, p. 199.

6 *Ibid.*, p. 200.

7 *Ibid.*

8 *Ibid.*

9 *Ibid.*, p. 202.

10 *Ibid.*

11 *Ibid.*, p. 203.

12 *Ibid.*, p. 204.

13 *Ibid.*, p. 207.

14 *Ibid.*, p. 209.

15 *Ibid.*

16 *Ibid.*, p. 210.

17 *Ibid.*

18 *Ibid.*, p. 211.

19 *Ibid.*

20 Horkheimer's early writings are generally assumed to be Marxist, and to differ in this respect from his writings in the 1940s. My arguments, however, whilst not denying a change of emphasis in Horkheimer's work, are concerned more with the continuity of his concerns.

21 Horkheimer, *op. cit.*, p. 226.

22 *Ibid.*, p. 230.

23 *Ibid.*, p. 226.

24 *Ibid.*, p. 229.

25 *Ibid.*

26 *Ibid.*

27 *Ibid.*, p. 233.

28 *Ibid.*, p. 230.

29 *Ibid.*, p. 231.

30 *Ibid.*

31 *Ibid.*

32 Cf. G. Lukács, *History and Class Consciousness* (London, Merlin Press, 1971), especially the article 'Reification and the consciousness of the proletariat'.

33 To examine Lenin's arguments on this matter would entail an examination on the one hand of his conception of socialist theory and his critique of 'spontaneity', and on the other hand his conception of the organisational form of the party and its relationship to socialist theory. Cf., amongst other pieces, 'What is to be done?', in V. I. Lenin, *Selected Works* (Moscow, Progress Publishers) (in three volumes), vol. 1.

34 Horkheimer, 'Traditional and critical theory', *op. cit.*, p. 247.
35 *Ibid.*, p. 249.
36 Cf. M. Jay, *The Dialectical Imagination* (London, Heinemann Education, 1973) p. 255. Jay is concerned to chart the shifts which take place in critical theory away from its early and more Marxist orientation. D. Held, *Introduction to Critical Theory* (London, Hutchinson, 1980) chapter 1, provides a clear account of the geographical movements of Horkheimer *et al.* during this period.
37 Max Horkheimer, *Eclipse of Reason* (New York, Oxford University Press, 1947), p. 3.
38 *Ibid.*, p. 4.
39 'Traditional and critical theory', op. cit.
40 Horkheimer, *Eclipse of Reason*, p. 5.
41 *Ibid.*
42 *Ibid.*, p. 9.
43 Cf. Lukács, *op. cit.*
44 Jay, *op. cit.*, remarks that 'Horkheimer had in fact always been an interested reader of Weber' (p. 259). Cf. M. Weber, *The Protestant Ethic and the Spirit of Capitalism* (London, Allen & Unwin, 1965). The extent of Weber's arguments concerning the process of 'rationalisation' are exemplified in his discussion of 'Occidental music and its instruments' in M. Weber, *The Rational and Social Foundations of Music* (Carbondale, Illinois, Southern Illinois University Press, Arcturus Books edn, 1969).
45 Cf. Max Scheler, *Die Wissensformen und die Gesellschaft* (Leipzig, 1926).
46 Cf. Michael Oakeshott, *Rationalism in Politics and Other Essays* (London, Methuen, 1962).
47 Horkheimer, *Eclipse of Reason*, p. 44.
48 *Ibid.*, p. 43.
49 *Ibid.*, p. 56.
50 *Ibid.*, p. 93.
51 *Ibid.*
52 *Ibid.*, p. 97.
53 *Ibid.*, p. 111.
54 *Ibid.*, p. 128.
55 *Ibid.*, p. 135.
56 *Ibid.*, p. 135.
57 *Ibid.*, p. 141.
58 *Ibid.*, p. 141.
59 'Traditional and critical theory', *op. cit.*
60 Horkheimer, *Eclipse of Reason*, p. 141.
61 *Ibid.*, pp. 160–1.
62 *Ibid.*, p. 171.
63 *Ibid.*, p. 175.
64 *Ibid.*, p. 171.
65 The notion of dialectics seems destined to remain one of the perennials of Marxist and neo-Marxist debate. This extends from Lenin's *Philosophical Notebooks*, vol. 38 of V. I. Lenin, *Collected Work* (Moscow, Progress Publishers, 1972), to much of the debates in contemporary journals such as *Radical Philosophy*. It should be added, however, that the latter witnesses a diverse range of concerns, many of them at odds with a 'dialectical' tradition.
66 Horkheimer, *Eclipse of Reason*, p. 177.

67 *Ibid.*
68 *Ibid.*
69 *Ibid.*
70 *Ibid.*, p. 187.
71 *Ibid.*, p. 178.
72 'The concept of man', in M. Horkheimer, *Critique of Instrumental Reason* (New York: Seabury Press, 1974).
73 *Ibid.*, p. 4.
74 *Ibid.*, p. 4.
75 M. Horkheimer, op. cit.
76 *Ibid.*, p. 156.
77 In the following I refer to the English translation of Horkheimer's contribution entitled 'Authority and the Family', which appears in M. Horkheimer, *Critical Theory*, *op. cit.*
78 Horkheimer, 'Authority and the Family, *op. cit.*, p. 53.
79 Goran Therborn, 'A critique of the Frankfurt School', *New Left Review*, no. 63 (1970).
80 Horkheimer, 'Authority and the Family', *op. cit.*, p. 54.
81 *Ibid.*
82 *Ibid.*, p. 56.
83 It is interesting that when Althusser discusses such institutions he seeks to incorporate them within the apparatus of the state. Cf. L. Althusser, 'Ideology and Ideological State Apparatuses' in *Lenin and Philosophy* (London, New Left Books, 1971).
84 Horkheimer, 'Authority and the Family', *op. cit.*, p. 69.
85 *Ibid.*
86 *Ibid.*, p. 70.
87 *Ibid.*
88 *Ibid.*, pp. 70–1.
89 *Ibid.*, p. 71.
90 *Ibid.*, p. 85.
91 *Ibid.*, p. 91.
92 *Ibid.*, p. 92.
93 *Ibid.*
94 *Ibid.*
95 *Ibid.*, p. 97.
96 *Ibid.*
97 *Ibid.*, pp. 97–8.
98 *Ibid.*, p. 98.
99 *Ibid.*, p. 99.
100 *Ibid.*, p. 100.
101 *Ibid.*
102 *Ibid.*, p. 101.
103 *Ibid.*, p. 102.
104 *Ibid.*
105 *Ibid.*
106 *Ibid.*, p. 109.
107 Quoted in *ibid.*, p. 111.
108 *Ibid.*, p. 111.
109 *Ibid.*, p. 112.
110 *Ibid.*, p. 114.
111 *Ibid.*
112 Cf. G. W. F. Hegel, *The Phenomenology of Mind*, translated J. B. Baillie (London, Allen & Unwin, 1966).
113 Cf. F. Engels, *The Origin of the Family, Private Property and the State* (London, Lawrence & Wishart, 1973), p. 120.
114 Horkheimer, 'Authority and the Family', *op. cit.*, p. 118.
115 *Ibid.*, p. 120.
116 *Ibid.*, p. 122.
117 *Ibid.*, p. 128.
118 *Ibid.* Cf. Hegel's discussion of the notions of 'Universality, particularity and individuality' in G. W. F. Hegel, *Hegel's Logic*, Part One of the *Encyclopaedia of the Philosophical Sciences* (Oxford University Press, 1975).

CHAPTER 2 HERBERT MARCUSE AND SUBJECTIVITY AS NEGATION

1 Cf. H. Marcuse 'The concept of essence' in *Negations* (Harmondsworth, Penguin, 1968).
2 *Ibid.*, p. 44.
3 *Ibid.*
4 *Ibid.*, pp. 44–5.
5 *Ibid.*, p. 49.
6 *Ibid.*, p. 51.
7 *Ibid.*
8 Cf. M. Horkheimer, 'Traditional and critical theory', in *Critical Theory* (New York: Seabury Press, 1972); see also the 'Postcript' to this article.
9 Cf. M. Foucault, *The Order of Things* (London: Tavistock, 1974), chapter 9, especially the section 'The "cogito" and the unthought'. G. Canguilhem in an excellent article on *The Order of Things* places great emphasis on the shift from Descartes to Kant in respect of Foucault's thesis concerning 'the birth of man'; cf. G. Canguilhem, 'Mort de l'homme ou épuisement du cogito', *Critique*, vol. 23, no. 242 (1967).
10 H. Marcuse, 'The concept of essence', *op. cit.*, p. 54.
11 *Ibid.*, p. 62.
12 *Ibid.*, p. 72.
13 *Ibid.*
13 *Ibid.*
14 *Ibid.*, p. 78.
15 *Ibid.*, p. 67.
16 The *Science of Logic* was first published in three parts in 1812, 1813, and 1816. The *Phenomenology of Spirit* appeared in 1807. The former is sometimes considered to have been superseded by the *Logic* of the *Encyclopaedia of the Philosophical Sciences* which first appeared in 1817. Without doubt the *Logic* of the *Encyclopaedia* is the more accessible of the later works. References to it in the following are from the Oxford University Press (1975) version.
17 H. Marcuse, *Reason and Revolution* (Boston: Beacon Press, 1960), p. 5.
18 *Ibid.*, p. 6.
19 *Ibid.*, p. 9.
20 *Ibid.*, p. 6.
21 *Ibid.*, p. 9.
22 *Ibid.*
23 *Ibid.*, p. 64.
24 *Ibid.*
25 *Ibid.*, p. 65.
26 *Ibid.*, p. 71.
27 *Ibid.*, p. 73.
28 Cf. G. W. F. Hegel, *The Phenomenology of Mind*, translated J. B. Baillie (London, Allen & Unwin, 1966).
29 H. Marcuse, *Reason and Revolution*, *op. cit.*, p. 120.
30 *Ibid.*, p. 113.
31 *Ibid.*, p. 134.
32 *Ibid.*, p. 135.
33 *Ibid.*
34 Hegel, *Science of Logic*, vol. 1, quoted in Marcuse, *Reason and Revolution*, p. 136.
35 Marcuse, *Reason and Revolution*, p. 136.
36 *Ibid.*, p. 137.
37 *Ibid.*
38 *Ibid.*, p. 138.
39 *Ibid.*
40 Hegel, *Science of Logic*, vol. 1, quoted in *ibid.*, p. 138.
41 *Ibid.*, p. 139.
42 *Ibid.*, p. 140.
43 Hegel, *Logic* (Oxford

University Press, 1975), p. 141.
44 Marcuse, *Reason and Revolution*, p. 143.
45 Cf. V. I. Lenin, *Philosophical Notebooks*, vol. 38 of *Collected Works* (London, Lawrence & Wishart, 1972). Dialectics, Lenin argued, 'in the proper sense is the study of contradiction *in the very essence of objects*' (*ibid.*, pp. 253–4; emphasis in original).
46 Lenin, *op. cit.*, quotes Hegel approvingly on this point; see *ibid.*, p. 138.
47 Marcuse, *Reason and Revolution*, p. 147.
48 *Ibid.*, pp. 147–8.
49 *Ibid.*, p. 148.
50 See chapter 1 above.
41 Marcuse, *Reason and Revolution*, p. 153.
52 *Ibid.*, p. 154.
53 The notion of 'transition' from one mode of production to another which I am referring to here owes much to the works of Louis Althusser and Etienne Balibar, especially *Reading Capital* (London, New Left Books, 1970).
54 For a criticism of Balibar's notion of transition, see B. Hindess and P. Q. Hirst, *Pre-Capitalist Modes of Production*, (London: Routledge & Kegan Paul, 1975).
55 Cf. G. Lukács, 'Class consciousness' in *History and Class Consciousness* (London: Merlin Press, 1971).
56 Marcuse, *Reason and Revolution*, p. 154.
57 *Ibid.*, emphasis in original.
58 *Ibid.*, p. 155.
59 *Ibid.*
60 *Ibid.*
61 *Ibid.*
62 *Ibid.*, p. 143.
63 *Ibid.*, p. 140.
64 Lenin, *op. cit.*, proposes such a reading of Hegel on the notion of dialectics. See also Lucio Colletti, *From Rousseau to Lenin* (London, New Left Books, 1972) and *Marxism and Hegel* (London, New Left Books, 1973). In the former see the article 'From Hegel to Marcuse'.
65 Cf. P. Slater, *Origin and Significance of the Frankfurt School* (London, Routledge & Kegan Paul, 1977), and P. Anderson, *Considerations on Western Marxism* (London, New Left Books, 1976) for different versions of such an account.
66 Marcuse, *Reason and Revolution*, p. 227.
67 *Ibid.*, p. 228.
68 *Ibid.*, p. 229.
69 *Ibid.*
70 *Ibid.*, p. 230.
71 *Ibid.*, pp. 230–1.
72 *Ibid.*, p. 231.
73 *Ibid.*
74 *Ibid.*
75 *Ibid.*
76 *Ibid.*, p. 315.
77 H. Marcuse 'Existentialism; Remarks on Jean-Paul Sartre's *L'Être et le néant*', in *Philosophy and Phenomenological Research*, vol. 8, no. 3 (1949); reprinted as 'Sartre's existentialism' in H. Marcuse, *Studies in Critical*

Philosophy (London, New Left Books, 1972).

78 H. Marcuse 'Industrialization and Capitalism in the Works of Max Weber' in *Negations* (Harmondsworth: Penguin, 1968).

79 H. Marcuse, *Reason and Revolution*, p. ix.

80 *Ibid.*, p. xi.

81 H. Marcuse, *One-Dimensional Man* (London: Routledge & Kegan Paul, 1964), p. 1.

82 *Ibid.*, p. 1.

83 *Ibid.*, p. 2.

84 *Ibid.*, p. 3.

85 *Ibid.*, p. 5.

86 *Ibid.*

87 *Ibid.*, p. 6.

88 *Ibid.*, p. 10; emphasis in original.

89 *Ibid.*, p. 12.

90 *Ibid.*

91 *Ibid.*, p. 31.

92 Cf. G. Lukács, 'Reification and the consciousness of the proletariat', in *History and Class Consciousness* (London, Merlin Press, 1971).

93 Marcuse, *One Dimensional Man*, p. 33.

94 *Ibid.*

95 *Ibid.*, p. 35.

96 *Ibid.*, p. 48; emphasis in original.

97 *Ibid.*, p. 52.

98 *Ibid.*, p. 51.

99 *Ibid.*, p. 52.

100 *Ibid.*, p. 56.

101 *Ibid.*

102 *Ibid.*, p. 57.

103 *Ibid.*

104 *Ibid.*, p. 58.

105 *Ibid.*

106 *Ibid.*, p. 61.

107 *Ibid.*

108 *Ibid.*, p. 64.

109 *Ibid.*, p. 72.

110 *Ibid.*

111 *Ibid.*

112 *Ibid.*, p. 73.

113 *Ibid.*

114 *Ibid.*, emphasis in original.

115 *Ibid.*, p. 75.

116 *Ibid.*, p. 78.

117 *Ibid.*, p. 6.

118 *Ibid.*, p. 7; emphasis added.

119 P. Slater, *op. cit.*, provides something of a defence of Marcuse's political integrity. He argues that Marcuse retained his radical opposition to contemporary capitalism, yet without subscribing to a Leninist conception of an avant-garde of intellectuals. But Slater's account of the nature of Marcuse's position is far from convincing. He argues that 'Marcuse's radicalised theoretical activity has not produced any "definitive" revolutionary strategy, since his theory is a dialectical response to an emerging new praxis' (*ibid.*, p. 91). I suggest that this explains nothing.

120 Marcuse, *One-Dimensional Man*, p. 245.

121 *Ibid.*, p. 252.

122 *Ibid.*, p. 253.

123 *Ibid.*, p. 255.

124 *Ibid.*

125 *Ibid.*, p. 256.

126 *Ibid.*, p. 257.

127 Marcuse, 'Philosophy and critical theory' (1936) in *Negations* (Harmondsworth: Penguin, 1968), p. 154.

128 *Ibid.*, p. 153.

129 Cf. P. Connerton, *The Tragedy of Enlightenment* (Cambridge

University Press, 1980), p. 86 for one example of this line of argument.

130 P. Anderson, *Considerations on Western Marxism*, *op. cit.*, provides an instructive example of this argument. Referring to Marcuse, Anderson states that 'The rupture between theory and practice that had silently started in practice in Germany in the later twenties was clamantly consecrated in theory in the mid sixties, with the publication of *One-Dimensional Man*' (*ibid.*, p. 34).

CHAPTER 3 JURGEN HABERMAS: HUMAN INTERESTS, COMMUNICATION AND LEGITIMATION

1 P. Connerton in the introduction to *Critical Sociology* locates Habermas as the fourth stage of critical theory – cf Connerton *op. cit.*, p. 30. D. Held, *Introduction to Critical Theory* (London, Hutchinson, 1980) provides a useful overview of Habermas's works, citing the recent proposals for a universal pragmatics as the more concerted attempt at 'reformulating' critical theory.

2 Between 1803 and 1806 Hegel gave lectures on the 'Philosophy of Nature and of Mind' at Jena. Rather than view these as precursors to the *Phenomenology* Habermas takes them as offering 'a distinctive, systematic basis for the formative processes of the spirit, which he later abandoned (Habermas, *Theory and Practice* (London, Heinemann, 1974), p. 142).

3 J. Habermas, *Knowledge and Human Interests* (London, Heinemann, 1972).

4 Habermas, *Theory and Practice*.

5 Habermas, 'Dogmatism, Reason and Decision: on theory and praxis in our scientific civilization', in *ibid.*, p. 262.

6 Habermas, 'Introduction: Some difficulties in the attempt to link theory and praxis', in *ibid.*, p. 1.

7 Deleuze, locating Kant in opposition to both empiricism and rational dogmatism, refers to this notion of the 'interests of reason'. G. Deleuze, *La philosophie critique de Kant* (Paris, Presses Universitaires de France, 1963).

8 Habermas, *Knowledge and Human Interests*, p. 205.

9 *Ibid.*

10 *Ibid.*, p. 206.

11 *Ibid.*

12 *Ibid.*, p. 210.

13 Habermas, 'Labour and Interaction: Remarks on Hegel's Jena *Philosophy of Mind*' in his *Theory and Practice*, pp. 144–5.

14 *Ibid.*, p. 151.

15 Cf. my discussion in the previous chapter of Marcuse's attempt to take the notion of the Master-Slave relation from the *Phenomenology* as the basis for a 'dialectical' account of subjectivity. As noted at the

beginning of this chapter, Habermas places greater weight on the notion of intersubjectivity.

16 Habermas, *Knowledge and Human Interests*, p. 195.
17 *Ibid.*
18 *Ibid.*, p. 196.
19 *Ibid.*
20 *Ibid.*, p. 198.
21 *Ibid.*, p. 312.
22 *Ibid.*, p. 314.
23 *Ibid.*
24 *Ibid.*
25 *Ibid.*, p. 228.
26 *Ibid.*, p. 229.
27 *Ibid.*, p. 233.
28 *Ibid.*, p. 245.
29 *Ibid.*, pp. 247–8.
30 One could, for instance, oppose to it Lacan's account of psychoanalysis. Thus Lacan argues, referring to the process of analysis, that 'nothing could be more misleading for the analyst than to seek to guide himself by some supposed "contact" experienced with the reality of the subject.' Lacan, 'The function and field of speech and language in psychoanalysis' in *Ecrits* (London, Tavistock, 1977), p. 44. For an introduction to the works of Lacan, see Anika Lemaire, *Jacques Lacan* (London, Routledge & Kegan Paul, 1977; trans. D. Macey).
31 Habermas, *Knowledge and Human Interests*, p. 257.
32 *Ibid.*, p. 259.
33 *Ibid.*, p. 260.
34 There is a perverse sense in which Coward and Ellis attempt something similar in their proposals for a Lacanian version of an Althusserian Marxist account of ideology. Of course it should be noted that they do so in resolute opposition to a unitary notion of the subject. Cf. R. Coward and J. Ellis, *Language and Materialism* (London, Routledge & Kegan Paul, 1977).
35 Habermas, *Knowledge and Human Interests*, p. 281.
36 *Ibid.*, p. 282.
37 *Ibid.*, p. 283.
38 J. Habermas, 'Introduction: some difficulties in the attempt to link theory and praxis', in his *Theory and Practice*.
39 Cf. P. Hirst and P. Woolley, *Social Relations and Human Attributes* (London, Tavistock, 1982) for a discussion of the concepts of person, individuality and rationality.
40 Habermas, *Theory and Practice*, p. 10.
41 *Ibid.*, p. 11.
42 *Ibid.*, p. 13.
43 *Ibid.*
44 Cf. D. Held, *Introduction to Critical Theory*, p. 326. Held provides a useful discussion of such criticisms. See also F. Dallmayr, 'Critical Theory criticised: Habermas' *Knowledge and Human Interests* and its aftermath', in *Philosophy of the Social Sciences*, vol. 2, no. 3 (1972).
45 Held makes a criticism which has similarities to that advanced here. He argues that 'Transcendental reflection on the general conditions of knowledge and action is inadequately distinguished

from critical self-reflection'; Held, *op. cit.*, p. 326.

46 Habermas, *Theory and Practice*, p. 32.

47 *Ibid.*

48 *Ibid.*, p. 36.

49 *Ibid.*, p. 37.

50 *Ibid.*, p. 40.

51 *Ibid.*

52 Cf. A. Wellmer, 'Communication and emancipation: reflections on the linguistic turn in critical theory' in J. O. Neill (ed.), *On Critical Theory* (London, Heinemann, 1977).

53 Quoted in Held, *Introduction to Critical Theory*, p. 331.

54 Cf. J. L. Austin, *How to do Things with Words* (London, Oxford University Press, 1962). For a general discussion of the philosophy of language see B. Harrison, *An Introduction to the Philosophy of Language* (Basingstoke, Macmillan, 1979); see also I. Hacking, *Why does Language Matter to Philosophy?* (Cambridge University Press, 1975).

55 Cf. J. Searle, *Speech Acts* (Cambridge, Cambridge University Press, 1969), and 'What is a speech act?' in M. Black (ed.), *Philosophy in America* (London, Allen & Unwin, 1964).

56 Cf. N. Chomsky, *Language and Mind* (Cambridge, Mass., MIT Press, 1965), and *Reflections on Language* (New York/London, Temple Smith/Fontana, 1976).

57 For an easily readable overview of sociolinguistics see P. Trudgill, *Sociolinguistics* (Harmondsworth, Penguin, 1974). Sociolinguistics covers a very broad area of concerns, and Habermas in fact pays very little attention to this variety. One of the more interesting examples of sociolinguistics is the work of W. Labov; cf. in particular his 'The study of language in its social context' and 'The logic of nonstandard English' in P. P. Giglioli (ed.), *Language and Social Context* (Harmondsworth, Penguin, 1972).

58 J. Habermas, 'What is universal pragmatics?' in *Communication and the Evolution of Society* (trans. T. McCarthy, London, Heinemann, 1979), p. 31.

59 J. Habermas, 'Towards a theory of communicative competence' in *Inquiry*, 13 (Winter 1970), p. 367.

60 J. Habermas, 'What is a universal pragmatics?' in *Communication and the Evolution of Society*, p. 6.

61 *Ibid.*, p. 1.

62 *Ibid.*, p. 26.

63 *Ibid.*, p. 13.

64 *Ibid.*, p. 17.

65 I discuss this question in the following section in relation to the notion of the 'end of the individual' as raised by Habermas.

66 Habermas, 'What is universal pragmatics?', *op. cit.*, p. 58.

67 *Ibid.*, p. 42.

68 *Ibid.*, p. 44.

69 *Ibid.*, p. 34.

70 *Ibid.*

71 *Ibid.*, p. 48.

72 *Ibid.*

73 *Ibid.*, p. 60.

74 Habermas is, at least in part, arguing here against those aspects of Austin and Searle's views which include reference to contexts or institutionally bound norms of speech. Searle, for instance, argues that in the 'analysis of illocutionary acts, we must capture both the intentional and the conventional aspects and especially the relationship between them.' Searle, *Speech Acts*, p. 45.

75 Habermas, 'What is universal pragmatics?', *op. cit.*, p. 62, emphasis in original.

76 *Ibid.*, p. 63; emphasis in original.

77 *Ibid.*

78 Cf. for a quite different position within the philosophy of language M. Pecheux, *Les Vérités de la Palice* (Paris, Maspéro, 1975); see also R. Robin, *Histoire et Linguistique* (Paris, Armand Colin, 1973).

79 I have not pursued the question of the extent to which Habermas tries to develop a general theory of social action on the basis of his proposals for a universal pragmatics. This would be an interesting question to follow through, in view of statements of his such as the following: 'I start from the assumption (without undertaking to demonstrate it here) that other forms of social action – for example, conflict, competition, strategic action in general – are derivatives of action oriented to reaching understanding (*verständigungsorientiert*).' Habermas, 'What is universal pragmatics?', *op. cit.*, p. 1.

80 Habermas, 'What is universal pragmatics', *op. cit.*, p. 22.

81 *Ibid.*, p. 23.

82 *Ibid.*, pp. 23–4.

83 Habermas, 'Towards a theory of communicative competence', *op. cit.*, p. 372.

84 Habermas, 'What is universal pragmatics?', *op. cit.*, p. 5.

85 J. Habermas, *Legitimation Crisis* (trans. T. McCarthy, London, Heinemann, 1976).

86 Cf. Part III of *Legitimation Crisis*. It is worth emphasising that even here it is primarily a set of general concepts of crisis tendencies, rather than an account of how such tendencies operate in a particular society, which Habermas attempts to elaborate.

87 Habermas, *Legitimation Crisis*, p. 1.

88 *Ibid.*

89 *Ibid.*

90 *Ibid.*

91 Here the most obvious point of reference is the work of Niklas Luhmann. For a useful commentary on the debate between Habermas and Luhmann cf. F. W. Sixel, 'The problem of sense: Habermas v. Luhmann' in J. O'Neill (ed.), *On Critical Theory* (London, Heinemann, 1977).

92 Habermas, *Legitimation Crisis*, p. 4.

93 *Ibid.*

94 *Ibid.*

95 *Ibid.*

96 *Ibid.*

97 *Ibid.*, p. 3.

98 *Ibid.*

99 *Ibid.*, p. 17.
100 *Ibid.*, p. 111.
101 This, in outline is Luhmann's account. Luhmann attempts to remain at the level of a systems analysis of the social world, and to suggest that legitimation is not limited to a model of rationality. For the initial debate between Habermas and Luhmann cf. J. Habermas and N. Luhmann, *Theorie Der Gesellschaft oder Sozialtechnologie* (Frankfurt, Suhrkamp, 1971).
102 Habermas, *Legitimation Crisis*, p. 97.
103 *Ibid.*
104 *Ibid.*, p. 100.
105 *Ibid.*, p. 101.
106 *Ibid.*
107 *Ibid.*, p. 102.
108 *Ibid.*, pp. 107–8.
109 *Ibid.*, p. 108.
110 *Ibid.*, p. 109.
111 *Ibid.*
112 *Ibid.*, p. 111.
113 *Ibid.*, p. 113, emphasis in original.
114 *Ibid.*
115 *Ibid.*, p. 114.
116 *Ibid.*, p. 107.
117 *Ibid.*, p. 117.
118 *Ibid.*, p. 122.
119 *Ibid.*, p. 128.
120 *Ibid.*, p. 130.
121 See above, notes 92 and 102. See also N. Luhmann, *Trust and Power* (Chichester, Wiley, 1979).
122 Quoted in Habermas, *Legitimation Crisis*, p. 130.
123 *Ibid.*, p. 131.
124 *Ibid.*, p. 133.
125 *Ibid.*, p. 139.
126 *Ibid.*, p. 142.
127 R. Bubner, 'Habermas' concept of critical theory', in J. B. Thompson and D. Held (eds), *Habermas: Critical Debates* (London, Macmillan, 1982).
128 J. B. Thompson, 'Universal pragmatics', *op. cit.*
129 *Ibid.*
130 J. Habermas, *Theorie des kommunikativen Handelns* (2 vols), (Frankfurt, Suhrkamp, 1981). Translated as *The Theory of Communicative Action*, trans. T. McCarthy (London, Heinemann, 1984).
131 J. B. Thompson, 'Universal pragmatics', p. 126.
132 J. Habermas, *The Theory of Communicative Action*, London, Heinemann, 1984, p. 278.
133 *Ibid.*, p. 288; emphasis in original.
134 *Ibid.*, p. 295; emphasis in original.
135 *Ibid.*, p. 331.
136 R. Bubner, *Modern German Philosophy* (Cambridge University Press, 1981), p. 187.

CHAPTER 4 UNREASON TO MADNESS: THE KNOWLEDGE OF SUBJECTIVITY

1 A useful account of *Histoire de la Folie* is provided in P. Hirst and P. Woolley, *Social Relations and Human Attributes* (London, Tavistock, 1982).
2 It is worth noting that Foucault does not erect a rigid distinction between psychology and psychiatry. They are seen to cohere around the project to

produce a knowledge of the individual. For an opposing view cf. J. Ben-David and R. Collins, 'Social Factors in the origins of a new science: the case of psychology', in *American Sociological Review*, vol. 31, no. 4, (August 1966).

3 On the notion of 'surfaces of emergence' cf. M. Foucault, *The Archaeology of Knowledge* (London, Tavistock, 1972), p. 41.

4 On the notion of government cf. M. Foucault, 'On governmentality', *Ideology and Consciousness*, no. 6 (Autumn 1979).

5 Foucault provides an incisive account of the relation between a psychiatry in the process of establishing itself and the judicial apparatus in 'About the concept of the "dangerous individual" in 19th century legal psychiatry', *International Journal of Law and Psychiatry*, vol. 1 (1978), pp. 1–18. R. Castel, *L'Ordre Psychiatrique* (Paris, Editions de Minuit, 1976) deals with these themes also.

6 A. Scull, *Museums of Madness* (London, Allen Lane, 1979) tends to account for psychiatry's rise to a position of dominance in the care of the insane in these terms. For a different interpretation cf. P. Miller and N. Rose (eds), *The Power of Psychiatry* (Cambridge, Polity Press, 1986).

7 Cf., for instance Klaus Doerner, *Madmen and the Bourgeoisie* (Oxford, Blackwell, 1981); George Rosen, *Madness in Society* (Chicago and London, University of Chicago Press/ Routledge & Kegan Paul, 1968); Robert Castel, *L'ordre psychiatrique* (Paris, Editions de Minuit, 1976); R. Castel, F. Castel and A. Lovell, *The Psychiatric Society* (Columbia University Press, 1982). See also M. Donnelly, *Managing the Mind* (London, Tavistock, 1983).

8 Erwin H. Ackerknecht, *A Short History of Psychiatry*, (New York, Hafner Publishing Company, 1968).

9 *Ibid.*, p. 10.

10 *Ibid.*, p. 34.

11 Cf., in particular, his *Medicine in the Paris Hospital 1794–1848* (Baltimore, Johns Hopkins University Press, 1966).

12 Cf. his article 'Psychopathology, primitive medicine and primitive culture' in *Bulletin of the History of Medicine*, 14, (1943), pp. 30–67.

13 Ackerknecht, *A Short History of Psychiatry*, p. 3.

14 *Ibid.*, p. 18.

15 G. Zilboorg and G. W. Henry, *A History of Medical Psychology* (New York, 1941).

16 *Ibid.*, p. 21.

17 A. Sheridan, *Michel Foucault: the will to truth* (London, Tavistock, 1980) provide some useful biographical details on Foucault's approach to the study of madness. He notes also the various editions of *Histoire de la Folie* (*ibid.*, p. 11).

18 In *Des Chercheurs Français S'interrogent* (1957).

19 M. Foucault (ed.), *I, Pierre Rivière* (Harmondsworth, Penguin, 1978).

20 On this shift in the mode of functioning of psychiatry cf. R. Castel, F. Castel and A. Lovell, *The Psychiatric Society* (New York, Columbia University Press, 1982); R. Castel, *La Gestion des risques* (Paris, Editions de Minuit, 1981); D. Armstrong, 'Madness and coping', *Sociology of Health and Illness*, vol. 2, no. 3 (November 1980). See also Miller and Rose (eds), *The Power of Psychiatry*.

21 This concern is not witnessed only in the sphere of psychiatry. Industrial psychology is equally concerned with the individual in this sense, as witnessed on the one hand in organisations such as the Tavistock Institute of Human Relations, and on the other hand in the utilisation of the latest psychological techniques in staff training schemes. On the former see the brief account in Cyril Sofer, *Organisations in Theory and Practice* (London, Heinemann, 1972), chapter 10. Examples of the latter can be found in A. Wagner, *The Transactional Manager* (Englewood Cliffs, NJ, Prentice-Hall, 1981) and M. Woodcock and D. Francis, *The Unblocked Manager* (London, Gower, 1981).

22 A. Scull, 'The social history of psychiatry in the Victorian era', in A. Scull (ed.), *Madhouses, Mad-Doctors, and Madmen* (London, Athlone Press, 1981), p. 5.

23 Hirst and Woolley, *op. cit.*, provide a useful account.

24 The law/psychiatry relation is perhaps one of the more interesting of such questions.

25 H. C. Erik Midelfort, 'Madness and civilisation in early modern Europe: a reappraisal of Michel Foucault' in B. C. Malament (ed.), *After the Reformation: Essays in Honor of J. H. Hexter* (Manchester, Manchester University Press, 1980).

26 P. Sedgwick, *Psycho Politics* (London, Pluto Press, 1982) basing himself on Midelfort, *op. cit.*, refers to 'Foucault's empirical deficiencies' (p. 272). Needless to say, Sedgwick's account of Foucault is based on the shortened English edition.

27 R. Descartes, 'Meditations' in *Discourse on Method and the Meditations* (Harmondsworth, Penguin, 1968), pp. 95–8.

28 M. Foucault, *Histoire de la Folie* (Paris, Gallimard, 1972), p. 57.

29 It is worth remarking on the impression which has sometimes been portrayed of Foucault's putatively idyllic depiction of the status of the mad before the mid-sixteenth century. On this point one can compare a sentence from the English translation referring to the fifteenth century with that of the original French: 'Madmen then led an easy wandering existence' (London,

Tavistock, 1967, p. 8). In the French this appears as 'Les fous alors avaient une existence facilement errante' (Paris, Gallimard, 1972, p. 19). An existence in which madmen wandered freely has become in translation a carefree, undisturbed, bohemian life-style. I would like to thank Colin Gordon for drawing my attention to this point.

30 J. Derrida, 'Cogito and the history of madness' in J. Derrida, *Writing and Difference* (London, Routledge & Kegan Paul, 1978).

31 *Ibid.*, p. 32.

32 *Ibid.*, p. 33; emphasis in original.

33 Foucault was to reply to Derrida in an article entitled 'Mon corps, ce papier, ce feu' published as an appendix to the second edition (Paris, Gallimard, 1972) of *Histoire de la Folie*. This is translated as 'My body, this paper, this fire' in *The Oxford Literary Review*, vol. 4, no. 1 (Autumn 1979). See also the other appendix to the second edition of *Histoire de la Folie* entitled 'La folie, l'absence d'oeuvre' which originally appeared in May 1964 in *La Table Ronde*.

34 Derrida, 'Cogito and the history of madness' in *Writing and Difference*, p. 24.

35 *Ibid.*, p. 40.

36 *Ibid.*, p. 41.

37 M. Foucault, *Histoire de la Folie*, p. 61.

38 *Ibid.*, p. 67.

39 M. Foucault, 'My body, my paper, this fire' in *op. cit.*, p. 16.

40 Derrida, *op. cit.*, p. 53.

41 M. Foucault, 'My body, my paper, this fire', in *op. cit.*, p. 17.

42 *Ibid.*

43 *Ibid.*, p. 27.

44 *Ibid.*

45 *Ibid.*

46 *Ibid.*

47 M. Foucault, *Histoire de la Folie*, p. 82.

48 *Ibid.*

49 *Ibid.*, p. 84.

50 *Ibid.*

51 *Ibid.*, p. 86.

52 *Ibid.*, p. 87.

53 Despite Foucault's occasional references to developments in other countries, *Histoire de la Folie* should be regarded as a history of the conditions of possibility of psychiatry in France rather than Europe as a whole.

54 M. Foucault, *Histoire de la Folie*, p. 88.

55 On this notion of 'police' see: P. Pasquino, 'Theatrum politicum. The Geneaology of capital – police and the state of prosperity', in *Ideology and Consciousness*, no. 4 (Autumn 1978); K. Tribe, 'Introduction in Knemeyer' and Franz-Ludwig Knemeyer, 'Polizei' both in *Economy and Society*, vol. 9. no. 2 (May 1980).

56 M. Foucault, *Histoire de la Folie*, p. 89.

57 Delamare, *Traité de Police*, 4 vols, Paris 1738.

58 M. Foucault, *Histoire de la Folie*, p. 90.

59 *Ibid.*, p. 96.

60 *Ibid*., p. 97.
61 *Ibid*.
62 *Ibid*., p. 102.
63 On the later medicalisation of the modern family and its implicit moralisation cf. J. Donzelot, *La Police des familles* (Paris, Editions de Minuit, 1977).
64 For a discussion of French nineteenth-century psychiatry see R. Castel, *L'ordre psychiatrique* (Paris, Editions de Minuit, 1976). See also my extended review of this text, 'The territory of the psychiatrist' in *Ideology and Consciousness*, no. 7, Autumn 1980.
65 M. Foucault, *Histoire de la Folie*, p. 104.
66 *Ibid*., p. 107.
67 *Ibid*., p. 111.
68 *Ibid*.
69 *Ibid*., p. 97.
70 *Ibid*., p. 113.
71 I.e. in the nineteenth century; cf. R. Castel, *L'ordre psychiatrique*, especially chapter 2.
72 M. Foucault, *Histoire de la Folie*, p. 113.
73 *Ibid*., p. 115.
74 *Ibid*., p. 117; emphasis in original.
75 *Ibid*., pp. 186–31 on examples of the individualisation of madness prior to the nineteenth century.
76 Zacchias (1584–1659) published his *Questions médico-légales* from 1624–1650. Cf. Zacchias, *Questions médico-légales*, 2 vols, Avignon, 1660–1.
77 Cf. Falret, *Des maladies mentales et les asiles d'aliénés* (Paris, 1864), and *Formalités à remplis pour l'admission des insensés à Bicêtre*, both cited by Foucault, *op. cit*., p. 141.
78 R. Castel, in *L'ordre psychiatrique* examines the implications for a nascent psychiatry of the abolition of the *lettre de cachet* in 1790. Cf. ch. 1., 'Le défi de la folie'.
79 *Ibid*., pp. 25 ff.
80 M. Foucault, *Histoire de la Folie*, p. 143.
81 *Ibid*., p. 144.
82 *Ibid*.
83 *Ibid*., p. 145.
84 *Ibid*.
85 *Ibid*., p. 146.
86 Cf. E. H. Ackerknecht, *A Short History of Psychiatry*, (New York, Hafner Publishing Co., 1968) ch. 6 for a useful account of Pinel's psychiatry.
87 Cf. J. De Ferrière, *Dictionnaire de droit et de pratique* (Paris, 1769), article 'Folie' cited in Foucault, *op. cit*., p. 154.
88 M. Foucault, *Histoire de la Folie*, p. 156.
89 *Ibid*.
90 *Ibid*., p. 166.
91 *Ibid*., p. 167.
92 *Ibid*., p. 168.
93 *Ibid*.
94 *Ibid*.; emphasis in original.
95 *Ibid*., p. 174.
96 *Ibid*., p. 177.
97 D. Jonston, *Idée universelle de la médecine*, (1644); Boissier de Sauvages, *Nosologie methodique* (1763); K. Linné, *Genera morborum* (1763); M. A. Weickhard, *Der philosophische Arzt* (1790).

98 M. Foucault, *Histoire de la Folie*, p. 203.
99 Cited in *ibid.*, p. 204.
100 Willis, *De morbis convulsivis* (1681) still spoke of morbific substances; cf. *ibid.*, p. 205.
101 *Ibid.*, p. 205.
102 Cf. M. Foucault, *The Birth of the Clinic* (London, Tavistock, 1973), p. 4 ff, on the role of symptomatology in eighteenth century medicine.
103 M. Foucault, *Histoire de la Folie*, p. 206.
104 Cf. Berg, *Linné et Sauvages* (Lychnos, 1956) cited in *ibid.*, p. 206.
105 M. Foucault, *Histoire de la Folie*, pp. 208–9.
106 *Ibid.*, p. 212.
107 *Ibid.*
108 *Ibid.*, p. 213.
109 P. Pinel, *Dictionnaire des sciences médicales* (1819), cited in *ibid.*, p. 214.
110 *Ibid.*
111 *Ibid.*, p. 215.
112 Cf. *Histoire de la Folie* Pt 2, ch. 2 for a more detailed discussion of the role of the notion of passion in the classical age.
113 *Ibid.*, p. 216.
114 *Ibid.*
115 *Ibid.*, p. 220.
116 *Ibid.*, p. 219.
117 Cf. Cullen, *Institutions de médecine pratique* (1785) cited in *ibid.*, p. 221.
118 *Ibid.*, p. 222.
119 On the question of the cure in relation to medicine cf. G. Canguilhem, 'Une pédagogie de la guérison est-elle possible?', translation forthcoming in *Ideology and Consciousness*, 10/11, 1987.
120 M. Foucault, *Histoire de la Folie*, p. 222.
121 Cf. Hanway, *Réflexions sur l'aération* (1766) and Genneté, *Purification de l'air dans les hopitaux* (1767), both cited in *ibid.*, p. 379.
122 *Ibid.*, p. 375.
123 On the question of the hospital as site of contagion cf. François Béguin, 'La machine à guérir' in M. Foucault *et al.*, *Les machines à guérir* (1976), pp. 56 ff.
124 M. Foucault, *Histoire de la Folie*, p. 378.
125 *Ibid.*, pp. 378–9.
126 *Ibid.*, p. 383.
127 Cf. Buffon, *Histoire Naturelle* in *Oeuvres complètes* (1848), cited in *ibid.*, p. 385.
128 *Ibid.*, p. 391.
129 Cf. G. Canguilhem, 'Une pédagogie de la guérison est-elle possible?' on the notion of milieu as applied to physiology. See also his article 'Le vivant et son milieu' in *La Connaissance de la vie* (Paris, Vrin, 1980).
130 Cf. E. H. Ackerknecht, *A Short History of Psychiatry*. Ackerknecht remarks that 'The real creator of the degeneration theory was Benedict Augustin Morel' (p. 55).
131 M. Foucault, *Histoire de la Folie*, p. 396.
132 Tissot, cited in *ibid.*, p. 395.
133 *Ibid.*, p. 396.
134 It is worth remarking that the French term *aliéné* does not entail the philosophical trappings of a humanism as invoked for example in the early works of Marx.

135 *Ibid.*, p. 400.
136 *Ibid.*, p. 404.
137 *Ibid.*, p. 405.
138 *Ibid.*, p. 406.
139 *Ibid.*, p. 409.
140 Foucault, *op. cit.*, p. 416 notes the outrage expressed at the conditions in the hospitals in the early years of the nineteenth century. Castel, in *L'Ordre Psychiatrique*, shows how this served to 'modernise' the hospital (*ibid.*, pp. 82–5).
141 M. Foucault, *Histoire de la Folie*, p. 418.
142 *Ibid.*, p. 420.
143 *Ibid.*, p. 422.
144 Cf also Labrousse, *La Crise de l'économie francaise à la fin de l'Ancien Régime* (Paris, 1944).
145 On political economy and the concept of poverty see G. Procacci, 'Social economy and the government of poverty' in *Ideology and Consciousness*, no. 4, (Autumn 1978). On the birth of economic discourse see K. Tribe, *Land, Labour and Economic Discourse* (London, Routledge & Kegan Paul, 1978).
146 On this point see also R. Castel, *L'ordre psychiatrique*, p. 71.
147 M. Foucault, *Histoire de la Folie*, p. 435.
148 *Ibid.*, p. 436.
149 *Ibid.*, p. 439.
150 *Ibid.*, p. 445.
151 *Ibid.*, p. 446.
152 *Ibid.*
153 *Ibid.*, p. 447.
154 *Ibid.*, p. 449.
155 *Ibid.*, p. 452.
156 *Ibid.*, p. 453.
157 *Ibid.*, p. 456.
158 *Ibid.*, p. 457.
159 Cf. the following comments by Scull in his *Museums of Madness* (London, Allen Lane, 1979):

> During the nineteenth century, mad-doctors manoeuvred to secure such a position for themselves and acceptance of their particular view of the nature of madness, seeking to transform their existing foothold in the marketplace into a cognitive and practical monopoly of the field, and to acquire for those practising this line of work the status prerogatives 'owed' to professionals – most notably autonomous control by the practitioners themselves over the conditions and conduct of their work. [p. 129] . . . . For professionalization to occur, one group had to succeed in driving out all its competitors or in subordinating all who persisted in this line of work to its authority (p. 130).

160 *Ibid.*, p. 457.
161 *Ibid.*, p. 460.
162 Cf. *ibid.*, p. 462.
163 *Ibid.*, p. 463.
164 See the attempt by P. Berger and S. Pullberg to develop a humanist concept of alienation and objectification in 'Reification and the sociological critique of consciousness' in *New Left Review*, no. 35 (January–February, 1966); see also the response by Ben Brewster in the same issue. There is, of course, no

suggestion that Foucault is proposing an account of the formation of the category of mental illness in the same terms as Berger and Pullberg.

165 M. Foucault, *Histoire de la Folie*, p. 463.
166 Des Essarts, *Dictionnaire de police* (Paris, 1786) cited in *ibid.*, p. 464.
167 *Ibid.*
168 Cited in *ibid.*, p. 464.
169 *Ibid.*, p. 465.
170 *Ibid.*, p. 466.
171 J.-P. Brissot de Warville, *Théorie des lois criminelles*, 2 vols, (Paris, 1781).
172 M. Foucault, *Histoire de la Folie*, p. 469.
173 *Ibid.*, p. 470.
174 Cf. N.-F. Bellart, *Oeuvres* (Paris, 1827).
175 Foucault, *Histoire de la Folie*, p. 474.
176 *Ibid.*, p. 475.
177 *Ibid.*, pp. 475–6.
178 *Ibid.*, p. 479.
179 *Ibid.*, p. 480.
180 *Ibid.*
181 *Ibid.*, p. 481.
182 On the 'golden age' of psychiatry cf. R. Castel, *L'ordre psychiatrique*.
183 Cf. S. Tuke, *Description of the Retreat* (York, Alexander, 1813); on Tuke's doctrine of moral treatment see A. Scull, 'Moral treatment reconsidered: some sociological comments on an episode in the history of British psychiatry' in A. Scull (ed.), *Madhouses, Mad-Doctors, and Madmen* (London, Athlone Press, 1981).
184 K. Doerner, *Madmen and the Bourgeoisie* (Oxford, Blackwell, 1981) discusses this aspect of the *Retreat*, *op. cit.*, pp. 77 ff.
185 M. Foucault, *Histoire de la Folie*, p. 503.
186 *Ibid.*, p. 504.
187 *Ibid.*, p. 510.
188 *Ibid.*, p. 514.
189 *Ibid.*, p. 515.
190 *Ibid.*
191 *Ibid.*
192 *Ibid.*
193 Cf. *ibid.*, pp. 515–23 for Foucault's discussion of these three mechanisms. It would be interesting to pursue the issues Foucault raises here, particularly with regard to such questions as Pinel's use of showers as a judicial measure. On this particular question see the remarks by Colin Gordon in his review of P. Sedgwick, *Psycho Politics* (London, Pluto Press, 1982) in the *Times Literary Supplement*, 16 July 1982.
194 M. Foucault, *Histoire de la Folie*, pp. 522–3.
195 *Ibid.*, p. 525.
196 *Ibid.*, pp. 526–7.
197 Doerner points out that others before Pinel had 'removed the chains' from the insane (Doerner, *op. cit.*, p. 119).
198 M. Foucault, *op. cit.*, p. 533.
199 One can speculate that one of the crucial features of the development of a psychological culture is the face-to-face relation of doctor and patient, however this may be construed. Castel suggests, in *La Gestion des Risques*, that this face-to-face relation is, at least in France, being gradually

supplanted by a decomposition of the subject into a number of 'risk' factors.

200 Foucault, *op. cit.*, p. 535.
201 *Ibid.*, p. 534.
202 *Ibid.*, p. 543.
203 *Ibid.*, p. 544.
204 *Ibid.*
205 *Ibid.*
206 *Ibid.*, p. 548.
207 *Ibid.*, pp. 548–9.
208 *Ibid.*, p. 557.
209 Cf. J. Coulter, *The Social Construction of Mind* (London, Macmillan, 1979), chapter 8.
210 Cf. M. Foucault, 'Questions of method: an interview' in *Ideology and Consciousness*, no. 8, Spring 1981. Here Foucault defines the object of his studies not as discourses and their relation to extra-discursive practices, rather as 'regimes of practices'.
211 Cf. M. Foucault, 'On governmentality' in *Ideology and Consciousness*, no. 6, Autumn 1979.
212 Despite his criticisms of Foucault this is what Sedgwick does in his recent book *Psycho Politics*. Sedgwick's dream is of a collectivist and organised treatment of the mad.
213 On this notion of surfaces of emergence cf. M. Foucault, *The Archaeology of Knowledge* (London, Tavistock, 1972. First published in French, 1969), p. 41.

CHAPTER 5 THE BIRTH OF MEDICINE AND THE INDIVIDUALISATION OF THE BODY

1 Cf. E. H. Ackerknecht, *Medicine at the Paris Hospital, 1794–1848* (Johns Hopkins University Press, 1967).
2 M. Foucault and R. Sennett, 'Sexuality and Solitude' in *London Review of Books*, 21 May–3 June 1981, p. 3.
3 Cf. the introduction to this section.
4 M. Foucault, *The Birth of the Clinic* (London, Tavistock, 1973), p. 198.
5 *Ibid.*
6 *Ibid.*
7 *Ibid.*
8 I am thinking here in particular of the works of Gaston Bachelard on the history and philosophy of science. Cf. G. Bachelard, *Le nouvel esprit scientifique* (Presses Universitaires de France, 1934); *Le rationalisme appliqué* (Paris, Presses Universitaires de France, 1949); *Le Matérialisme rationnel* (Paris, Presses Universitaires de France, 1953).
9 Quoted in A. Treacher and G. Baruch, 'Towards a critical history of the psychiatric profession' in D. Ingleby (ed.), *Critical Psychiatry* (Harmondsworth, Penguin, 1981), p. 136. On Virchow see E. H. Ackerknecht, *Rudolf Virchow: Doctor, Statesman, Anthropologist* (Madison, University of Wisconsin Press, 1953).
10 M. Foucault, 'The politics of health in the eighteenth century' in C. Gordon (ed.),

Power/Knowledge (Brighton, Harvester, 1980). This article originally appeared in M. Foucault (ed.), *Les machines à guérir* (1976).

11 M. Foucault, 'The politics of health in the eighteenth century' in *op. cit.*, p. 166.

12 Cf. the discussion of Tuke and the York *Retreat* in the previous chapter. There it is 'mental' health rather than physical health which is at issue.

13 M. Foucault, 'The politics of health in the eighteenth century' in *op. cit.*, pp. 167–8.

14 *Ibid.*, pp. 168–9.

15 *Ibid.*, p. 169.

16 *Ibid.*

17 *Ibid.*, p. 170.

18 Delamare, *Traité de police*, 4 vols, (Paris, 1738).

19 K. Doerner, *Madmen and the Bourgeoisie* (Oxford, Blackwell, 1981) provides a brief discussion of the German system of medical police (Pt. 3, ch. 1). See also G. Oestreich, *Neostoicism and the Early Modern State* (Cambridge University Press, 1982).

20 Cf. F. Guery and D. Deleule, *Le Corps productif* (Paris, Maison Mame, 1972). See also G. Canguilhem, 'Machine et organisme' in his *La Connaissance de la Vie* (Paris, Vrin, 1980).

21 On the *enquêtes* of the late eighteenth century in France see: J. Meyer, 'Une enquête de l'Académie de médecine sur les épidemies (1774–1794)' in *Annales E.S.C.* July–August 1966; C. Hannaway, 'The Société Royale de Médecine and epidemics in The Ancien Régime' in *Bulletin of the History of Medicine*, vol. 56, 1972; J.-P. Peter, 'Les mots et les objets de la maladie' in *La Revue Historique*, July 1971.

22 I. Hacking, 'How should we do the history of statistics?' in *Ideology and Consciousness*, no. 8 (Spring, 1981).

23 *Ibid.*, p. 16.

24 *Ibid.*

25 M. Foucault, 'The politics of health in the eighteenth century' in *op. cit.*, p. 172.

26 M. Foucault, *The Birth of the Clinic*, p. ix.

27 On this question of visibility and of 'rendering the visible' it is worth noting Foucault's references to Paul Klee. Cf. Foucault's comments in 'L'Homme est-il mort? Un entretien avec Michel Foucault' (interview with Claude Bonnefoy) in *Arts et Loisirs*, no. 35, May 25–31, 1966.

28 Boissier de Sauvages, *Nosologie méthodique*, 10 vols, 1772.

29 Ph. Pinel, *Nosographie philosophique*, (Paris, year VI).

30 M. Foucault, *The Birth of the Clinic*, p. 4.

31 Cf. the previous chapter where the role of this 'botanical model' is discussed in relation to the question of madness.

32 Th. Sydenham, *Médecine pratique* (1784), quoted in M. Foucault, *The Birth of the Clinic*, p. 7.

33 M. Foucault, *The Birth of the Clinic*, p. 8.

34 *Ibid.*, p. 10.

35 *Ibid.*, p. 15.

36 *Ibid.*
37 *Ibid.*
38 *Ibid.*
39 *Ibid.*
40 *Ibid.*, p. 16.
41 *Ibid.*
42 On the displacement of the eighteenth-century nosographies cf. the previous chapter and the same shift as it occurs with reference to a theoretical reflection on madness.
43 Cf. C. C. Hannaway, 'The Société Royale de Médecine and epidemics in the Ancien Régime' in *Bulletin of the History of Medicine*, vol. 46 (1972); J. Meyer, 'Une enquête de l'Académie de médecine sur les épidemies (1774–1794)' in *Annales E.S.C.* July–August, 1966.
44 Cf. C. C. Hannaway *op. cit.*
45 Cf. J. Meyer *op. cit.* Meyer notes the strategic role which metereological instruments played in this *enquête*; he notes also the unreliability of many of those employed, and the difficulties which many doctors had in replying to the questionnaires sent them.
46 Cf. Hannaway, *op. cit.*
47 M. Foucault, *The Birth of the Clinic*, p. 26.
48 *Ibid.*, p. 34.
49 J.-P. Peter, 'Les mots et les objets de la maladie' in *La Revue Historique* (July, 1971), p. 33.
50 J.-P. Peter, 'Le grand rêve de l'ordre médical, en 1770 et aujourd'hui' in *Autrement*, no. 4 (Winter, 1975–6), p. 185. Emphasis in original.
51 G. Canguilhem, *Le Normal et le Pathologique* (Paris, Presses Universitaires de France, 1966), p. 75.
52 Cf. T. Gelfand, 'The hospice of the Paris College of Surgery (1774–1793) "A unique and valuable institution" ', in *Bulletin of the History of Medicine*, vol. 47 (1973).
53 Gelfand, *op. cit.*, remarks that 'Apparently, the hospice, because of its small size, had only one position for a resident surgical student or *interne*, also known as a student "wearing a *tablier*" ' (p. 384).
54 Cf. Anne Thalamy, 'La médicalisation de l'hopital' in M. Foucault (ed.), *Les Machines à guérir* (1976).
55 M. Foucault, *The Birth of the Clinic*, p. 51.
56 Foucault notes that it was in the military hospitals that clinical teaching was first organised; in *ibid.*, p. 58.
57 Cf. in addition to Foucault, *op. cit.*, E. H. Ackerknecht, *Medicine at the Paris Hospital, 1794–1848.*
58 M. Foucault, *op. cit.*, p. 68.
59 *Ibid.*, p. 69.
60 *Ibid.*, p. 64; emphasis in original.
61 Cf. E. H. Ackerknecht, *op. cit.*, p. 32.
62 M. Foucault, op. cit., p. 70.
63 Ackerknecht, *op. cit.*, p. 32.
64 The law was enacted on 14 Frimaire, Year III.
65 Cf. Ackerknecht, *op. cit.*, p. 32.
66 Foucault, *Birth of the Clinic*, p. 71.
67 *Rapport de J.-M. Calès sur les Écoles spéciales de Santé*, (12

Prairial Year IV), cited in Foucault, *op. cit.*, p. 75.

68 Foucault, *Birth of the Clinic*, p. 76.
69 *Ibid.*, p. 77.
70 *Ibid.*
71 *Ibid.*, p. 78.
72 *Ibid.*
73 *Ibid.*
74 *Ibid.*, p. 79.
75 Cf. Ackerknecht, *op. cit.*, pp. 38–9.
76 Foucault, *op. cit.*, p. 81.
77 *Ibid.*
78 *Ibid.*
79 *Ibid.*
80 *Ibid.*, p. 82.
81 *Ibid.*, p. 83.
82 *Ibid.*, p. 84.
83 On Chambon cf. T. Gelfand, 'A clinical ideal: Paris 1789' in *Bulletin of the History of Medicine*, vol. 51, 1977.
84 Cf. the memoir on clinical medicine written by Chambon in 1789 and discussed in Gelfand, *op. cit*. The quote in the text is from Gelfand, *op. cit.*, p. 406.
85 Gelfand, *op. cit.*, p. 407.
86 Cf. Roy Porter, *English Society in the Eighteenth Century* (Harmondsworth, Penguin, 1982), p. 303 on English hospitals around this period.
87 Chambon, quoted in Gelfand, *op. cit.*, p. 407.
88 Gelfand, *op. cit.*, p. 408.
89 *Ibid.*; emphasis in original.
90 *Ibid.*, p. 409.
91 Foucault, *The Birth of the Clinic*, p. 84.
92 *Ibid.*, p. 85.
93 *Ibid.*, p. 89.
94 *Ibid.*
95 *Ibid.*
96 *Ibid.*, p. 90.
97 *Ibid.*, pp. 97–8.
98 *Ibid.*, p. 105.
99 *Ibid.*, p. 109.
100 *Ibid.*, p. 115.
101 On the question of language and medical observation cf. R. Barthes, 'Sémiologie et médecine' in *Les Sciences de la Folie* (Paris, Mouton, 1972); J.-P. Peter, 'Les mots et les objets de la maladie' in *La Revue Historique* (July 1971).
102 M. Foucault, *The Birth of the Clinic*, p. 115.
103 *Ibid.*, p. 114.
104 *Ibid.*, p. 115.
105 X. Bichat, *Anatomie générale appliquée à la physiologie et à médecine*, 3 vols, (Paris, 1801); *Traité des membranes* (Paris, 1807). On Bichat's 'vitalism' cf. E. Haigh, 'The roots of the vitalism of Xavier Bichat' in *Bulletin of the History of Medicine* vol. 49, 1975. Haigh argues that Bichat's tissue theory 'quite clearly sprang from and was supported by Bichat's vitalist assumptions' (*op. cit.*, p. 72). This is, of course, contrary to Foucault's interpretation.
106 M. Foucault, *The Birth of the Clinic*, p. 125.
107 *Ibid.*, p. 128.
108 *Ibid.*, p. 129.
109 F. Jacob, *The Logic of Living Systems* (London, Allen Lane, 1974), p. 113.
110 M. Foucault, *The Birth of the Clinic*, p. 136.
111 *Ibid.*, p. 137.
112 *Ibid.*, p. 139.
113 Cf. Bichat, *Anatomie générale*,

vol. I, p. xcix, cited in *ibid.*, p. 140.

114 Cf. Bichat, *Recherches Physiologiques sur la Vie et la Mort* (Paris, Magendie, 1796) pp. 234, 238, 251, 253.

115 M. Foucault, *The Birth of the Clinic*, p. 142.

116 *Ibid.*

117 *Ibid.*, p. 117.

118 Cf. the previous chapter of this study.

119 Cf. Bichat, *Recherches physiologiques sur la vie et la mort* (Paris, Marabout, 1793) quoted in M. Foucault (ed.), *Les Machines à guérir*, p. 26.

120 M. Foucault, *The Birth of the Clinic*, p. 149.

121 *Ibid.*, p. 155.

122 Cf. the previous chapter where the concept of degeneration is discussed in relation to the emergence of psychiatry.

123 M. Foucault, *The Birth of the Clinic*, p. 158.

124 *Ibid.*, p. 137.

125 Cf. Barthes, 'Sémiologie et médecine' in *op. cit.*

126 M. Foucault, *The Birth of the Clinic*, p. 159.

127 *Ibid.*

128 *Ibid.*, p. 161.

129 *Ibid.*, p. 162.

130 *Ibid.*, p. 167.

131 Cf. Foucault's discussion of the moral problems posed by auscultation, particularly in the case of women. The stethoscope was to provide a solution to these difficulties; it was, Foucault argues, 'the measure of a prohibition transformed into disgust, and a material obstacle' (*ibid.*, p. 163).

132 *Ibid.*, p. 168.

133 *Ibid.*, pp. 168–9.

134 *Ibid.*, p. 170.

135 Cf. F. Dagognet, 'Archaeologie ou histoire de la médecine' in *Critique*, vol. 21 (1965), p. 444.

136 On the theory of fevers of the late eighteenth century and early nineteenth century see W. F. Bynum, 'Cullen and the study of fevers in Britain, 1760–1820' in W. F. Bynum and V. Nutton (eds), *Theories of Fever from Antiquity to the Enlightenment* (London, Wellcome Institute for the History of Medicine, 1981); D. C. Smith, 'Medical science, medical practice, and the emerging concept of typhus in mid-eighteenth century Britain', *ibid.*

137 M. Foucault, *The Birth of the Clinic*, p. 180.

138 E. H. Ackerknecht, *Medicine at the Paris Hospital, 1794–1848*, p. 61 Ackerknecht has remarked also on the revolution brought about by Broussais's conception of fevers that

> Irritation was always a local phenomenon that turned into general inflammation, which could, in turn, be observed in the form of anatomical lesions. Fever was only a symptom of inflammation. 'Essential fevers' were therefore non-existent; they could always be reduced to local lesions. Anatomical lesions had to be studied according to tissues (*ibid.*, p. 68).

139 M. Foucault, *The Birth of the Clinic*, p. 188.
140 *Ibid.*
141 *Ibid.*, p. 189.
142 *Ibid.*, p. 192.
143 On this notion of 'technologies' cf. C. Gordon, 'Other Inquisitions' in *Ideology and Consciousness*, no. 6, 1979, p. 38.
144 Cf. the previous chapter. There Foucault's account is distinguished from a humanist account of the process whereby subjects are held to be reduced to objects.
145 Cf. G. Canguilhem, 'Le normal et le pathologique' in G. Canguilhem, *La Connaissance de la Vie* (Paris, Vrin, 1980). Canguilhem remarks that 'Sans les concepts de normal et de pathologique la pensée et l'activité du médecin sont incompréhensibles' (*ibid.*, p. 155). Cf. also his *Le Normal et la Pathologique* (Paris, Presses Universitaires de France, 1966).

CHAPTER 6 THE HUMAN SCIENCES AND THE BIRTH OF MAN

1 Cf. I. Hacking, 'Michel Foucault's Immature Science', *Nous*, 13 (1979), Indiana University.
2 On this notion of 'event' and what Foucault terms 'eventalisation' see his comments in 'Questions of method: an interview' in *Ideology and Consciousness*, no. 8 (Spring 1981), pp. 6 ff.
3 I have deliberately avoided any attempt to assess the difficulties which might be raised against the notion of *episteme*. My concern in this study is not to assess the adequacy of Foucault's conceptual schema in this respect. Suffice it to say that I regard a reasonably limited notion of *episteme*, understood as the interlocking system of conceptual possibilities between specified bodies of knowledge, as far from a hindrance to the sort of enquiry Foucault undertakes in *The Order of Things*.
4 An example of such criticism can be found in the article by G. Huppert, '*Divinatio et Eruditio*: thoughts on Foucault' in *History and Theory*, vol. 13, no. 3, 1974, pp. 191–207.
5 M. Foucault, *The Order of Things* (London, Tavistock, 1970), p. ix.
6 *Ibid.*
7 *Ibid.*, p. x.
8 *Ibid.*, p. xi.
9 *Ibid.*
10 *Ibid.*
11 In previous chapters I have presented Foucault's account of the formation of modern medicine and psychiatry in terms of the notion of *conditions of possibility*. It would, however, not be unfair to imply that in places Foucault utilises there a weak notion of causality in respect of certain changes

which made possible medicine and psychiatry.

12 Foucault has spoken of 'lightening the weight of causality' in 'Questions of method: an interview', *op. cit.*, p. 6.

13 M. Foucault, *The Order of Things*, p. xiv.

14 I. Hacking, *The Emergence of Probability* (Cambridge University Press, 1975).

15 Francois Jacob, *The Logic of Living Systems: a history of heredity* (London, Allen Lane, 1974).

16 Jacob, *op. cit.*, pp. 20–1.

17 M. Foucault, *The Order of Things*, p. 56.

18 *Ibid.*, p. 59.

19 *Ibid.*

20 *Ibid.*, p. 71.

21 M. Foucault, *The Order of Things*, p. 62.

22 Jacob, *op. cit.*, p. 29.

23 Jacob, *op. cit.*, p. 32.

24 M. Foucault, *The Order of Things*, p. 63. On the linguistic sign in the classical age cf. R. Donzé, *La Grammaire générale et raisonnée de Port-Royal*, Pt 2, ch. 1.

25 For a discussion of the emergence of probability which, for its general approach, owes something to *The Order of Things*, cf. I. Hacking, *The Emergence of Probability op. cit.* See also the brief account in K. M. Baker, *Condorcet: from Natural Philosophy to Social Mathematics* (University of Chicago Press, 1975), pp. 155 ff.

26 M. Foucault, *The Order of Things*, p. 63.

27 *Ibid.*, p. 63; emphasis in original.

28 *Ibid.*, pp. 63–4.

29 *Ibid.*, p. 65.

30 *Ibid.*

31 *Ibid.*, p. 67.

32 This figure is taken from *The Order of Things*, p. 72.

33 J. Culler, *Saussure* (London, Fontana, 1976), pp. 55–6; emphasis added.

34 M. Foucault, *The Order of Things*, p. 73.

35 On language in the classical age see also Foucault's discussion of general grammar in his 'Introduction' to Arnauld et Lancelot, *Grammaire Générale et Raisonnée* (Paris, Republications Paulet, 1969). Secondary sources which have proved helpful for an understanding of language in the classical age are: J.-Cl. Chevalier, *Histoire de la Syntaxe: naissance de la notion de complément dans la grammaire francaise, 1530–1750* (Genève, Librairie Droz, 1968); R. Donzé, *La Grammaire Générale et Raisonnée de Port-Royal* (Editions Francke, Berne, 1967); G. Mounin, *Histoire de la Linguistique* (Paris, Presses Universitaires de France, 1974); R. H. Robins, *A Short History of Linguistics* (London, Longman, 2nd edn, 1979).

An interesting further aspect of general grammar is the question of pedagogy. On this see Chevalier, *op. cit.*, pp. 497 ff.; see also J.-Cl. Chevalier, 'La grammaire générale et la pédagogie au XVIIIe siecle' in

Le Francais moderne, January 1972; T. Hordé, 'La théorie du signe/du sujet et l'organisation de l'école. Notes sur les Idéologues' in *Cahiers critiques de la litterature* no. 5, (Autumn 1978).

36 M. Foucault, *The Order of Things*, p. 78.
37 *Ibid.*
38 *Ibid.*
39 *Ibid.*, p. 79.
40 *Ibid.*, p. 81.
41 *Ibid.*, p. 82.
42 *Ibid.*, pp. 82–3.
43 Foucault, *The Order of Things*, p. 83; emphasis in original.
44 On the shift from general grammar to comparative grammar cf. G. Mounin, *op. cit.*, chs 3 and 4; see also R. H. Robins, *op. cit.*
45 Foucault, *op. cit.*, p. 91.
46 On this point cf. the comments by Donzé in *La Grammaire générale et raisonnée de Port-Royal*, p. 35. See also Chevalier, *Histoire de la syntaxe*, pp. 498–9 where he distances himself a little from Foucault's account by identifying in the Port-Royal approach a notion similar to Chomsky's concept of 'deep structure'.
47 Foucault, *op. cit.*, p. 91.
48 On the classification of the parts of discourse proposed in the Port-Royal 'Grammar' cf. R. Donzé, *La Grammaire générale et raisonnée de Port Royal*, p. 60 ff.
49 M. Foucault, *The Order of Things*, p. 92.
50 *Ibid.*, p. 93.
51 *Ibid.*, p. 94.
52 *Ibid.*
53 *Ibid.*
54 The disappearance of general grammar is generally identified by means of the appearance of comparative grammar, which in turn is located with the European 'discovery' of Sanskrit. Referring to this shift R. H. Robins in his *A Short History of Linguistics* remarks that:

> The European discovery of Sanskrit was the primary source of this development, and a number of the early scholars in historical linguistics were themselves Sanskritists, such as the brothers A. W. and F. Schlegel (1767–1845 and 1772–1829), F. Bopp (1791–1867), and A. F. Pott (1802–87) (*ibid.*, pp. 169–70).

Robins notes that the study of Sanskrit took place before the nineteenth century (*ibid.*, p. 104), although the first Sanskrit grammar in English was published early in the nineteenth century (*ibid.*, p. 135).

55 M. Foucault, *The Order of Things*, p. 96.
56 *Ibid.*, p. 103.
57 *Ibid.*, p. 104.
58 *Ibid.*, p. 105.
59 Cf. Georges Mounin, *Histoire de la linguistique*, p. 131.
60 M. Foucault, *The Order of Things*, p. 112.
61 *Ibid.*
62 *Ibid.*, p. 113.
63 *Ibid.*, p. 114.
64 *Ibid.*, p. 117.

65 *Ibid.*
66 *Ibid.*, p. 119.
67 *Ibid.*, p. 120.
68 *Ibid.*, p. 132. On natural history in seventeenth- and eighteenth-century France see J. Roger, *Les Sciences de la vie dans la pensée Francaise du XVIIIe siècle* (Paris, Armand Colin, 1963; second edn 1971).
69 *Ibid.*, p. 131.
70 *Ibid.*, p. 158.
71 *Ibid.*, p. 159.
72 F. Jacob, *The Logic of Living Systems*, pp. 47–8.
73 *Ibid.*, p. 87.
74 M. Foucault, *The Order of Things*, p. 161.
75 *Ibid.*
76 *Ibid.*
77 *Ibid.*, p. 177.
78 *Ibid.*
79 On this topic cf. K. Tribe, *Land, Labour and Economic Discourse* (London, Routledge & Kegan Paul, 1978).
80 M. Foucault, *The Order of Things*, p. 202.
81 *Ibid.*
82 *Ibid.*, p. 203.
83 *Ibid.*
84 *Ibid.*
85 *Ibid.*, p. 208.
86 *Ibid.*, p. 218.
87 *Ibid.*
88 On this aspect of *The Order of Things* see G. Canguilhem, 'Mort de l'homme ou épuisement du cogito' in *Critique*, vol. 23, no. 242 (1967). It is worth noting the following comment by Keith Michael Baker on this issue, especially since Baker is generally sympathetic to Foucault's account:

> In many ways, the view of Condorcet's thought set forth here corresponds closely to Foucault's analysis of the fundamental mode of Enlightenment thinking. His argument that a human science was simply unthinkable in this period, on the other hand, seems to be sheer intellectual provocation. Logically, it rests on an ironclad definition of the human sciences that simply refuses the name to other possible conceptions. Historically, it flies in the face of the evidence of all those writers, great and small, for whom the attempt to create a science of man represented the opportunity to become the Newton of the moral world (K. M. Baker, *Condorcet*, p. viii).

89 On the role of Smith in relation to modern economic discourse, see Keith Tribe, *Land, Labour and Economic Discourse*. Tribe suggests that Smith's removal of the category circulation was central to the 'disarray' introduced into economic discourse by *The Wealth of Nations*.
90 G. Mounin, *Histoire de la linguistique* remarks on this displacement as it appears in early nineteenth-century linguistics that 'The key word of the new linguistic science will be much less the word *system* or *structure* (already in

common use), than the word *organism*' (*ibid.*, p. 162).
91 This transformation is central also to the shifts identified in *The Birth of the Clinic*. On this see the previous chapter of this study.
92 F. Jacob, *The Logic of Living Systems*, p. 85.
93 This is similar to Foucault's argument in *The Birth of the Clinic*: see in particular chapter 9, 'The visible invisible'.
94 On vitalism cf. G. Canguilhem, 'Aspects du vitalisme' in his *La Connaissance de la Vie* (Paris, Vrin, 1980).
95 Foucault attributes this to the fundamental position of language analysis in the classical episteme: 'Of all the forms of non-quantitative order it was the most immediate, the least deliberate, the most profoundly linked to the movement of representation itself' (M. Foucault, *The Order of Things*, p. 232).
96 J. Culler, *Saussure*, pp. 60–1.
97 M. Foucault, *The Order of Things*, p. 235.
98 *Ibid.*
99 *Ibid.*, p. 236.
100 *Ibid.*, pp. 280–1.
101 *Ibid.*, p. 238.
102 *Ibid.*, p. 242.
103 *Ibid.*
104 *Ibid.*
105 *Ibid.*, p. 243.
106 *Ibid.*, p. 244.
107 *Ibid.*, pp. 248–9; emphasis added.
108 *Ibid.*, p. 250.
109 *Ibid.*, p. 252. On this point see also G. Canguilhem, 'Mort de l'homme ou épuisement du cogito', *op. cit.*
110 *Ibid.*, p. 296.
111 *Ibid.*, p. 309.
112 Jacob, *The Logic of Living Systems*, p. 33.
113 M. Foucault, *The Order of Things*, p. 310.
114 *Ibid.*, p. 311.
115 *Ibid.*, p. 312.
116 *Ibid.*, pp. 313–14.
117 *Ibid.*, p. 319.
118 *Ibid.*
119 *Ibid.*
120 Cf. Foucault's comments on his approach in *The Order of Things* in M. Foucault, 'Truth and power', in M. Morris and P. Patton (eds), *Michel Foucault: Power, Truth, Strategy* (Sydney, Feral Publications, 1979).
121 M. Foucault, *The Order of Things*, p. 324.
122 *Ibid.*, p. 325.
123 On this point see the discussion of *Histoire de la Folie* in chapter 4 of this study. There it is a question of a knowledge of the 'interior' of the subject.
124 M. Foucault, *The Order of Things*, p. 326.
125 *Ibid.*, p. 327.
126 *Ibid.*, p. 328.
127 *Ibid.*
128 *Ibid.*, p. 329.
129 *Ibid.*, p. 330.
130 *Ibid.*, p. 331.
131 *Ibid.*, pp. 334–5.
132 *Ibid.*, p. 335.
133 *Ibid.*, p. 338.
134 *Ibid.*, p. 347.
135 *Ibid.*
136 *Ibid.*
137 *Ibid.*, p. 348.
138 *Ibid.*, p. 352.

139 *Ibid.*, p. 353.
140 *Ibid.*, p. 356.
141 *Ibid.*, p. 357.
142 *Ibid.*
143 *Ibid.*, p. 358.
144 *Ibid.*, p. 360.
145 Cf. K. Goldstein, *The Organism* (American Book Company, 1939); *Human Nature in the Light of Psychopathology* (New York, Schocken, 1940; paperback edn, 1963).
146 Cf. M. Mauss, *Sociologie et Anthropologie* (Paris, Presses Universitaires de France, 1968). This is a collection of essays which covers the period 1902–38.
147 Cf. G. Dumezil, *Mythe et Épopée*, vol. 1, 'L'idéologie des trois fonctions dans les épopées des peuples indo-européens' (Paris, Gallimard, 1968) and vol. 3, 'Histoires Romaines' (Paris, Gallimard, 1973).
148 Cf. in particular, E. Durkheim, *The Division of Labour in Society* (New York, Macmillan, 1964).
149 M. Foucault, *The Order of Things*, pp. 360–1.
150 *Ibid.*, p. 362.
151 *Ibid.*
152 *Ibid.*, p. 363.
153 *Ibid.*, p. 364.
154 *Ibid.*
155 *Ibid.*
156 *Ibid.*
157 On this notion of 'mature' science cf. I Hacking, 'Michel Foucault's immature science' in *Nous*, vol. 13 (1979); see also H. Putnam, *Meaning and the Moral Sciences* (London, Routledge & Kegan Paul, 1978).
158 M. Foucault, *The Order of Things*, p. 366.
159 *Ibid.*
160 *Ibid.*, pp. 366–7.
161 *Ibid.*, p. 373.
162 *Ibid.*, p. 376. On Foucault's account of psychoanalysis in *The Order of Things* as well as in his more recent work, cf. J. Forrester, 'Michel Foucault and the history of psychoanalysis' in *History of Science*, vol. 18 (1980).
163 M. Foucault, *The Order of Things*, p. 374.
164 *Ibid.*, p. 375.
165 *Ibid.*
166 *Ibid.*, p. 377.
167 *Ibid.*, p. 378.
168 *Ibid.*
169 *Ibid.*, p. 379.
170 *Ibid.*, p. 380.
171 *Ibid.*, p. 381.
172 *Ibid.*
173 See also Foucault's discussion of general grammar in the 'Introduction to Arnauld et Lancelot, *Grammaire générale et raisonnée* (Paris, Republications Paulet, 1969).
174 M. Foucault, *The Order of Things*, p. 382.
175 *Ibid.*, p. 383.
176 *Ibid.*, p. 384.
177 *Ibid.*, p. 386.
178 Cf. M. Foucault, 'Entretien' in *La Quinzaine littéraire* (1–15 March 1968), p. 20.
179 M. Foucault, *The Order of Things*, p. 387.
180 See above, chapters 5 and 6.
181 The effect of *Histoire de la Folie* on the critical examination of psychiatry is so pervasive that it is almost irrelevant to cite individual studies. Cf. however

the recent book by Peter Sedgwick, *Psycho Politics* in which the title of his chapter which discussed *Histoire de la Folie* is called 'Michel Foucault: the anti-history of psychiatry'. The discussion of *Histoire de la Folie* in Britain has tended to be limited to the shortened edition.

182 Perhaps the best current example of this is I. Illich, *Limits to Medicine* (Harmondsworth, Penguin, 1977). See also I. Kennedy, *The Unmasking of Medicine* (London, Allen & Unwin, 1981).

183 M. Foucault, 'Truth and Power', in M. Morris and P. Patton (eds), *Michel Foucault: Power, Truth, Strategy* (Sydney, Feral Publications, 1979), p. 32.

184 M. Foucault, 'L'homme est-il mort? Un entretien avec Michel Foucault' in *Arts et Loisirs*, no. 35 (25–31 May 1966), p. 8.

185 Cf. J.-P. Sartre, *Critique de la raison dialectique* (Paris, Gallimard, 1960); translated as *Critique of Dialectical Reason* (London, New Left Books, 1976).

186 G. Canguilhem, 'Mort de l'homme ou épuisement du cogito?' in *Critique*, vol. 23, no. 242 (July 1967).

187 *Ibid.*, pp. 614–15.

188 *Ibid.*, p. 618.

189 M. Foucault, 'L'homme est-il mort? Un entretien avec Michel Foucault', *op. cit.*, p. 9.

190 R. Castel in *La Gestion des risques* (Paris, Editions de Minuit, 1981) suggests that the category of subject is being partially broken down in current shifts in French psychiatric 'administration'. The individual patient of classical psychiatry – the 'dangerous individual' – is, he argues, being supplanted by the category of 'risks' which permits a decomposition of the subject into a number of 'risk factors' which can then be administered outside the framework of the doctor-patient relation.

191 As remarked above, note 3, I have omitted discussion of the desirability of talking in terms of the notion of *episteme*. I suggested that for the purposes of this study it could be deemed to have a definite utility in demonstrating the connections between determinate bodies of knowledge.

192 M. Foucault, 'L'homme est-il mort? Un entretien avec Michel Foucault', *op. cit.*, p. 8.

193 Cf. M. Foucault, 'Questions of method: an interview' in *Ideology and Consciousness*, no. 8 (Spring 1981), p. 5.

194 Cf. P. Berger and S. Pullberg, 'Reification and the sociological critique of consciousness' in *New Left Review*, no. 35 (January–February 1966).

CHAPTER 7 FROM DISCIPLINARY POWER TO GOVERNMENTALITY

1 Cf. Alan Sheridan, *Michel Foucault: The Will to Truth* (London/New York, Tavistock, 1980). For a more sensitive account of the effect of political events on Foucault's writings cf. Paul Patton, 'Of Power and Prisons', in M. Morris and P. Patton (eds), *Michel Foucault: Power, Truth, Strategy* (Sydney, Feral Publications, 1979).
2 For a discussion of the notion of genealogy Cf. M. Foucault, 'Nietzsche, Genealogy, History', in D. F. Bouchard (ed.), *Michel Foucault: Language, Counter-Memory, Practice* (Oxford, Blackwell, 1977).
3 M. Foucault, 'Truth and Power' in C. Gordon (ed.), *M. Foucault, Power/Knowledge* (Brighton, Harvester Press, 1980).
4 On this question cf. the discussion by P. Patton, 'Of Power and Prisons'.
5 This view of the disparity of Foucault's studies is suggested in M. Cousins and A. Hussain, *Michel Foucault* (Basingstoke, Macmillan Education, 1984).
6 At the time of writing only Volumes One and Two have been translated. These are: *Volume One: An Introduction* (Harmondsworth, Penguin, 1981); *Volume Two: The Use of Pleasure* (New York, Viking, 1986). Volume Three is *Le Souci de Soi* (Paris, Gallimard, 1984).
7 Published in English as: 'The Order of Discourse', in R. Young (ed.), *Untying the Text* (London, Routledge & Kegan Paul, 1981).
8 On *Discipline and Punish* see the discussions in A. Sheridan, *Michel Foucault*, and M. Cousins and A. Hussain, *Michel Foucault*. See also P. Patton, 'Of Power and Prisons'.
9 Gilles Deleuze, 'Ecrivain non: un nouveau cartographie', in *Critique*, no. 343, December 1975, pp. 1207–27. Republished in G. Deleuze, *Foucault* (Paris, Editions de Minuit, 1986). See also F. Ewald, 'Anatomie et corps politiques', in *Critique*, no. 343 (December 1975), pp. 1228–65.
10 Such an interpretation is suggested in D. Melossi, 'Institutions of social control and the capitalist organization of work' in B. Fine *et al.* (eds), *Capitalism and the Rule of Law* (London, Hutchinson, 1979). See also the essay by J. Lea, 'Discipline and capitalist development', in Fine *et al.*, *op. cit.*
11 Cited in M. Foucault, *Discipline and Punish* (London, Allen Lane, 1977), p. 16.
12 M. Foucault, *Discipline and Punish*, p. 17.
13 Cf. P. Pasquino, 'Criminology: the birth of a special savoir', in *Ideology and Consciousness*, no. 7 (Autumn 1980), pp. 17–32.
14 On the interrelation between legal and psychiatric forms of

judgment cf. M. Foucault, 'About the concept of the "dangerous individual" in 19th century legal psychiatry', *International Journal of Law and Psychiatry*, vol. 1, pp. 1–18, 1978.

15 M. Foucault, *Discipline and Punish*, p. 23.

16 *Ibid.*, p. 24.

17 *Ibid.*, p. 126.

18 *Ibid.*, p. 137.

19 *Ibid.*, p. 304.

20 On the notion of regulatory practices of the self and the ways in which it can be understood in relation to psychiatry cf. P. Miller and N. Rose (eds), *The Power of Psychiatry* (Cambridge, Polity Press, 1986). See also R. Castel, F. Castel and A. Lovell, *The Psychiatric Society* (New York, Columbia University Press, 1982).

21 M. Foucault, *Discipline and Punish*, p. 256.

22 F. Chatelet and E. Pisier-Kouchner, *Les Conceptions Politiques du XXe Siecle* (Paris, Presses Universitaires de France, 1981).

23 M. Foucault, 'Questions of method: an interview', *Ideology and Consciousness*, no. 8 (Spring 1981), pp. 3–14.

24 P. Patton, 'Of Power and Prisons', pp. 123–4.

25 *Ibid.*, p. 124.

26 Cf. N. Rose, *The Psychological Complex: Social Regulation and the Psychology of the Individual* (London, Routledge & Kegan Paul, 1985). See also D. Armstrong, *Political Anatomy of the Body*, (Cambridge University Press, 1983).

27 Cf. P. Miller, 'Psychotherapy of Work and Unemployment', in P. Miller and N. Rose (eds), *The Power of Psychiatry*.

28 Richard Sennett in M. Foucault and R. Sennett, 'Sexuality and Solitude', *London Review of Books* (21 May–3 June 1981), p. 3.

29 M. Foucault, *The History of Sexuality, Volume One: An Introduction* (Harmondsworth, Penguin, 1981).

30 M. Foucault, 'The life of infamous men', in M. Morris and P. Patton, *Michel Foucault: Power, Truth, Strategy*.

31 M. Foucault, 'The life of infamous men', p. 89.

32 M. Foucault, *The History of Sexuality, Volume One*, p. 93.

33 They have been criticised particularly in D. Lecourt, *Dissidence ou révolution?* (Paris, Maspéro, 1978); and N. Poulantzas, *State, Power, Socialism* (London, New Left Books, 1978).

34 On this question cf. my comments in the Introduction.

35 M. Foucault, 'Omnes et Singulatim: towards a criticism of "political reason" ', reprinted in S. McMurrin (ed.), *The Tanner Lectures on Human Values* II (Salt Lake City, University of Utah Press, 1981).

36 On these two sets of doctrines cf. the excellent discussion in G. Oestreich, *Neostoicism and the early modern state*

(Cambridge University Press, 1982).

37 On the question of political arithmetic and statistics cf. M. J. Cullen, *The Statistical Movement in Early Victorian Britain* (Brighton, Harvester Press, 1975).

38 On the notion of 'police', in addition to the discussion by Oestreich, *Neostoicism and the early modern state* see also: P. Pasquino, 'Theatrum politicum: the genealogy of capital – police and the state of prosperity', *Ideology and Consciousness*, no. 4 (Autumn 1978); K. Tribe, 'Introduction to Knemeyer' and F. L. Knemeyer, 'Polizei', in *Economy and Society*, vol. 9, no. 2 (May 1980), pp. 168–96.

39 Cited in M. Foucault, 'Omnes et Singulatim', p. 248.

40 Cf. my discussion of the notion of population in chapter 5.

41 Cf. Colin Gordon's remarks on this issue in C. Gordon, 'Introduction' to G. Burchell, C. Gordon and P. Miller, *The Foucault Effect*, Harvester Press, forthcoming.

42 Foucault draws attention to the 'virility' of the prescriptions he refers to. For this reason I have used masculine pronouns throughout this section.

43 G. Oestreich, *Neostoicism and the early modern state*, p. 271.

CONCLUSION

1 Cf. for example the special issue of *Critique*, no. 471–2 (August–September 1986) devoted to Foucault.

2 M. Foucault, 'Structuralism and post-structuralism: an interview with Michel Foucault', by G. Raulet, *Telos* no. 55 (Spring 1983).

3 *Ibid.*, p. 200.

4 M. Foucault, 'Un course inédit', *Magazine littéraire*, no. 207, Paris (May 1984), pp. 35–9. Translated as 'Kant on Enlightenment and Revolution', in *Economy and Society*, vol. 15, no. 1 (February 1986), pp. 88–96. See also the commentary on that article: C. Gordon, 'Question, Ethos, Event', *Economy and Society*, vol. 15, no. 1 (February 1986), pp. 71–87.

5 J. Habermas, 'Une flèche dans le coeur du temps présent', *Critique*, no. 471–2 (August–September 1986).

6 M. Foucault, 'Structuralism and post-structuralism', pp. 203–4.

7 See for instance the issues addressed in: P. Miller and N. Rose (eds), *The Power of Psychiatry* (Cambridge, Polity Press, 1986); P. Miller and T. O'Leary, 'Accounting and the construction of the governable person', *Accounting, Organizations and Society* (vol. 12, 1987), pp. 235–65.

8 See the comments in the introduction to P. Miller and N. Rose, (eds), *The Power of Psychiatry*.

SELECTED BIBLIOGRAPHY

•

The following is a selection of those key works referred to in the text, and of some of the recent commentaries and discussions of the works of critical theory and Foucault. It is in no sense intended to be complete. More detailed bibliographies can be found in C. Gordon (ed.), *Power/Knowledge*, Brighton: Harvester, 1980 and M. Clark, *Michel Foucault: An Annotated Bibliography*, New York: Garland, 1983. See also D. Held, *Introduction to Critical Theory*, London: Hutchinson, 1980.

AARSLEFF, H., *The Study of Language in England: 1786–1860*, Princeton University Press, 1967.

ADORNO, T. and HORKHEIMER, M., *Dialectic of Enlightenment*, London: Verso, 1979. Originally published 1944.

ALTHUSSER, L., *Lenin and Philosophy and other essays*, London: New Left Books, 1971.

ALTHUSSER, L. and BALIBAR, E., *Reading Capital*, London: New Left Books, 1970.

ARATO, A. and GEBHARDT, E. (eds), *The Essential Frankfurt School Reader*, Oxford: Blackwell, 1978.

BOUCHARD, D. (ed.), *Language, Counter-Memory, Practice*, Oxford: Blackwell, 1977.

BUBNER, R., *Modern German Philosophy*, Cambridge University Press, 1981.

BURCHELL, G., GORDON, C. and MILLER, P. (eds), *The Foucault Effect*, Brighton: Harvester Press, 1987, forthcoming.

CANGUILHEM, G., *La connaissance de la vie*, Paris: Vrin, 1980. First published 1952.

CANGUILHEM, G., *Le normal et le pathologique*, Paris: Presses Universitaires de France, 1966.

CANGUILHEM, G., 'Mort de l'homme ou épuisement du cogito', *Critique*, vol. 23, no. 242 (1967).

CANGUILHEM, G., *Études d'histoire et de philosophie des sciences*, Paris: Vrin, 1983. First published 1968.

CASTEL, R., *L'ordre psychiatrique*, Paris: Editions de Minuit, 1976.

CASTEL, R., CASTEL, F. and LOVELL, A., *The Psychiatric Society*, New York: Columbia University Press, 1982. First published as *La société psychiatrique avancée*, Paris: Editions Grasset et Fasquelle, 1979.

CAVAILLES, J., *Sur la logique et la théorie de la science*, Paris: Vrin, 1976. First published Paris: Presses Universitaires de France, 1947.

CHATELET, F., *Les idéologies*, vol. 3, 'De Rousseau à Mao', Verviers: Marabout, 1981. First published 1978, Paris: Librairie Hachette.

CHATELET, F. and PISIER-KOUCHNER, E., *Les conceptions politiques du XX*e siècle, Paris: Presses Universitaires de France, 1981.

CLARK, M., *Michel Foucault: An Annotated Bibliography*, New York: Garland, 1983.

CONNERTON, P. (ed.), *Critical Sociology*, Harmondsworth: Penguin, 1976.

COUSINS, M. and HUSSAIN, A., *Michel Foucault*, Basingstoke: Macmillan Education, 1984.

CRITIQUE, *Michel Foucault: du monde entier*, vol. 42, no. 471–2 (August–September, 1986).

DELEUZE, G., *Foucault*, Paris: Editions de Minuit, 1986.

DESCOMBES, V., *Le Même et l'autre*, Paris: Editions de Minuit, 1979.

DONZELOT, J., *The Policing of Families*, London: Hutchinson, 1980.

DREYFUS, H. L. and RABINOW, P., *Michel Foucault: Beyond Structuralism and Hermeneutics*, Brighton: Harvester Press, 1982.

FOUCAULT, M., *Madness and Civilization*, London: Tavistock, 1965. An abridged version of *Histoire de la folie*.

FOUCAULT, M., *The Order of Things*, London: Tavistock, 1970. First published as *Les mots et les choses*, Paris: Gallimard, 1966.

FOUCAULT, M., *Histoire de la folie à l'âge classique*, Paris: Editions Gallimard, 1972. Originally published as *Folie et déraison: histoire de la folie à l'âge classique*, Paris: Plon, 1961.

FOUCAULT, M., *The Birth of the Clinic*, London: Tavistock, 1973. First published as *La naissance de la clinique*, Paris: Presses Universitaires de France, 1963.

FOUCAULT, M., *Mental Illness and Psychology*, New York: Harper & Row, 1976. Revised edition of *Maladie mentale et personnalité*, Paris: Presses Universitaires de France, 1954.

FOUCAULT, M. *et al.*, *Les machines à guérir*, Paris: Dossiers et Documents d'Architecture, Institut de l'Environnement, 1976.

FOUCAULT, M., *Discipline and Punish*, London: Allen Lane, 1977. First published as *Surveiller et punir: naissance de la prison*, Paris: Gallimard, 1975.

FOUCAULT, M. (ed.), *I, Pierre Rivière*, Harmondsworth: Penguin, 1978. First published as *Moi, Pierre Rivière, ayant égorgé ma mère, ma soeur et mon frère*, Paris: Gallimard/Julliard, 1973.

FOUCAULT, M. (ed.), *Power/Knowledge*, C. Gordon (ed.), Brighton: Harvester, 1980.

FOUCAULT, M., 'The order of discourse', in R. Young (ed.), *Untying the Text*, London: Routledge & Kegan Paul, 1981. Originally published as *L'ordre du discours*, Paris: Gallimard, 1971.

FOUCAULT, M., *The History of Sexuality*, vol. 1, Harmondsworth: Penguin,

1981. First published as *La volonté de savoir; histoire de la sexualité*, vol. 1, Paris: Gallimard, 1976.

FOUCAULT, M., 'Sexuality and solitude', discussion with R. Sennett, *London Review of Books*, 21 May–3 June, 1981.

FOUCAULT, M., 'An exchange' (with Lawrence Stone), *New York Review of Books*, vol. 30, no. 5 (March 31, 1983), pp. 42–4.

FOUCAULT, M., *L'usage des plaisirs; histoire de la sexualité*, vol. 2, Paris: Gallimard, 1984.

FOUCAULT, M., *Le souci de soi; histoire de la sexualité*, vol. 3, Paris: Gallimard, 1984.

GEUSS, R., *The Idea of a Critical Theory: Habermas and the Frankfurt School*, Cambridge University Press, 1981.

HABERMAS, J., *Towards a Rational Society*, London: Heinemann, 1970.

HABERMAS, J., *Knowledge and Human Interests*, London: Heinemann, 1972. First published as *Erkenntnis und Interesse*, 1968.

HABERMAS, J., *Theory and Practice*, London: Heinemann, 1974. Abridged edition of 4th German edition of *Theorie und Praxis*, Frankfurt: Suhrkamp, 1971.

HABERMAS, J., *Legitimation Crisis*, London: Heinemann Education, 1976. First published as *Legitimationsprobleme im Spätkapitalismus*, Frankfurt: Suhrkamp, 1973.

HABERMAS, J., *Communication and the Evolution of Society*, London: Heinemann Education, 1979.

HABERMAS, J., *Theorie des Kommunikativen Handelns*, 2 vols, Frankfurt: Suhrkamp, 1981.

HABERMAS, J., *Philosophical-Political Profiles*, London: Heinemann, 1983.

HABERMAS, J., *The Theory of Communicative Action, vol. I: Reason and the Rationalization of Society*, London: Heinemann Education, 1984. Translation of vol. I of *Theorie des Kommunikativen Handelns*.

HABERMAS, J., *Autonomy and Solidarity: Interviews*, P. Dews (ed.) and intro., London: Verso, 1986.

HELD, D., *Introduction to Critical Theory*, London: Hutchinson, 1980.

HORKHEIMER, M., *Eclipse of Reason*, New York: Oxford University Press, 1947. Reprinted New York: Seabury Press, 1974.

HORKHEIMER, M., *Critical Theory: Selected Essays*, New York: Seabury Press, 1972.

HORKHEIMER, M., *Critique of Instrumental Reason*, New York: Seabury Press, 1974. Originally published as *Zur Kritik der Instrumentellen Vernunft*, Frankfurt, 1967.

HORKHEIMER, M., *Dawn and Decline, Notes 1926–1931 and 1950–1969*, New York: Seabury Press, 1978. Previously published as *Notizen und dämmerung*, Frankfurt: Fischer, 1974.

JACOB, F., *The Logic of Living Systems*, London: Allen Lane, 1974. First published as *La logique du vivant*, Paris: Gallimard, 1970.

JAY, M., *The Dialectical Imagination: A History of the Frankfurt School and the Institute of Social Research 1923–1950*, London: Heinemann Educational, 1973.

LUHMANN, N., *Trust and Power*, Chichester: Wiley, 1979. Translation of *Vertrauen*, Stuttgart: Ferdinand Enke, 1973; and *Macht*, Stuttgart: Ferdinand Enke, 1975.

LUKES, S., *Power: A Radical View*, London: Macmillan, 1974.

McCARTHY, T., *The Critical Theory of Jurgen Habermas*, Cambridge: Polity Press, 1984. First published in America 1978.

MAJOR-POETZL, P., *Michel Foucault's Archaeology of Western Culture: Towards a New Science of History*, Chapel Hill: University of North Carolina Press, 1983.

MARCUSE, H., *Reason and Revolution: Hegel and the Rise of Social Theory*, Boston: Beacon Press, 1960. First published New York: Oxford University Press, 1941.

MARCUSE, H., *One-Dimensional Man*, London: Routledge & Kegan Paul, 1964.

MARCUSE, H., *Five Lectures*, London: Allen Lane, 1970.

MARCUSE, H., *Negations*, Harmondsworth: Penguin University Books, 1972.

MARCUSE, H., *Studies in Critical Philosophy*, London: New Left Books, 1972.

MILLER, P., 'The territory of the psychiatrist: review of Robert Castel's *L'ordre psychiatrique*', *Ideology and Consciousness*, no. 7 (Autumn 1980).

MILLER, P., 'Psychiatry – the renegotiation of a territory: review of F. Castel, *et al.*, *La société psychiatrique avancée*', *Ideology and Consciousness*, no. 8 (Spring 1981).

MILLER, P. and ROSE, N. (eds), *The Power of Psychiatry*, Cambridge: Polity Press, 1986.

MILLER, P. and O'LEARY, T., 'Accounting and the construction of the governable person', *Accounting, Organizations and Society*, vol. 12, 3 (1987), pp. 235–65.

MORRIS, M. and PATTON, P., *Michel Foucault: Power, Truth, Strategy*, Sydney: Feral Publications, 1979.

POSTER, M., *Foucault, Marxism and History*, Cambridge: Polity Press, 1984.

POULANTZAS, N., *State, Power, Socialism*, London: New Left Books, 1978.

RABINOW, P., *The Foucault Reader*, London: Pantheon, 1984.

RACEVSKIS, K., *Michel Foucault and the Subversion of Intellect*, Ithaca, NY: Cornell University Press, 1983.

RODERICK, R., *Habermas and the Foundations of Critical Theory*, Basingstoke: Macmillan Education, 1986.

ROGER, J., *Les sciences de la vie dans la pensée francaise du XVIIIe siècle*, Paris: Armand Colin, 1963.

SCHROYER, T., *The Critique of Domination: The Origins and Development of Critical Theory*, New York: Braziller, 1973.

SEARLE, J. R., *Speech Acts*, Cambridge: Cambridge University Press, 1969.

SENSAT, J., *Habermas and Marxism*, Beverley Hills, CA: Sage Publications, 1979.

SHERIDAN, A., *Michel Foucault: The Will to Truth*, London: Tavistock, 1980.
SMART, B., *Foucault, Marxism and Critique*, London: Routledge & Kegan Paul, 1983.
THERBORN, G., 'A critique of the Frankfurt School', *New Left Review*, no. 63 (1970).
THERBORN, G., 'J. Habermas: the new eclecticism', *New Left Review*, no. 67 (1971).
THOMPSON, J. B. and HELD, D., *Habermas: Critical Debates*, London: Macmillan Press, 1982.
VEYNE, P., *Comment on écrit l'histoire*, Paris: Éditions du Seuil, 1971.

INDEX